Troublemakers

To Elena

looking forward to more stories

Troublemakers
The Best of South Africa's
Investigative Journalism

x Margaret Renn

October 2010 .

edited by
Anton Harber
&
Margaret Renn

JACANA

First published by Jacana Media (Pty) Ltd in 2010

10 Orange Street
Sunnyside
Auckland Park 2092
South Africa
(+27 11) 628-3200
www.jacana.co.za

ISBN 978-1-77009-893-0

Cover design by publicide
Set in Ehrhardt 11/15pt
Printed and bound by Ultra Litho (Pty) Limited, Johannesburg
Job no. 001309

See a complete list of Jacana titles at www.jacana.co.za

Our thanks to all those who gave us permission to use their work.

The Taco Kuiper Award recognises excellence in South African investigative reporting. Launched in 2006, it is funded by The Valley Trust, in memory of the late publisher Taco Kuiper. It is run by Wits Journalism.

The Valley Trust trustees: Dion de Beer (chairman), Leslie Jamieson, the Rev. Dr D. Alan Maker, Mrs Janet Cloete, Mrs Sinah Tshabalala

The Taco Kuiper Award judges: Justice Tom Cloete, Professor Anton Harber, Charlayne Hunter-Gault, Justice Malala, Margaret Renn.

Winners:
2006 – Adriaan Basson and Carien du Plessis of *Die Beeld* and *Die Burger*
2007 – Brett Horner, Chandré Prince and Ntando Makhubu of the *Daily Dispatch*
2008 – Sam Sole, Stefaans Brümmer and Adriaan Basson of the *Mail & Guardian*
2009 – Rob Rose of the *Financial Mail* and the *Sunday Times*

For further information visit www.journalism.co.za

Note on text

The articles in this book were entries for the Taco Kuiper Awards in 2010. Some minor edits have been made, particularly where a series of articles over a number of days or weeks included repeats or were very long. Readers who would like to read the full text and updates to the stories are referred to Sources on page 238.

Contents

Introduction

This collection of investigative reporting should sharpen debate over South Africa's journalism and the role it is playing in this new democracy.

Our journalism has been lambasted from all sides since the country was liberated from apartheid in 1994. Critics from the left and the right, and journalists themselves, have lamented a lack of accuracy, balance, diversity, independence and ethics in our news media, and more generally a failure to deliver on the promise of media freedom enshrined in our Constitution.

In February this year, two of the country's most respected editors spoke at a colloquium on the State of Our Journalism, hosted by Wits Journalism. Ferial Haffajee, until recently editor of the *Mail & Guardian* and now at *City Press*, said:

"I think in South Africa we confuse [journalism and public relations], which is why journalists can be a PR one day and a journalist the next, and we flip-flop so easily between these two worlds. I think all of travelling, motoring, lifestyle and entertainment journalism today is very seriously embedded. Those kinds of journalism take up many more column inches than do political journalism and developmental journalism.

"I have many friends in public relations who measure how many times we use their releases, lock, stock and barrel, to use their words. That is, in turn, how they are measured, how they are paid and how they get their bonuses.

"And you'll understand that we have basically become slaves to the PR machine because their effectiveness rate is extremely high and all you need to do is ask PRISA, the PR association, about just how effective it is.

"So every week in my paper I am used to scribbling 'this is PR bullshit' across many pages that describe cars costing well over one million rand as 'affordable sedans' – this in a country where most people earn about R850 a month.

"The seductive world of free trips, of expensive hotels, of champagne and bling has enticed an entire generation of young journalists who have become mere appendages of PR …

"Read the social columns and the lifestyle pages – on the whole our journalists write without the cynicism, without a tongue-in-cheek quality, without the recognition that these are worlds so far removed from the daily reality to be quite ridiculous. It's all 'gosh, gosh, gosh' embeddedness."[i]

And Tim du Plessis, who moved recently from the editorship of *Rapport*, the country's biggest Afrikaans voice, to *Beeld*, the prestigious daily, told this story:

"I don't know if many of you remember the famous reference: 'a generally corrupt relationship existed between Schabir Shaik and Mr Jacob Zuma'? For a full 18 months, that was never checked. It was reported in editorials, in various articles. They said it was found in Schabir Shaik's corruption trial that a 'generally corrupt relationship' existed between him and Jacob Zuma.

"And then after 18 months of this story doing the rounds, and even being mentioned in the Appeal Court, the judge wrote a letter to *Business Day* and said: 'I noticed that you used the phrase "a generally corrupt relationship existed between Shaik and Zuma". I just wish to point out' – and I'm paraphrasing – 'just wish to point out that I never said those words, they are not in the judgment.'

"Then someone went through the judgment – a very long judgment – and they found it wasn't there. Nobody had bothered to check.

"Now that has nothing to do with media bosses squeezing newsrooms and forcing editors to lay off people. That's simply an example of lazy journalism."[ii]

The criticism of our media has taken various forms. Some argue there has not been enough transformation from the pre-1994 racial structures inherited from apartheid, while others say the pressure for fast change has come at a great cost in skills and experience. Few would take issue with the problem set out by the soon-to-be president, Nelson Mandela, in 1994:

"The tragic absence of diversity in the South African media has been a matter of grave concern to us over a number of years ... South African media are still largely dominated by persons drawn almost exclusively from one racial group. With the exception of the *Sowetan*, the senior editorial staffs of all South Africa's daily newspapers are cast from the same racial mould. They are white, they are male, they are from a middle-class background, they tend to share a very similar life experience. The same holds true for the upper echelons of the electronic media, again with a very few recent exceptions."[iii]

In its "Ready to Govern" document of 1992, a time when it was positioning itself for the first democratic elections, the ANC declared its media policy in entirely positive tones: South Africa had to move from a closed to an open society based on a culture of debate; democracy demanded citizens had access to the media and to government information; media diversity had to be encouraged; and public media had to be independent.

On coming to power, the ANC made it clear that it viewed media transformation as a priority, given that the media needed to reflect the new order and also had a key role to play in driving change in the rest of society. In the 15 years since then, there have undoubtedly been significant shifts in the racial and age representivity of media owners and senior staff [iv] – though less in the gender make-up – and the ANC acknowledged this:

"The considerable progress made and some significant milestones achieved within the communications industry particularly with regard to ownership patterns, the licensing of new media at commercial and community levels, the increase of black and women journalists, editors and managers, as well as the repositioning of the SABC to play a role of being a public broadcaster, driven by a public mandate as opposed to a party political role, has to an extent introduced a measure of diversity in ownership, with black empowerment groups and union funds controlling some of the assets."[v]

But the ANC has taken up two further lines of argument. The first is to suggest that the change has been cosmetic. Black individuals in editorial seats have failed to change the old "white liberal" culture of many of these newsrooms, and have taken on the same middle-class, middle-of-the-road values. The media is still serving narrow financial and political interests which make it preternaturally hostile to the ANC and its transformation project. Journalists, the argument goes, are stuck in a neo-liberal posture of hostility to government and fail to grasp the kind of journalism required to contribute to a democratic and developmental state. In 2007, an ANC policy document said:

"The behaviour of media during the apartheid years left a legacy that has not been eradicated nor properly discussed … most of the decision makers during these repressive years have continued doing what they were doing then. It is therefore not surprising that sections of the media continue to act in a manner that resists meaningful transformation of our country. Opponents of transformation regard state structures over which they do not have any influence as a threat to the maintenance of the status quo."[vi]

This crosses the line from criticism of the faults of the media to the serious accusation that journalists actively resist transformation and are therefore ideological and strategic foes of the government.

Just recently, ANC secretary-general Gwede Mantashe responded to a black journalist in a media conference who asked about the singing of the liberation song with the lines "Kill the Boer", by saying: "I call that a coconut approach, where you have a black face, but your interest is white."[vii] This contempt for the media began to show itself in much of the ruling party's relations with the media. It became routine to picture the media as only interested in making money and driven by greed – a difficult thing for most underpaid, underappreciated and often risk-taking journalists to accept.

Ten years into democracy, at a time of national stock-taking, leading ANC policy-maker and thinker Joel Netshitenzhe made an important speech to editors in which he said our media were good at being critics, but less able to define a wider social role. Our newspapers still did not reflect the voices of many South Africans: "In its multiplicity of roles as court-jester, actor, trouble-stirrer, the nosy and noisy irritant and bearer of bad and (sometimes) good news, the South African media has acquitted itself well. As to whether the balance among these roles is appropriate; as to the demographics of the social actors whose pride and prejudice find voice in our news media, the jury is still out."[viii]

This leads us to the second line of argument: ownership is too concentrated, access to the media is limited, and commercialism dominates and distorts the media's social role. This is a substantive critique of the structure of the media in a society in which it has traditionally served narrow political and financial interests and the power of advertisers is increasingly subsuming any wider social and political roles for journalism.

"The ability of the media to collectively represent the broad range of views and interests present in society is limited by, among other things, the pressure of the market. While all South Africans have the right to freedom of expression, the capacity of the vast majority to exercise that right through the media is extremely limited … Driven by a need to gain market share in those sections of society to whom advertisers are more readily drawn, newspapers are under pressure to shape their content to meet a particular commercial goal. While editors may profess their independence – from both owners and advertisers – and their commitment first and foremost to comprehensive, accurate and fair coverage, there is significant pressure on newspapers to deliver a product that sells, and sells to the right portion of the market."[ix]

This situation has a number of effects. It tends to make the media lean towards those with wealth, and shuts out those without it, thus exacerbating the deep social inequalities which lie at the heart of the country's challenges. It is a view, though, which needs to take account of the rise of the tabloids, which – at least to some extent – give voice and coverage to working-class South Africans. In the *Daily Sun*, now by far the country's biggest newspaper (at least three times the size of the next-biggest daily), for example, one sees images and hears voices that were previously absent from most of our media: that of working-class township dwellers battling with the daily challenges of inefficient bureaucracy, cruel criminals and troublesome tokoloshes. This, however, is not the working-class voice envisaged by those in power.

It is also a view – a crude political economy of the media – which gives no agency to journalists within profit-making enterprises to act honourably or independently, portraying the media as a monolithic, single-minded institution. There may arguably be a lack of diversity in the media, and a predominance of establishment views, but the crude picture that was presented was at odds with reality.

The ANC's policy response to the inequalities in media access has been to call for greater funding for the national public broadcaster, the SABC, as well as support for community media through a statutory funder, the Media Development and Diversity Agency (MDDA). The SABC had led the way during the 1990s in a difficult transformation from an overwhelmingly white-managed propaganda voice to a diverse public broadcaster pursuing a wide-ranging social and cultural mandate. But it was dependent on advertising for over 80% of its revenue, which limited its capacity to fulfil its public mandate and left it permanently schizophrenic, uncertain which master to serve: the advertiser or the audience.

The SABC was also – quite naturally, given the fact that it so dominated the broadcasting industry[x] – the subject of constant political pressure and repeated threats to its independence. This culminated in the appointment of a former government spokesman, Snuki Zikalala, as head of news and the "deployment" of an unqualified cadre, Dali Mpofu, as group chief executive. In recent years, the SABC's news had deteriorated to a procession of boring ministers making dull, everyday speeches and the organisation had gone from healthy profit to major deficit and deep disfunctionality. This was a tragic decline for such an important institution. It hobbled what was by a long way the biggest and best-resourced news operation on the continent and the one best placed to pursue public service journalism free of commercial pressures. Government pressure on the rest of the media might have been lessened if the public broadcaster was better able to fill its social and political role.

The MDDA was set up to give support to community media, both print and broadcasting, with money from the state and the private sector, but its budget has never been big enough for it to make a major impact. The ANC government decried the commercial nature of the news media, promised alternatives, but failed to back them adequately. Both the MDDA and the SABC highlighted a government tendency to "talk left and walk right", as commentator Jane Duncan put it: they decry the impact of the market on the media, yet leave it to the market to sort out.

On the other side of the political spectrum, it is commonly argued that the drive for transformation, together with financial pressures, has led to shrinking newsrooms, poor working conditions for journalists, a loss of skills and experience, and a "juniorisation" of newsroom management. Certainly, many of the most experienced and skilled members of news and subs rooms fell foul of the push to end the dominance of middle-aged white men, and many have retired, emigrated or gone into public relations jobs. Young black journalists were sometimes hastily propelled into senior positions, with some sinking and some rising to the challenge. Newsrooms as well as editorial management became more representative, but age and experience levels dropped.

A second wave of departure from newsrooms came with the recruitment by government communication departments of some of the best journalism talent. In a bid to improve its shaky communications, government was able to use a combination of money (they paid relatively well), position (a director of communication enjoys perks not available to the average newsroom hack) and moral persuasion ("Come help us make this democracy work") to raid the ranks of the profession for many of its best and brightest. The SA National Editors' Forum (Sanef) was one of many bodies to bemoan the impact of the revolving door between journalism and government communicators on the depletion of newsroom personnel.

This view of deteriorating standards, though, tends to romanticise journalism under apartheid and suggest that universally high standards were set and maintained in that time. That would, of course, depend on one's view of what constitutes high standards. Spelling and grammar may have been better, but it is debatable whether coverage was more accurate or substantial. The media – even the most liberal media – were shaped and compromised by the experience of apartheid.

While there has been a tense relationship between government and media since 1994, no direct action was taken against the media, and indeed tough stories were uncovered and many journalists (and cartoonists in particular) were sharply outspoken without any fear of arrest, closure or other form of the kind of state action which had been common under apartheid. Debate was robust. The questions being asked by journalists of government were by no means unique to this country, but they came against the torrid background of a tense transition to democracy, a media in which many had been tainted by apartheid history, the fragility of an uncertain social compact, and a new government struggling to make progress under difficult circumstances.

A series of news stories that went awry and some controversial ethical conduct in the period 2006–8 fuelled the debate. One of the most common lines of attack was against the indiscriminate use of unnamed sources, particularly when this related to internal conflicts in the ruling party and among its allies. This criticism came from editors and journalists, as much as politicians and other subjects of discomforting media attention. It was acknowledged as a problem by Sanef, which published a pocket guide to sourcing and attribution.

There were hot-spots of controversy. When the *Sunday Times* accused the minister of health, Manto Tshabalala-Msimang, of being a kleptomaniac and drunkard while recovering from a liver transplant, there were calls from the presidency for government to cease advertising in what is one of the country's biggest newspapers, and the SABC – the country's biggest media institution – withdrew from the NEF. Prolific and relentlessly critical cartoonist Zapiro (Jonathan Shapiro), whose work appears in a number of newspapers, drew considerable ire, particularly for a series that accused then-aspirant president Jacob Zuma not just of raping women, but also of raping justice. Zapiro's relentless depiction of Zuma with a shower always hovering above his head, reminding everyone of his witness-box faux pas when he said he showered after sex to avoid HIV, has led to considerable pressure on both him and the newspaper to scrap the shower.

The media faced a torrent of abuse during the pre-presidential courtroom battles of Zuma, when he was accused in separate cases of rape and corruption. Journalists were charged with subjecting him to trial by media, and the incident, quoted above, in which newspapers for months quoted a judge wrongly on the case, was frequently cited as an example of bias and prejudice overshadowing journalistic judgment. Certainly, much of the media was hostile to Zuma, reflecting a middle-class angst around the traditionalism and populism he represented, and editors were slow in realising how much mass support he commanded.

Things were not helped by some serious factual and ethical lapses by the media. *Business Day* ran a front-page story about the president's controversial role in an ANC meeting, though it turned out he had never been present. An extraordinary top-of-front-page apology ensued. *Sunday Times* reporter Ranjeni Munusamy could not accept when the editor declined to run a story saying that the prosecutor pursuing Zuma and his friends for corruption had been suspected of being an apartheid-era spy. She gave the story to a rival newspaper, was fired, and went on to join Zuma's presidential campaign. (The spying allegations were subjected to a formal state inquiry and could not be sustained.) Another editor, Vusi Mona, breached the rules of an off-the-record briefing because he felt it was being abused by the authorities to tarnish Zuma. Mona was later fired for a conflict of interest over a public relations firm he was running on the side, while editing the paper. He too went on to work for Zuma's government.

And in 2008, the *Sunday Times* ran a serious of sensational stories of dubious provenance. These ranged from the claim that President Mbeki had himself taken some arms deal bribery money (it turned out the source for the information was dead and there was nothing else to back it up) to a report that the giant state transport company, Transnet, had "sold our se giving rights to a large part of Cape Town's most valuable asset to a foreign investor. The story was vastly exaggerated and included a front-page map which was shocking, particularly for Capetonians fond of their coastline, but had little resemblance to reality.

The situation was complicated by the new government's poor handling of communications and a keen sensitivity to criticism. The ANC, for many years the darling of the global anti-apartheid campaign, was taken aback at being in government and facing a media that was sharply critical, and even hostile. "We brought liberation, and we brought a constitution which protected media freedom and promoted access to information, and now you turn on us and treat us like the previous government," was what they said in private. Of course, those in the media, particularly those who had been in the anti-apartheid media, saw it differently. Liberation and media freedom were not something the ANC had "delivered"; they had come through hard-fought battles, including from sections of the media and some brave journalists. These individuals were not about to give up their hard-fought independence or right to criticise.

Poor communications from the new government led to constant frustration on its part that its message was not getting through to the public. The government felt that its voice was being drowned out by a constituency with access to the media who were nervous, suspicious of the new government and often outright cynical. As a result, it felt its successes were not being recognised and progress not sufficiently welcomed. Some of this was justified, but much of it was the result of poor handling of the media, and an unrealistic expectation of what the media might achieve.

In fact, by 2007 much of what the media had been saying about government's failure to deliver was being used as the reason to oust Mbeki from the presidency. What the media had been criticised for – its scepticism about government's effectiveness in dealing with social services – was now coming from within the ruling alliance itself. The ruling party ran its election campaign in 2008 based on the acceptance that it had fallen short of delivering on its promises,[xi] conveniently forgetting that it had lambasted the media for saying this for some years.

Nevertheless, dissatisfaction with coverage led to calls in the ruling party for the establishment of a statutory Media Appeals Tribunal. The ANC's Polokwane conference, seen as a landmark gathering for the ruling party and one where Zuma was anointed leader and future president, called for the investigation of such a measure, arguing that the existing self-regulatory bodies, such as the Press Council and Ombudsman, were inadequate to deal with the problem.

The conference resolution charged that "some fractions of the media continue to adopt an anti-transformation, anti-ANC stance". This was much more than a critique of media inadequacy or faults, as it identified what was seen as a hostile ideological onslaught by the ANC's enemies:

"The ANC is faced with a major ideological offensive, largely driven by the opposition and fractions in the mainstream media, whose key objective is the promotion of market fundamentalism, control of the media and the images it creates of a new democratic dispensation in order to retain old apartheid economic and social relations.

"This offensive against our movement, in its content and form, is part of a global offensive against progressive values and ideas."[xii]

A constant charge against the media was that journalists were using their rights to trample on the rights of others, notably the right to privacy and dignity. "The ANC notes", read the Polokwane resolution, "that in many instances the media in pursuit of the application of this freedom of expression principle, conducts itself to the detriment of the constitutional rights of others."

The call was for the media to play a more positive role in the developmental economy: "The ANC is of the view that the media needs to contribute towards the building of a new society and be accountable for its actions."

The print media responded by strengthening self-regulation.[xiii] The office of the Ombudsman was beefed up with the appointment of a senior and respected journalist, Joe Thloloe, and the Press Council was resuscitated. Strong calls were made for a new sense of ethics in the profession.

For some two years, the ANC did not take any action to implement the resolution and the organisation's communication staff privately gave assurances that the tribunal would never happen. That changed in 2010. First there was an increase in anti-media rhetoric. There followed a wave of proposed new legislation which sought to chip away at the free flow of information and threatened the independence of public and community media. A pornography Bill required newspapers to go through pre-publication vetting for material involving minors and sex. It was only after much lobbying, that it was agreed that publications accepting the authority of the Press Council would be exempt. But those that did not are still subject to this form of prior censorship.

A draft new Public Broadcasting Bill gave the minister direct powers of intervention in the SABC and proposed to tie local community stations to municipal authorities; a Bill on the broadcasting regulator likewise gave the minister direct powers to force them to act on his will; a Protection of Information Bill massively widened the capacity of all sorts of government and parastatal officials to classify documents as secret even if they "may" threaten the national interest – a scope so wide that it begged abuse.

Most significantly, there was a new push for the Media Appeals Tribunal. A policy document was tabled on this matter and leaders of the ruling alliance – notably from the SA Communist Party – suddenly spoke out in its favour. A host of motivations were given – such as the shoddiness of the media, its reluctance to correct errors and the weakness of the existing self-regulatory Ombudsman system – but it was no coincidence that those calling for it were almost all the subject of recent embarrassing exposés in the press. For example, SACP general secretary and minister of higher education and training, Blade Nzimande, was shown to have spent lavish amounts of taxpayers' money in a stay at Cape Town's ultra-posh Mount Nelson Hotel because his official home was not ready for him. A week after this was splashed in the papers, he called for the Media Appeals Tribunal. ANC Youth League leader, Julius Malema, who had been tied in media reports to a string of dubious state tenders, backed the tribunal, saying that "These people [journalists] … think [they] are untouchable and they can write about anything they like and about anybody anyhow". Those who engage in unethical activities, "must be locked up," he said.[xiv] Both Nzimande and Malema made clear their view that the media was an ideological enemy. Nzimande described the press as "bourgeois" and "our only opposition" and Malema said the press was "dangerous to the revolution".

Also repeatedly cited was an admission by former journalist Ashley Smith that the then-premier of the Western Cape, the ANC's Ebrahim Rasool, had paid him to help him fight political rivals. The ANC condemned this "brown envelope journalism" and said it strengthened the call for a statutory tribunal. It was a strange case to pick as the case had been exposed by the newspaper itself after a lengthy investigation, seemingly strengthening the argument for self-regulation, while the ANC had appointed Rasool to the prestigious position of Ambassador to Washington.

The ANC's discussion document on Media Diversity and Ownership[xv], which sets out the case for a tribunal, reflects an ideologically conflicted ANC. While it argues that journalists cannot be neutral, it complains that they are not. While it argues that journalists must be free and independent, it says they must be accountable to state structures. While it supports freedom of expression, it proscribes that "in our National Democratic Revolution, the media should contribute to the transformation of our country, [including] building social cohesion and promoting values of a caring society".

It describes the ANC's values as the "developmental state, collective rights, values of caring and sharing community, solidarity, ubuntu, non-sexism, [and] working together" and the mainstream media's as "neo-liberalism, a weak and passive state, and overemphasis on individual rights, market fundamentalism, etc". These descriptions of both parties are caricatures which bear little relationship to reality, but they do set up the ANC and the media as ideological foes on either side of the nation's political battlefield.

When journalists met to discuss how to oppose the tribunal in August 2010, police raided offices in the same building and arrested a journalist, Mzilikazi wa Afrika. While they said the arrest had nothing to do with his journalism, it was hard to ignore the fact that the journalist's name had been on a story that very week alleging massive wasteful expenditure by the Police Commissioner. Police presented no warrant, took all his computers and notebooks, held him without bail for two days, including waking him at 2am for interrogation, before charging him in court with fraud.

Temperatures rose considerably.

✳ ✳ ✳

The future of journalism and particularly of costly in-depth investigations is being debated around the world as newspapers decline in the Western world. As Charles Lewis put it in 2006:

"In recent years nearly all of our media corporations have been actually reducing their commitment to journalism, reducing their editorial budgets, early 'retiring' thousands of reporters and editors from their newsrooms, in order to keep their annual profit margins high and their investors happy, harvesting their investments from a 'mature' industry. The net result of this hollowing out process: There are fewer people today to report, write and edit original news stories about our infinitely more complex, dynamic world."[xvi] It was clear that the old model of advertising-driven media that paid for reporting was in collapse, and it is unclear what new model for funding the business of journalism will emerge within new media. In Europe, governments in Italy and France were keeping newspapers afloat at considerable cost;[xvii] in the US and the UK charitable foundations were trying to step into the breach to support the cost of good reporting.[xviii]

South Africa, like other developing countries, still had a growing newspaper environment, but the impact of new media was on the horizon, kept at bay only by the slowness of the government in introducing cheap broadband. And the growth was uneven: the older, traditional newspapers were at best stagnant, and it was the new tabloids that accounted for what growth there was.

The 2008–9 economic recession added to the burden. The downturn in advertising – as much as 25 per cent – had brought editorial cutbacks, a shrinking of the news space in papers, and the consolidation of newsrooms within the large groups. Media24 brought all the newsrooms of its five Afrikaans papers under centralised organisation, retrenching a number of older, and more senior, journalists. This, they said, was because the younger ones were more at ease with the transition to new media, but it was no coincidence that it was the more experienced and more expensive individuals who went. They also said it would allow them, for example, to hire a central team of investigative reporters to service the whole group, rather than the smaller and isolated initiatives which had come from some of the newsrooms. Indeed, they hired one of the country's most respected newshounds, Jacques Pauw, and they gave him a large budget to run investigations for their various publications.

Independent News and Media, which had already pared its staffing down well below what had been considered the minimum, created one national production room to replace all the localised subs rooms across the country. Specialised staff were increasingly shared across the group. Again, they initiated for the first time a group-wide investigations unit, led by controversial former police investigator Ivor Powell.

Avusa, a third large newspaper publisher, began to talk in 2010 of "centres of excellence", a polite way of introducing centralisation and consolidation. But a new investigative team was being re-formed at the *Sunday Times*. At the *Mail & Guardian*, their long-standing team of hot-shot investigators, led by Stefaans Brummer and Sam Sole, was hived off into a stand-alone unit with outside funding.

Paradoxically, newsrooms may have been shrinking but investment in investigations was increasing, at least in our newspapers. This may have been because editors saw the need to continue investing in unique content to hold on to readers. It was contrary to international patterns, where investigations were usually the first to suffer cutbacks.

❋ ❋ ❋

It was against this background that the judges sat down to consider entries for the 2009 Taco Kuiper Award for Investigative Journalism in early 2010. And we were very surprised by what confronted us.

Not only were there more entries than ever before, but the quality and range were like nothing we had seen in the previous three years of the competition. There were 44 entries from 16 outlets, including print, television, radio and online. This was more than three times the previous level of entry. For the first time entries came from *SABC* (the national broadcaster), *Radio 702* (a private talk station), Politicsweb (a website), Sake24 (the business section of the Afrikaans dailies), *Business Times* (business section of the *Sunday Times*) and a small-town community paper called the *Highlands Herald*. This was apart from the regular entrants: *Mail & Guardian*, *Daily Dispatch*, *Beeld/Die Burger* – all previous winners – as well as the *Sunday Times*, *Noseweek*, *Carte Blanche*, and others.

A short-listing panel had been asked to reduce the final list to a maximum of six, only the serious contenders. After long hours of debate, they came back with 10 and said they could take it no lower. They were uncomfortable even doing that. When we looked through this pile, we had to reluctantly agree. The top 20 entries were all good, the top 10 were all excellent – and they were certainly all contenders for the top prize.

When the judges met, it took a long time to get a "short short-list" of five entries. They all agreed that the difference between any of the top 10 was fractional. To get down to just two took more time, and then to choose between the winner and runner-up was excruciating. There could be no better testimony to the excellence of entries.

The judges made the obvious point that this was "the best evidence that pockets of journalistic excellence exist all over the country" and this reflected very positively on the state of our democracy. Justice Malala, former editor and one of the judges, put it this way: "I feel very positive about the future of South Africa after reading and watching these entries. Certainly, our democracy is vibrant and our media is even more so. If this country continues to produce this quantity and volume of investigative work, the politicians and shady businesspeople are in trouble."

Another judge, Charlayne Hunter-Gault said: "This year's submissions were so outstanding, we had to work harder and longer to choose a winner. But that's fine with me, because gratifyingly, it speaks to the journalists of South Africa taking seriously their roles as the guardians of their country's promise."

There were a number of other things that stood out. Entries did not just deal with the political and the usual flow of exposés of the corruption of officialdom, but also focused on white-collar crime, environmental issues and the socio-economic environment. It was clear that the scope and range of hard-nosed reporting were spreading.

The domination of print as the primary medium of investigative reporting was being challenged. There were a number of interesting television entries and one which had been published only on the Internet. The only medium that was under-represented was radio. *Radio 702* and *Eyewitness News* each put in one entry, and there was not a single one from the national public broadcaster, which dominates radio. It was a sign of the emerging power of the internet and the sad state of most of our radio journalism.

The judges noted that there was markedly better quality of presentation and editing in the print entries. "In previous years, we have had cause to bemoan the fact that some promising entries were harmed by shoddy editing and design, negatively affecting their readability. Not so this year."

Entries came from young and old, showing a good mix of experience as well as new enthusiasm and energy. Did this signal that the industry trend of losing older, more skilled journalists was at least slowing down? It certainly gave hope that fresh talent was coming in.

One had to ask why there had been such a boom in competition entries. Why were all the predictions of the demise of investigative reporting so off the mark? What accounted for such richness in in-depth, probing stories, most notably at a time when the media seemed to be under such political and financial pressure? There could not be many countries in the world that, within one year, could produce such a range and quality of investigative reporting.

Maybe the news media were settling down after the turmoil of the first years of transition? Could it be that journalists were finding their feet again and newspapers their voice? Was it possible that newspapers, having gone through something of a transformation, were regaining the confidence to take on authority and the skill to make their stories stick? Might it reflect the rise of a new generation of journalists whose formative years were in the post-apartheid period, with less historical baggage and less emotional commitment to the liberation movement?

Part of the reason might be that the Taco Kuiper competition had been running for four years, with a very generous cash prize, and was now establishing itself among journalists. The prize was created after the death of Kuiper, a financial publisher, who left a good deal of his considerable estate to The Valley Trust with the instruction that they should promote investigative reporting. Kuiper was a Dutch immigrant who had fallen in love with this country and made his fortune here, but was troubled in particular by white-collar crime and the need to keep a watch on it. The Trust, in partnership with Wits Journalism, started the award, a system of grants to support reporters doing investigative work, a Taco Kuiper Chair in Investigative Journalism at Wits University and the Wits Justice Project, which uses students as interns to investigate injustices in our legal and court systems.

The award certainly drew attention because it offered by far the biggest cash prize in the country (R200 000 for a winner and R100 000 for a runner-up), and also because it enjoyed long-term sustainability without the burden and unpredictability of commercial sponsorship.

Journalists would also have seen that the Afrikaans newspapers, which won the prize in its first year, were carving out a new position for themselves in the journalistic landscape, and tough investigative reporting was a key part in this. The second winner, the *Daily Dispatch*, used hard-hitting exposés to reach beyond their small footprint and make a national impact. And the *Mail & Guardian* had sustained itself against the odds by being a cheeky muckraker.

One thing became clear: it is not the wealthiest and best-resourced papers that lead the way in investigations. It seldom is. In South Africa's media history, it has usually been the smaller, under-resourced, often loss-making papers which put their energies into breaking investigative stories: the *Guardian* of the 1950s (on labour conditions), *Drum* magazine in the 1950s (on prison and labour conditions), the *Rand Daily Mail* in the 1960s and 1970s (prison conditions), the *Sunday Express* in the 1970s (Info Scandal), the *Vrye Weekblad* (death squads) and *Weekly Mail* (Inkathagate) in the 1990s, and the *Daily Dispatch* in the 1970s and now. The large and prosperous institutions – such as the SABC, the biggest newsroom in Africa by a long way – shied away from such troublesome stories. It is no coincidence. Smaller, more marginal papers wanted to make a mark and bold exposés were a way to do this. They are often best placed to take the risks, having less to lose. Larger and wealthier papers tended to be more cautious and middle-of-the-road, not least of all because they think investigations often made advertisers nervous.

Two community papers deserve special mention: a one-man Barberton operation, called the *Umjindi Guardian* (now renamed the *Guardian*), run by the indomitable Bheki Mashile, received special mention at the 2008 awards. And the *Highlands Herald* was spotlighted in 2009.

There are exceptions to this pattern. The *Sunday Times* – perhaps the most lucrative paper of all in this country – has had great episodes of investigative reporting. But it occurred only at distinct times, under certain editors – notably Joel Mervis in the 1970s and Mondli Makhanya more recently – who made their names on their courage and outspokenness.

One factor in the emergence of such impactful journalism in recent years was the divisions in the ruling party. It is when those in power are fighting among themselves that leaks tend to happen. Those fighting for political advantage throw mud at each other, and sometimes the media is the best catapult. Battles over state power and resources are reflected in the media, not necessarily as a result of the hard slog of investigation but often through timely and well-placed leaks. At times like this, a liberation movement in power loses its sheen and its moral authority – opening the way for more aggressive reporting.

Leaks designed to serve internal party political battles brought some criticism of journalists for allowing themselves to be used as fodder in such battles, serving one side rather than reporting from the sidelines. Leaks are almost always intended to serve the purpose of the source and there have certainly been instances where journalists have betrayed the bigger story by allowing themselves to be courted by one side, in exchange for leaks and leads. Using sources, and not having them use you, is a constant balancing act for journalists.

Two things happened in South Africa in recent years to feed the flow of information. First, doubts began to be aired about "delivery" – the capacity of the ANC government to achieve its bold promises. In 2009, the ANC campaigned on the basis that delivery of crucial services, like health and housing, had faltered and needed greater impetus. President Zuma rose to power on the promise of doing better on this front. The media, which had been critical about state service delivery and highlighted its failures, had been accused of being eager-to-criticise Afro-pessimists. Now this line of criticism had legitimacy – even the ruling party was saying it.

Secondly, there was also a creeping loss of confidence in many of the institutions of democracy. In the early years of transition, a number of bodies were set up to monitor governance, put a check on state power and prevent corruption: the Public Protector, the Human Rights and Gender commissions, the Constitutional Court, the Judicial Service Commission, Parliament itself, independent regulators in many sectors such as broadcasting, energy and banking, the special police force called the Scorpions, to name just a few. Great – and perhaps unrealistic – hope was placed in these important bodies, as well as resources, and they were seen as a crucial check on the power of a massive ruling party with a firm grip on power. Many of these bodies were new and energetic and had more promise in the early years than a media still burdened by its history and struggling with transformation.

That has changed. There has been an operational failure in at least some of these bodies, and a number have been compromised by the ANC's policy of "deployment" – systematically placing its loyal cadres, acting under its orders, in all the important institutions of government and the private sector. The news media have stepped into the breach, perhaps because of their greater relative independence. The private sector media may be the one pillar of democracy where it is most difficult for the ruling party to deploy its cadres and where an independence of spirit has flourished.

Parliament and the prosecuting authorities backed off from probing the arms deal shenanigans, but some newspapers stuck with the story. The presidency seemed to go soft on corruption, dismantling the Scorpions, and shackling the National Prosecuting Authority, but at least some journalists were relentless in pursuing tales of corruption. The prison authorities failed to act when the president's friend and convicted fraudster Schabir Shaik was shown to be flouting his parole; but reporters and photographers stuck with the story and splashed it over the front pages. When the government shunned a Cosatu call for "lifestyle audits" of political leadership that would show who was using their power to enrich themselves, the media did it anyway. The Judicial Service Commission faltered in calling to account judges who had political clout but flexible ethics, but the media watched their every move.

For all its faults and inadequacies, the private media has become the primary institution holding the government and the private sector to account, exposing corruption and the abuse of power, and keeping a torch shining into the dark areas of our society. Far from being the enemy of democracy described by many of its critics, the media in its reluctance to accept facile calls for national unity and to insist on the value of its muckraking, has become a bulwark against the potential abuse of power by a dominant ruling party.

This is largely due to a few individuals in a few of our newsrooms who have shown courage and consistency in investigative reporting, and to some editors and publishers/owners who have recognised the value – both journalistic and financial – of exposé, and backed their reporters. Nelson Mandela also recognised their value when he said: "A critical independent and investigative press is the lifeblood of any democracy. It must be free from state interference. It must have the economic strength to stand up to bullying by Government officials. It must be protected so that it can protect our rights as citizens."[xix]

This book is a tribute to them and, hopefully, an encouragement to others to join them.

The journalists featured here are our reportorial troublemakers – those who relentlessly disturb the complacency of people with power and wealth, making difficult their lives and limiting their opportunities to abuse their power and wealth. This book should make clear how valuable it is to have troublemakers in our newsrooms and editorial offices, and what an important social and political role they can play.

Anton Harber

Johannesburg, August 2010

i   The State of our Journalism: Colloquium at Wits University,
     8 February 2010. Available at www.journalism.co.za.

ii   ibid

iii Nelson Mandela, Speech to the IPI Congress, Cape Town,
     14 February 1994.

iv   See G. Berger, *Publishing for the People: The Alternative Press, 1980–1999*.

v   ANC Discussion Document 2002. Available at www.anc.org.za.

vi   ANC Media Policy 2007. Available at www.anc.org.za.

vii Quoted in *Business Day*, 9 April 2010, p.11.

viii Joel Netshitenzhe, Speech to Sanef, Johannesburg, 13 August 2004.

ix   ANC Media Freedom Day Statement, 2005. Available at www.anc.org.za.

x   In 2008, the SABC still enjoyed 53% of all television advertising revenue and
     42% of all radio advertising revenue.

xi   "Working together, we can do more" was their slogan.

xii ANC, Resolutions of the 52nd National Conference, Polokwane, 16-20
     December 2007. Available from www.anc.org.za.

xiii Interestingly, this was often the pattern under apartheid: government would
     make threats and the media would respond by tightening their self-regulation,
     leading to a climate of self-censorship.

xiv *Sunday Times* 8 August 2010, p10

xv   "Media Transformation, Ownership and Diversity", an NGC 2010 discussion
     document, available at www.anc.org.za.

xvi C. Lewis, *The Growing Importance of Non-Profit Journalism*, 2006.

xvii France developed an 800 million euro scheme to support subscriptions for
     young people, and Italy ploughed about 700 million euros into newspapers.

xviii www.editorsweblog.com.

xix Speech to the International Federation of Newspaper Publishers' conference,
     Prague, 1992, available at http://www.anc.org.za/show.php?include=docs/
     sp/1992/sp0526.html.

PART ONE

Shady Characters

Chapter 1

Exposed – SA's Madoff: The Barry Tannenbaum Story

Rob Rose

Financial Mail / Sunday Times

Winner of the 2009 Taco Kuiper Award for Investigative Journalism

Rob Rose heard a story through the grapevine of his business contacts that he thought was too ludicrous to be true: some of South Africa's wealthiest and most respected businessmen were being ripped off to the tune of billions of rand by South Africa's very own Madoff.

Investment adviser Bernie Madoff fleeced his American clients to the tune of $18 billion, through a Ponzi scheme – robbing Peter to pay Paul – and is now in prison. Rose believed he had found a similar scheme in South Africa, operated by Barry Tannenbaum.

"When I arrived at an investors' meeting at law firm Routledge Modise and saw 300 grim people who all believed they were part of a tiny investment group and were slowly grasping that they'd been conned, it was quite a bizarre moment that echoed what I had read of Madoff's investors," says Rose.

E-mails, invoices, prospectuses and other documents corroborated this unlikely story. To verify that some were actually forgeries used to dupe investors he took each document to the relevant institution – from the SA Reserve Bank to pharmaceutical firms like Aspen Pharmacare and Adcock Ingram.

Then he interviewed 30 investors, including top names like former Pick n Pay boss Sean Summers, ex-Bond Exchange CEO Tom Lawless and stockbrokers like Howard Lowenthal, to get a sense of how the scheme worked.

When the story finally hit the news-stands it made the headlines and was seized upon by newspapers, television and radio stations. But Rose was cautious, only claiming what he was sure he could prove – that R2 billion had gone missing. Since then finance minister Pravin Gordhan has put the figure at R12.5 billion.

Over the year 16 articles appeared – five are reproduced here. The story has travelled the world, with chief executives in London, the US and Australia exposed as investors. Arrest warrants have been issued for Barry Tannenbaum (now in hiding on Australia's Gold Coast) and lawyer Dean Rees, who was the scheme's agent and is now living in Switzerland.

The Taco Kuiper Award judges said this of the entry: "Financial journalists have been criticised in the last couple of years for the stories they missed. Rob came through with a really good tale, carefully pieced together and well told, exposing a major fraudster. Tannenbaum might have fooled some of South Africa's best-known investors, but not Rob Rose."

An interesting footnote, as Rose tells it, is that when he first heard the story, he googled Barry Tannenbaum to find out more. There was nothing. By early 2010 there were 932 000 results for "Barry Tannenbaum latest".

Rob Rose joined the *Sunday Times*' investigations team in 2009 and is the winner of the 2009 Taco Kuiper Award for Investigative Journalism. In 2010 he was also named Financial Journalist of the Year in the Sanlam Awards, won the overall award at the Citadel financial journalism awards, and was named Telkom business journalist of the year. He has a law degree but lasted only two weeks as an articled clerk before swapping law for journalism. He joined *Business Day* in 2002, before moving to *Financial Mail* magazine.

Duped

12 *June*

It was a meeting that could have taken place six months ago in a Manhattan law firm, as Bernard Madoff's shattered investors bemoaned their gullibility and contemplated how to recoup the millions they had sluiced into Madoff's Ponzi scheme.

But instead, it was 300 investors jostling for standing room in the auditorium of Sandton law firm Routledge Modise. And instead of Madoff, the man at the centre of arguably SA's largest-ever Ponzi scheme is Barry Tannenbaum, a 43-year-old South African who lives in Sydney's

St Ives suburb in Australia. With nearly R2bn already unaccounted for, and speculation that sums of up to R15bn are involved, Tannenbaum's investment scheme looks set to become SA's largest corporate scandal, dwarfing Fidentia and Masterbond.

Among those drawn into the scheme are former Pick n Pay boss Sean Summers, ex-Bond Exchange CEO Tom Lawless and former JSE chair Norman Lowenthal. At the same time, blue-chip JSE firms Adcock Ingram and Aspen Pharmacare have been dragged into Tannenbaum's slipstream, even though the CEOs – Jonathan Louw and Stephen Saad – did not invest personally.

The scale of losses is not yet clear: by Friday, the debtors' book (against which Tannenbaum "borrowed" from investors) officially stood at R1.76bn. The *FM* understands at least 400 investors – in SA and countries like the US and Australia – are involved. Among other investors, Qatar-based real estate company Barwa is said to have negotiated to invest $30m, and unconfirmed reports suggest one US-based lawyer entrusted more than $100m to Tannenbaum.

Warren Drue, an attorney at Routledge Modise who invested in the scheme, declared at last week's meeting: "We've all been devastated … it appears there was no fundamental business, so the money we've invested must be gone."

Another investor confessed: "I feel violated and stupid."

Though investors are now forming a committee to probe what happened, evidence gathered by the *FM* points to Tannenbaum's scheme as an old-school Ponzi scheme as used by Madoff. The US Securities and Exchange Commission defines Ponzi schemes as a pyramid scheme which "robs Peter to pay Paul". With the promise of stratospheric returns as bait, the scheme takes money from new investors and uses it to pay earlier investors. When no more new recruits are found, it collapses.

Here, Tannenbaum persuaded people to invest in his companies – Frankel International and Frankel Chemicals – by offering prodigious returns of up to 216% a year. Investors, who typically heard about the scheme from "friends", would transfer cash to Tannenbaum's RMB Private Bank account, believing it would be used in a legitimate business, and they'd be paid back a few months later. It worked fine, until all payments stopped last month.

Who is Barry?

Schooled in Krugersdorp, he obtained a BSc degree from Wits in 1987. Following a stint in the army, he worked as an advertising manager for Times Media (now Avusa) and joined EuroChemicals (which trades as Frankel Chemicals) in 1992. He purchased it in 1998, and it is now 100% owned through the Frankel Trust of which Tannenbaum is the sole beneficiary. Married with two children, he lives in St Ives in Sydney, Australia, but travels to SA frequently.

Tannenbaum, whose father was one of the founding Adcock Ingram shareholders, punted his scheme as a legitimate business buying APIs (active pharmaceutical ingredients) from foreign countries, which he then on-sold to generic drug makers like Aspen, Adcock and Novartis to make antiretroviral drugs.

Rather than the red tape involved with borrowing from banks, Tannenbaum said he would "borrow" the funds to buy APIs from investors, who would be paid handsome returns for deals typically lasting a few months. It was a scheme that extended beyond SA's borders, with Frankel having operations in Germany, Brazil, Australia and India.

But the actual business was a fraud. The *FM* is in possession of many documents which show the largest "purchase orders", meant to prove there was a pipeline of cash to repay investors, were forged. Also, auditors have confirmed the financial accounts of Tannenbaum's companies had been "altered and falsified".

For example, Tannenbaum produced documents allegedly showing incoming cash flows, such as one supposedly signed by Aspen's Bert Marais confirming that "an amount of R140m will be paid to [Tannenbaum's] nominated account, ANZ Bank Australia on May 18 2009". But these were also forged.

In response to queries by the *FM* and investors, Aspen confirmed that "the signature on the letter is false, together with the company letterhead".

Equally, an Aspen purchase order for five medical ingredients, including antiretroviral drug nevirapine, supposedly confirmed on an Aspen letterhead on December 4 that the medical company owed Frankel Chemicals R160m.

Yet, Aspen legal head Pieter van der Sandt describes this, and another purchase order for R8.5m in February, as a forgery. "Aspen does not order any of the chemicals as described ... in addition, there are subtle differences in the styling of the forged documents and an authentic Aspen purchase order."

This is crucial, considering Frankel's documents listed Aspen as its largest client for 2008, having bought R2.5bn worth of medical supplies. Sandoz Novartis was second, with orders allegedly totalling R351m, Revlon with R342m and Adcock Ingram with R178.4m.

In an e-mail in the *FM*'s possession, in March Tannenbaum told one of his business partners that "Aspen holds the largest value in my book, and that is based purely on the antiretrovirals and other such tender items that they [*sic*] rely on funding from the World Health Organization and government".

Yet Van der Sandt confirms that "there are no monies due and payable to Frankel Chemicals by Aspen Pharmacare". Aspen had apparently done some business with Tannenbaum in the past, buying coal tar prepared and betamethasone sodium phosphate from Frankel – but nothing near the amount claimed.

And it wasn't just Aspen that got entangled in this web of deceit. The *FM* obtained a purchase order, dated 12 March 2008, on an Adcock Ingram letterhead supposedly signed by an employee. This apparently confirmed that Adcock owed Tannenbaum and Frankel Chemicals R15.1m for a consignment of diphenhydramine (a potent antihistamine). Adcock CEO Louw confirmed to the *FM* this was false. "We don't even procure diphenhydramine for our critical care business."

Like Aspen, Adcock did some small business with Frankel. But, says Louw: "The numbers for those deals are less than R1.3m and nothing like the numbers on that purchase order."

It was the same story when the *FM* provided Novartis-Sandoz with three purchase orders between March 2008 and January 2009 for erthromycin phthalate and metformin. Sandoz SA has confirmed that the three orders were not issued by the company. "These purchase orders have been falsified. Sandoz will be investigating this matter further and will manage this accordingly."

It seems crime-fighting authorities may have been watching Tannenbaum for some time, but haven't acted. Millions in investor payments passed through his account at RMB Private Bank, which falls under First National Bank.

It is understood that in 2007, RMB Private Bank reported these transactions as "suspicious" to the Financial Intelligence Centre (FIC), a body tasked with cracking down on money laundering. The FIC told the *FM* it was "aware of the case, and the FIC is working with relevant law enforcement agencies on it".

While this appears to indicate that Tannenbaum's scheme is a fraud, some of the investors can't reconcile this with the person they knew – a story that resonates with many of Madoff's victims.

Wayne Gadden, investor and long-time friend, doesn't believe Tannenbaum orchestrated the scheme. "Barry's a great human being. He lives in a modest home and he's so trusting: if you tell him it's raining outside, he won't even go to the window to check. I just can't fathom that he was involved in this," he says.

Accountant Howard Lowenthal, who invested in Tannenbaum's scheme, told the *FM*: "Over the past few weeks, Barry and I have been in e-mail contact and he has continually said, 'Sorry about the mess, I'm busy raising money so please be patient.' Now I believe we've lost part of our capital."

Another Johannesburg businessman says: "Up until last week, my head was telling me it would never work, but my heart was saying please let it work. I had R3.2m invested with him after two years, even selling part of my business to raise the cash. Now I feel stupid. It's our life savings and wasn't easy to accumulate."

How did Tannenbaum get away with it? Partly because the scheme worked successfully for a while. People who invested were either paid back large returns or believed their money was safe with him and being "rolled" into new investments. He was a guy people trusted.

But in recent months, those asking to be repaid were met with excuses. In one e-mail, Tannenbaum explains the delay in getting funds from an overseas bank: "They wrote the incorrect date! Will get the new one this morning … It was meant to be May 5 2009. I am on it … never seems to end."

Yet the scheme was running at full tilt until a few days ago. One Johannesburg-based financier says: "As recently as 10 days ago, they were trying to get me to invest R3m, but it sounded like it was too good to be true, so I knew trouble was coming and I rejected the offer."

The *FM* has communicated with Tannenbaum in Australia over the past week and he has admitted to a degree of wrongdoing in telephonic conversations and on e-mail. "The debtors' book was overstated," he concedes, "but I have never said the Aspen invoices are frauds."

But when questioned about how this "overstatement" happened,

Tannenbaum promised to respond but hadn't done so at the time of going to print. One e-mail he sent to the *FM* said: "Been in meetings all day with very important guys. Looks like I'm winning the race!"

Tannenbaum hinted that "other parties" had orchestrated this situation, insinuating that lawyer Dean Rees was involved. But when asked to provide specifics, he was vague. "I am not sure who the responsible parties are, but intend finding out." Without admitting guilt, he adds: "If I go down, [Rees] is going with me." But then backtracks: "I deny the truth of the aspersions that have been levelled against me and the fanciful allegations."

To many investors, Rees is the man most under suspicion. Tannenbaum's brochures said Rees "has been involved in the business relationship with Frankel for the last 3½ years". Rees owns 100% of Abated Investments, which secures funding for Frankel Chemicals … via its SA subsidiary Suscito Investments.

"Frankel has appointed Abated Investments as its global partner in sourcing of funds and logistical services in securing funding for its ongoing deals," the brochures say. Rees owned 100% of Abated Investments (which is registered in the British Virgin Islands) through Madmacks Investments.

It was Rees who, speaking as the voice of Frankel International, assumed an increasingly large role in the days leading up to the scheme's apparent collapse.

On 23 May, Rees wrote to investors, saying there had been "unexpected delays" in the funds due to be disbursed as one of the banks was unhappy with the structure used to transfer funds into SA. "Due to the delays and late payments, I've been appointed as interim chief operating officer of [the wider] Frankel Group … [as] we feel it is necessary that someone is appointed to consider the interests of the investors, as I represent you in my capacity as an attorney."

On 28 May, Rees said some investors had formed a committee to audit and "reconcile debtors' books, based upon irregularities that came to light". He said Deloitte had been appointed to assist.

On 2 June, Rees wrote another letter, saying his status as chief operating officer had been "revoked", and Deloitte was prevented from gaining access. He said some debtors told him that purchase orders were "forged".

But at the investor meeting at Routledge Modise, Rees came under fire. One investor said: "I wrote to Dean three months ago, saying the pharmaceutical companies don't unilaterally extend credit terms [as

Tannenbaum suggested]. I didn't get a response."

Warren Goldblatt, head of SA's only private law enforcement agency, Specialised Services Group, which represents one of the investors, raised concerns about Rees's involvement. "I don't think Dean is in a position to spearhead this on behalf of investors … [he] emphatically informed us that [he] had successfully concluded two trades in Hong Kong and the funds would be available shortly."

Goldblatt said Rees may have benefited as he was central to Tannenbaum's operations and his involvement as the "white knight" was a conflict of interest.

However, attorney Drue defended him: "This is not a thing about Rees. Dean came forward as a white knight."

Though Rees describes himself as "an attorney acting for the investor base", he also earned "a large amount" in commissions for introducing investors. He and Darryl Leigh were allegedly paid 6% of amount invested.

But Rees denies he had any role in the scheme. "I'm as shocked as anyone by this," he told the *FM*. "If I believed it was a scam, why would I take two of my cars [Ferraris] and give them to my friends? Why would I put my own money into this?" Rees says he wrote off R7m, which he invested in the scheme, and having moved his family to Switzerland, "I now have to go back to SA."

Yet, as the Ferraris attest, Rees leads a lavish lifestyle, leading people to question where he gets the funds. "It's not about my lavish lifestyle," he says, "it's about getting down to brass tacks: it's about the fact that what appear to be genuine orders were actually fraudulent."

But Rees's Suscito Investments was used as a conduit for payments to investors. His Investec bank account statements, extracted from a due diligence report by PricewaterhouseCoopers (PwC), confirm that more than R152m moved through his various accounts between July 2007 and April 2008. This money was then paid out of Rees's accounts through either his trust account or Suscito.

The third player is 59-year-old retired advocate Darryl Leigh. As investor stories show, Leigh introduced a number of investors to Tannenbaum. He and Tannenbaum had other business links too: companies' office records show he and Tannenbaum are directors of a close corporation, Tann-Leigh Properties.

Leigh refused to answer the *FM*'s questions. "You're obviously not hearing me. At this stage, I'm not saying anything."

Like Rees, his lavish lifestyle has attracted attention. In March, Leigh's Lamborghini LP640 Roadster was involved in an incident in which the head of marketing for Ericsson, Jan Embro, died in his Ultima GTR. Newspapers reported that police were probing whether Leigh and Embro "were dicing" with each other.

If Tannenbaum's scheme relied on forged purchase orders and free marketing from participants, investors weren't helped by the fact that independent sources gave it a clean bill of health. The *FM* is in possession of a confidential report by PwC prepared in September to provide an assurance to one of Tannenbaum's funders.

PwC was asked to check a few things: first, that raw materials purchases were actually taking place and above board; and second, that funds were properly transferred between the Investec Private Bank accounts of Tannenbaum and Rees.

It wasn't a proper audit, but PwC did find a flaming red flag. Though it traced about R200m moving between Tannenbaum and Rees's accounts, PwC said: "This is substantially less than the indicated transaction values of the raw materials [bought]." PwC was told this was because "investment returns [were being] transferred while investment capital amounts are not transferred".

EuroChemicals (another name for Frankel Chemicals) also produced audited financials for the year to February 2007, which would have given investors some comfort. Auditors IAPA signed off the accounts, saying they "present fairly, in all material respects, the financial position of the company". These financials, in the *FM*'s possession, said Frankel was owed R566m in "trade and other receivables", had cash of R434m and inventories of R125m. At that stage, EuroChemicals apparently owed shareholders R693m.

But IAPA confirmed to the *FM* that "those financials have been altered, falsified and are incomplete". This "irregularity" was reported to the Independent Regulatory Board for Auditors.

In cases like this, people ask why the investment regulator, the Financial Services Board (FSB), didn't intervene. But neither Frankel nor Tannenbaum was registered with the FSB, as these entities just took "loans". FSB spokesman Russel Michaels says: "In a case like this, we can't do much other than refer this to the police commercial crimes unit."

Tannenbaum is likely to face fraud charges as it is believed several investors have spoken to the SA Police Service's commercial crimes unit. A website has also been set up for investors to get information.

Goldblatt says the solution is to apply urgently to court to sequestrate Tannenbaum's estate and liquidate his companies, allowing a liquidator access to books and bank accounts. "The liquidator may then be in a position to demand repayment of any benefit that any investor may have received."

The Tannenbaum revelations are likely to blow a hole through an SA business environment whose decision-makers are renowned for conservatism and sound judgment. In the same way it shocked America to learn that Madoff operated a thriving Ponzi scheme, Tannenbaum's success in duping SA's wealthy will puncture holes in SA's corporate façade.

Too good to be true

Accuse former Pick n Pay boss Sean Summers of bad judgment, but don't charge him with trying to hide the painful truth about his investment in what could turn out to be SA's biggest Ponzi scheme.

"Yes, I was a participant," says Summers, before adding: "But unlike in the matter of food inflation, we appear to know who the perpetrators are."

And Summers is fortunate in that, while he is believed to have put more than R20m into the scheme, he hasn't lost everything. Mervyn Serebro, the former head of OK Bazaars, told the investor meeting in Sandton, Johannesburg, last week that some of his relatives sold their houses to invest cash with Tannenbaum. Now it appears they've lost it all.

The question is, why did investors get involved in a scheme that clearly was too good to be true? Partly it was exactly because the returns were so good in a recession.

The *FM* has scoured long spreadsheets – apparently Tannenbaum's internal working documents – which contained records of the investments, interest rates, and payouts. This shows that there were at least 100 SA-based investors, some of whom have ploughed up to R9m into the scheme. In addition, certain overseas investors are believed to have put more than R300m into the scheme.

For example, in "deal ARV43" concluded on 15 November 2008, the DWP Trust put in R15m for 95 days. By 20 February this year, the trust was paid back its R15m, plus R3m interest – which works out to an annual interest rate of 76%.

In other deals, investors were paid annualised interest rates of 164%, 111% and even 216% on their investment.

The old cliché about "if it looks too good to be true, it probably is" didn't faze many of the investors. "We were told Frankel Chemicals was a high-margin business," says Howard Lowenthal, an accountant. "There are many lending businesses charging 5% interest a month, and so it seemed we were being paid a similar return for bridging finance. At the time, I thought being paid interest of 12% over three months was high, but not entirely unfeasible," he says. His father, Norman, a former chairman of the JSE, also invested in the scheme.

So what is the most likely outcome for investors? Under a typical Ponzi scheme, legal experts say, all the participants will need to return everything they got – capital and interest. This will then be divided between the participants. Either way, a protracted legal wrangle awaits the unfortunate investors, some of whom share their stories above.

It may be of little solace to Tannenbaum's investors to be told that they need not think of themselves as being "stupid" if the investment seemed legitimate.

University of Colorado psychiatry professor Stephen Greenspan recently wrote a book, *Annals of Gullibility*, about why people invest in Ponzi schemes. Speaking to the *FM* this week, Greenspan says: "The real problem is with those people who put 100% of their [funds] into these schemes."

His argument is that the real mistake is in throwing caution to the wind, like those investors who put every last cent with Madoff – and with Tannenbaum. Ironically, Greenspan lost a chunk of his own savings when Madoff's Ponzi scheme was exposed. "I invested in Madoff through a hedge fund, and when you're investing through a hedge fund that is supposedly reputable, you have a right to expect those people to look out for you," he says.

In this case, not only was Tannenbaum's scheme not regulated by the Financial Services Board, but the investment scheme relied heavily on trust. Those with all their eggs in that basket can't be too surprised to see the yolk dripping out.

Claims and Counterclaims   *19 June*

The *FM* has obtained a letter that was purportedly sent from the Reserve Bank to First National Bank (FNB) on 15 May 2009. It discusses how an application to have funds released to a Hong Kong bank account was "being fast tracked and should be released within the next four working days".

This letter was shown to Qatar-listed real estate company Barwa, and was meant to confirm a payment from Aspen. Reliable sources confirm Barwa put US$30.3m into Frankel in two tranches for two specific transactions. The letter was used to show that the purchase of drugs overseas was legitimate. When contacted in Qatar, Barwa refused to comment.

But when the *FM* showed this document to the Reserve Bank spokeswoman, Samantha Henkeman, she said: "It is our letterhead and it is the signature of [former exchange control head] Alick Bruce-Brand, but this was cut and pasted from another document. The reference numbers aren't ours and we don't deal with individual bank branches."

For one thing, the document supposedly dates from May, yet Bruce-Brand retired at the end of October.

Who forged the documents, and who exactly is responsible for what appears to be SA's biggest financial scam? Fingers are being pointed at Tannenbaum as well as at attorney Dean Rees (who was paid commission for introducing investors to the scheme).

At his Rivonia office last week, Rees said Tannenbaum admitted the Aspen orders were forgeries. "This was during a telephone conference call [on 28 May] with me, James Patterson [who invested through Frankel's international business] and one of my employees."

Contacted in France, Patterson confirmed this version of events: "We had a conference call with Barry, and he admitted that the invoices were forgeries." Patterson said Tannenbaum did not reveal why the invoices were forged, nor the extent of the fraud.

Rees's employee, who does not want to be named but participated in that call, also said: "Barry said the first Aspen invoices were forged, and the debtors book wasn't what he showed us."

Though these claims look bad for Tannenbaum, this is possibly evidence from parties with interests to protect. It is likely to come down to finger-pointing, with Tannenbaum blaming Rees for conspiring to set him up as the fall guy.

When asked about this by the *FM* last week, Tannenbaum denied saying the Aspen invoices were forged, but admitted the debtors book was "overstated". He did not explain how.

Darryl Ackerman, Tannenbaum's attorney, arrived back in SA on Sunday after days of poring over documents. "What I've seen and what I've heard reaffirm that Barry is innocent," he said. When asked why Tannenbaum hadn't presented any evidence that he'd been set up, Ackerman said: "I don't think people are interested in the truth."

Despite the fact that Rees returned from London last week, he is still under suspicion, partly because of his flashy lifestyle.

Investor Christopher Leppan, who had Tannenbaum's SA estate sequestrated last week, wrote in an affidavit: "I am reliably informed that Rees currently rents a property in Zurich, Switzerland, at a cost of R1m/month, and owns several Ferrari sports vehicles as well as a Mercedes [McLaren] super sports car, with a value in excess of R18m in Switzerland." Leppan adds that Rees also lives in a R60m property in Johannesburg, and questions where he got the money for this.

Rees dismisses these claims: "I was independently wealthy before this scheme arose, due to property deals. The house in Johannesburg he refers to has a bond over it, and I personally put about R3m of my own cash into Frankel."

He is adamant that he was an unwitting pawn of Tannenbaum, and produces an e-mail to substantiate this statement.

That e-mail, ostensibly from Tannenbaum to Rees on Thursday 28 May, apparently makes some damning admissions. According to it, Tannenbaum says: "The reality is that the book debt of Frankel Chemicals cannot survive scrutiny on the basis of what has been represented … the investor funds have flowed to building up Frankel International. It is for this reason that you cannot allow an audit into Frankel SA's books: that is not where the solution or payment for investors sits."

Tannenbaum writes there is a need for an "audit process", and to "negotiate amounts to be paid and the timeline of each investor … It is probably a good time to come clean, and move forward together without any hidden agendas and secrets," he says.

Without conceding that Tannenbaum was in fact the author of that communication, Ackerman told the *FM* that "in the fullness of time, you'll understand the thinking and reasoning for that e-mail".

Ponzi Scheme:
The Dirty E-mail Trail

In a 42-page affidavit admitted to a London court, lawyer Dean Rees has painted a damning picture of how Barry Tannenbaum set up his South African Ponzi scheme.

The Rees papers suggest that investors may have pumped R3bn into the scheme – far more than the R2bn a government task team estimated.

Tannenbaum's Frankel Chemicals, which promised investors returns of more than 200% for financing the trade of pharmaceutical ingredients to buyers like Aspen and Adcock Ingram based on forged invoices, is the largest investment scam uncovered in SA.

Rees's assets were frozen by UK High Court judge Andrew Smith on 22 June. Now Rees is asking that the freezing order be dismissed, saying he stands to lose $75m.

In his affidavit, Rees rounded on Tannenbaum, calling him a "self-confessed fraudster and demonstrable liar" who is trying to "extricate himself from a massive fraud by seeking to lay blame on [me]". He said he too was duped by Tannenbaum and "I have lost a considerable amount of money".

Specifically, Rees rejected an affidavit signed by Tannenbaum in which he admitted "a number of documents including invoices, bills of lading and e-mails were altered or fabricated by me", but said this was done "with the active encouragement and full knowledge of Dean Rees".

Tannenbaum's affidavit was used by Qatari investor Barwa, which invested R250m with Frankel, to obtain the freezing order against Rees.

Rees said the freezing order means he cannot pay mortgage bonds of R380 000 on seven properties in South Africa.

This will ring hollow with angry investors who saw evidence of Rees's flashy lifestyle on the Facebook website, which boasted pictures of him driving a Ferrari and travelling in a private jet.

Barwa has also produced damning e-mails which it said shows that Rees and Tannenbaum colluded to create fictional invoices.

In an e-mail exchange on 31 March, Rees wrote to Tannenbaum: "Hi mate, hope all OK. I need an order and invoice on a 60-day payment basis for $3.1m. Can you send to me today? Just doing admin."

Tannenbaum responded: "I assume invoice value around 3.1m? South African customer, or can it be South American? No problem, cheers mate."

Rees replied: "Either mate."

But Rees denied that this was a request for Tannenbaum to "create a fictitious order", saying he simply received money from investors who wanted a return over 60 days.

"What I was asking for from Mr Tannenbaum was an order that would match such an investment – it did not matter where the order emanated from, but what was important was to obtain an order that matched the investment criteria."

He said he "did not vet and analyse the documentation pertaining to every order" as there were too many orders.

The number of investors grew so fast that, in some cases, Rees said, "I had available investors' money without Tannenbaum having arranged a specific trade, and in those circumstances I would have to ask him to undertake a particular trade to meet the investors' investment criteria."

Rees's court papers confirmed that Nick Pagden, current chairman of banking at Citigroup's South African office, also invested with Tannenbaum. Of the $30.3m paid by Barwa to Tannenbaum, a large chunk went to repay existing investors, including $2.6m directly into Pagden's bank account.

This adds to the list of wealthy South Africans stung by the scheme. The court papers reveal that one of the world's biggest hedge funds came close to being scammed too.

Rees said Och–Ziff, the New York Stock Exchange-listed company with assets of more than $20bn, negotiated with him "with a view to entering into an ongoing financing arrangement". But when the markets turned, Och–Ziff pulled the plug on the deal.

In his papers, Rees relied on an e-mail "confession" from Tannenbaum on 28 May. In it, Tannenbaum wrote: "I cannot carry on like this" and "it is probably a good time to come clean and move forward without any hidden agendas and secrets". Tannenbaum added that "the reality is that the book debt of Frankel Chemicals cannot survive scrutiny on the basis of what has been represented".

But many investors believe Rees was integral to the scheme.

In July, orthopaedic surgeon Julius Preddy, who invested R875 020 in Tannenbaum's scheme, applied to the South Gauteng High Court for Rees's sequestration.

In Preddy's court papers, he said Rees was a "bona fide agent" of Tannenbaum who earned more than R180m in commissions "out of the fraudulent scheme".

Preddy said Rees bought a number of expensive assets with the commissions he earned, including a property in Switzerland, several Ferraris and a collection of watches worth more than R2.5m.

Preddy said Rees bought the Swiss house "because he knew that the scheme would eventually collapse ... and he wanted to protect himself from the investors in the scheme by relocating to Switzerland, which is known to be a tax haven for wrongdoers".

In his new papers, Rees admitted receiving money: "My clients were at all times aware that I charged a fee for representing them, introducing them to these transactions and arranging for the performance of the administrative functions."

Though Tannenbaum and Rees are now blaming each other, the relationship was once close.

In an e-mail to Rees on 8 December last year, Tannenbaum said Rees was to be his "main partner".

"I trust you equally with my life and am very comfortable with how our relationship has progressed over the last two years."

Tannenbaum: Rees to Blame   16 August

Barry Tannenbaum, the man accused of running South Africa's biggest investment scam, said he "stands by" his accusation that lawyer Dean Rees was his accomplice in an audacious R250m fraud against Qatari property company Barwa.

The high-living Rees claims he was also duped by Tannenbaum.

However, a scathing judgment this week in the UK's Royal Courts of Justice by Justice David Steele dismantled Rees's claim to being a Tannenbaum victim.

It is the first time a court has made a finding on responsibility for the scam.

Steele said he was "satisfied that there is a good, arguable case that Mr Rees was a party – and a successful party – to the conspiracy to defraud Barwa".

He said it is clear Rees was "prima facie involved in that fraud, was in receipt of substantial sums [from Barwa] and that those monies were then distributed through various entities in which Mr Rees had an interest".

The court case stemmed from Rees's bid to have a worldwide freezing order on his assets – obtained by Barwa in July – dismissed. Rees argued that he has no assets in the UK.

Steele, despite his pointed comments about Rees' involvement, said that "with some regret, I have come to the conclusion that it is not appropriate to continue this worldwide freezing order".

However, he did agree with Barwa that because Rees has an "ill-defined" residence – with houses in Switzerland and Johannesburg – there is a "real risk" that assets will be sold.

The victory for Rees is bittersweet as the judge's comments about his involvement will probably be used in other court applications against him.

Barwa will appeal the ruling, so the freezing order stays in place for at least 21 days. And it is likely Barwa will now launch a court action in South Africa, where Rees has at least seven properties and various businesses.

In the court hearing, damning evidence of the investment scheme emerged.

In an unsigned affidavit, Tannenbaum reported a telephone conversation in which Rees allegedly asked how to get round the problem of Barwa not transferring cash until it knew pharmaceuticals had been bought for a specific deal.

Tannenbaum answered: "We can just tell them we've paid."

Rees replied: "They'll want documentation, just get something going."

Rees's lawyer said this proves nothing, as the conversations are based on the word of "a self-confessed fraudster".

Though $12.7m of the $31.3m paid to Tannenbaum's companies by Barwa went to Rees, he argued that this "does not in any way show or prove that Mr Rees had knowledge of the fraud".

The London court case seemed to confirm that Tannenbaum's scheme – at least when it came to Barwa – was a classic Ponzi scheme in which "Peter was robbed to pay Paul".

Barwa lent $31.3m to Tannenbaum's company Frankel International, believing the cash would be used to buy pharmaceuticals for a specific deal with Aspen Pharmacare and Pharma-Q.

But, as Steele asked in court, "How is it that the monies ... do not go to pharmaceutical companies but to Mr Rees?"

Rees's lawyer said this was because the pharmaceuticals had already been bought using other money, so Barwa's cash was used to repay investors owed cash.

But the Aspen and Pharma-Q deal never proceeded and Tannenbaum forged invoices which he showed to Barwa.

The issue is who is responsible.

In a signed affidavit Tannenbaum confessed that "a number of documents including invoices, bills of lading and e-mails were altered or fabricated by me". But he also said this was done "with the active encouragement and full knowledge of Dean Rees".

Rees responded in his papers that Tannenbaum was a "self-confessed fraudster and demonstrable liar" who is trying to "extricate himself from a massive fraud by seeking to lay blame on [me]".

This week, Tannenbaum told *Business Times* that Rees did not tell the truth in his legal papers.

He said the reason he did not respond to Rees's claims was because, "strangely and inexplicably", he was not allowed a copy of the court papers.

While the legal papers were given to his lawyer, Tannenbaum said this was "on the strict understanding that he was prohibited from providing me with a [copy] so that I could carefully work through it to answer all the allegations.

"It was on the strength of allegations by me, contrary to those which Rees now makes, that a freezing order [against him] was granted in the first place," he says.

He said he had been "tried and pilloried in the media", which was not the right forum "to debate all the complex issues".

With Barwa's action in the UK thwarted, the battleground is set to shift to SA.

Rees – against whom two sets of criminal charges have already been laid in South Africa – is now in the spotlight.

Lawyer Loses $825m
in SA's Biggest Ponzi Scam

1 November

Meir Levin, a New York-based South African lawyer, is "owed" $825m by the man dubbed South Africa's Bernie Madoff: Barry Tannenbaum.

Levin, who emigrated to the US 20 years ago, has offered to meet investigators in South Africa to help bring Tannenbaum to book.

And in a further twist it has emerged that Tannenbaum's brother Michael – the finance director of a London-listed property company – was sucked into the fraud. Michael Tannenbaum provided guarantees to Levin, before he, too, was allegedly conned by his brother. Michael claims his signature was forged.

Levin first invested $425 000 in Tannenbaum's business – supposedly buying "medical ingredients" to be sold on to pharmaceutical firms – in August 2004. Though he was repaid with interest, Levin, like many investors, kept "rolling" this cash into new investments.

Now, a government task team believes that when Tannenbaum's scheme was exposed in June as SA's biggest investment scam, Levin was owed around $825m (R6bn), including "interest", making him the biggest investor, when the bubble burst.

This has been confirmed by insiders in the criminal investigation and Tannenbaum's associates.

Rumours of Levin's exposure had circulated for months, but phone calls and e-mails to his Staten Island house by the *Sunday Times* in recent months have gone unanswered.

But Levin's South African advocate, Mannie Witz, said he believed the figure overstates Levin's investment. "We are still quantifying his investment, but he initially invested far less.

"The $825m includes all the interest payments he was owed, so the amount he actually lost was far smaller," Witz added.

He said part of the problem in tracking Levin's investment was that while the initial amounts were transferred through Tannenbaum's South African bank accounts at RMB Private Bank, the largest portion was put through Tannenbaum's Australian bank account.

"Meir has really been devastated by this, so he has offered to come to South Africa to assist the task team to bring Tannenbaum to book," he said.

Finance minister Pravin Gordhan this week put the size of the scheme at R12.5bn – much more than the R1bn lost by investors in Fidentia, or the R900m at LeisureNet.

Gordhan added that warrants of arrest had been issued for Tannenbaum, who lives in the upmarket suburb of St Ives in Sydney, Australia, and lawyer Dean Rees, who is now in Switzerland. The warrants accuse Tannenbaum and Rees of racketeering, money laundering, fraud and theft. Charges of contravening the Banks Act are likely to follow.

Tannenbaum's attorney Darryl Ackerman said: "I know nothing about the arrest warrant, I've heard what everyone else has heard."

However, Willie Hofmeyr, the deputy director of the National Prosecuting Authority, said: "Now that we have the arrest warrant, the police will ask Interpol to list it internationally, and we will apply for Tannenbaum's extradition in Australia."

Levin's lawyer claims that his client only signed for the scheme because of the guarantees provided in 2004 by Michael Tannenbaum, who is the financial director of the London Stock Exchange-listed property firm Westcity. Drawn up by legal firm Edward Nathan Friedland, the guarantees confirmed that Michael Tannenbaum would stand surety for his brother's debts.

Said Witz: "Meir only invested on the basis that Michael Tannenbaum provided those guarantees. When it came to the later investments, Barry delivered the guarantees to Meir himself."

When he was contacted about this by the *Sunday Times* in July, Michael Tannenbaum denied signing any guarantees, specifically for five "investments" made by Levin worth $47m in 2006.

"I didn't sign anything. I don't know whose signature was on those documents, but it wasn't mine," he said.

This week, however, Michael Tannenbaum admitted to the *Sunday Times* that he did sign "certain guarantees".

"Many years ago, Barry asked me to give one, perhaps a couple, of modest personal guarantees in respect of Levin's loans, as part of the company's expansion. I did this in good faith, and was told at the time that the loans were repaid and the guarantees fell away," he said.

But Michael Tannenbaum said he discovered in recent months that more "guarantees" were given in his name to Levin. "It is obvious that the signatures on these documents are not mine, and bear no relation to my signature," he said. This suggests he was conned by his brother.

Chapter 2

Tearful Niehaus Admits Fraud

Pearlie Joubert
Mail & Guardian

In early 2009 a former colleague told Pearlie Joubert that Carl Niehaus owed him some money, around R2000. It was a relatively small sum for a man who was then the chief spokesperson for the ANC, but he apparently seemed reluctant to pay the money back.

A week later, unprompted, another friend told Pearlie of more money owed. This time the sum was much greater, and not only was there a reluctance to pay it back, but Niehaus was refusing to take any calls about it.

Pearlie was intrigued. But those two snippets of information led her to a story she could hardly have guessed at. For three weeks she spoke to former employers, colleagues and comrades of Carl Niehaus. She asked him directly for his CV – and got a rebuff.

Gradually a story emerged of this much-respected ANC representative and a trail of serious debt and deception. Her first significant breakthrough was getting the detail of Niehaus's money borrowing from the Rhema Church. Her first contact said he had left "owing a bit of money". More digging, and this "bit of money" turned into R1m (the figure she quotes in the published article) but eventually became more than R4m.

Niehaus's dealings with the Rhema Church, and with the Gauteng Economic Development Agency, where he forged signatures to raise more money for himself, turned the initial bit of gossip into a really damning story. Except that no one would go on the record.

"Four days before deadline I still didn't have a single person on the record," says Pearlie. Her sources were heavily involved in ANC politics and influential captains of industry. They were very reluctant to speak publicly against the spokesperson for the ANC.

She had enough to publish, albeit a story littered with "alleged" and "according to sources".

"I had known Niehaus since I interviewed him and his wife on their release from prison in March 1991 [having served seven years for underground ANC activities]. I admired him. He was a hero in my world.

"Our professional and friendly relationship stretched over many years, which made this story difficult for me. I sent him an e-mail, with 15 questions, and gave him 24 hours to respond."

Her decision to confront Niehaus paid off. He phoned her and agreed to meet.

"It was almost unbearable." He burst into tears. "Niehaus confessed to all that I wrote." There were no challenges to the honesty, accuracy or fairness of the story. As the award judges said: "This was perhaps the first of the lifestyle audits of prominent politicians, conducted by the media when the authorities have failed to do it."

On Tuesday 17 February the ANC announced that Carl Niehaus had resigned.

Pearlie Joubert works for the *Mail & Guardian* in their Cape Town office as part of their investigative unit. She started working as a journalist in 1989 at the *Vrye Weekblad* newspaper. Shortly before its closure in 1992, she moved into television, spending 12 years as a researcher, producer and director of documentary films. She covered the arrival and withdrawal of the American marines and United Nations troops in Somalia, genocide in Rwanda, and South African involvement in Angola, and reported from Zimbabwe and Botswana for a variety of news outlets, including Independent Television News (ITN), Channel Four and Sky. She joined the *Mail & Guardian* in 2006.

Tearful Niehaus Admits Fraud   *13 February*

He has been entrusted by the ANC with the strategic job of spokesperson. But Carl Niehaus has left a broad trail of bad debt and broken promises behind him.

Confronted this week with allegations that he owed hundreds of thousands of rands to politicians and influential businessmen and committed fraud while working for the Gauteng provincial government, a tearful Niehaus admitted that he:

- Forged signatures while he was chief executive of the Gauteng Economic Development Agency (Geda) before resigning in December 2005;

- Borrowed money over a six-year period from some of the brightest stars of the ANC and business galaxy, much of which he has not paid back;

- Asked to be connected to Brett Kebble because he was "desperate for financial help";

- Had to leave a top job at Deloitte & Touche in 2003 after his financial woes became embarrassing;

- Owed the Rhema Church more than R700 000 when he was asked to resign from his post as chief executive and spokesperson by a full board meeting in 2004; and

- Had to repay R24 000 to director-general in the presidency Frank Chikane when he left his job there under a cloud in 2004.

Niehaus, appointed ANC spokesperson in November 2008, also admitted to using the Rhema Church's travel agent to book a holiday for himself and his wife in Zanzibar and to using the presidency's travel agent to book flights and a trip to Durban for his former wife.

But he denied allegations by his co-workers at the time that he intended to pass off the trips as work expenses. He disputed accounts that he left the presidency amid claims of financial impropriety and ran up implausible expense accounts at Deloitte.

Among those he asked for financial assistance from are arts and culture minister Pallo Jordan, ANC empowerment magnates Saki Macozoma, Tokyo Sexwale and Cyril Ramaphosa, Absa chair and former deputy governor of the Reserve Bank Gill Marcus, and mining tycoon Rick Menell.

When powerful friends could not rescue him from what he described as "the devastation of debt", he drifted into seemingly outright criminal conduct.

In 2005, after just seven months as Geda chief executive, responsible for handling millions of rands of transactions, he wrote a fraudulent letter and forged the signatures of then finance minister and now Gauteng premier Paul Mashatile, transport minister Ignatius Jacobs, education minister and now ANC Women's League president Angie Motshekga and agriculture minister Khabisi Mosunkutu.

The letter was intended to secure a loan for Niehaus from a businessman who hoped to use it to ensure favourable treatment from the Gauteng government on property deals.

Niehaus confessed this fraud to Mashatile, who told him to quit or face a disciplinary inquiry. Niehaus resigned on 9 December 2005.

Told this week of a long list of former employers and creditors who told the *Mail & Guardian* about their dealings with him, Niehaus broke down.

"Most of what you've confronted me with is true. I wish it wasn't. I've made massive mistakes and I've disappointed a lot of people terribly. I've no illusions that if you publish this article it will mean the end of my career," he said, weeping.

"I asked people like Saki Macozoma, Cyril Ramaphosa, Tokyo Sexwale, Gill Marcus, Pallo Jordan and Rick Menell to help me financially.

"I was down and out. Some of them gave me money and some didn't. I am terribly indebted. I also received money from Brett Kebble," Niehaus said.

Niehaus said he asked Macozoma to introduce him to Kebble. "I asked for the meeting. Saki was my friend and I asked him to help me out. I asked to be introduced to Kebble and I met him three times.

"Kebble gave me R70 000 for communications work. He still owed me money. I'm paying R100 000 back because I can't fight the liquidators – there was no contract, only a verbal agreement. I can't prove anything and I don't have the money to go to court," he said.

Niehaus is locked in a battle with the ANC's other spin doctor, Jessie Duarte, who is said to be extremely unhappy with the circumstances of his appointment.

Party insiders say he was headhunted for the role by ANC secretary-general Gwede Mantashe, angering Duarte, the incumbent. She is understood to be reluctant to stay on after the elections.

Those who have worked with Niehaus over the past 14 years and lent him cash to fund his and his former wife, Linda Thango's, extravagant lifestyle say they are not surprised things turned sour.

Niehaus has always "over-promised and under-delivered", they say.

Over the past decade he has resigned from most jobs under pressure or earlier than his contract stipulated because of debt or unhappiness with the management of his financial affairs.

Niehaus became a household name when, as an anti-apartheid activist, he was found guilty of high treason and sentenced to 15 years in jail in 1983.

He became Nelson Mandela's spokesperson in 1994 and was then ambassador to the Netherlands.

On his return to South Africa he briefly worked at the NGO Nicro before his relationship with Mandela helped him secure a job at audit firm Deloitte & Touche in Gauteng and in the Netherlands.

While at Deloitte he was embroiled in legal action after failing to honour an offer to purchase an expensive house on Prinzen Gracht, one of Amsterdam's most prestigious addresses. The penalty for cancellation was more than R1m. This debt sent him into a financial tailspin.

"I felt I had to resign because Deloitte have strong ethics around their partners – they must have their financial dealings in order," Niehaus said.

A former partner at Deloitte, who asked not to be named, said Niehaus was "always" in financial crisis and that the Prinzen Gracht débâcle had not led to his ousting.

"He borrowed money from partners at Deloitte. He also asked me for money but I told him I'm not a bank.

"He once booked a helicopter to fly from Sun City to Johannesburg at huge expense. He claimed to have lost his credit cards on at least two occasions [when improper expenses appeared on the statement] and asked people to help him out [with hotel bills]. He also knew somebody in Nedbank who helped him out.

"He insisted on a huge salary – more than others on the same level. We paid him because he promised to bring political work to the company. That didn't materialise."

Another source, also a partner when Niehaus worked at Deloitte, said that when Niehaus resigned, the firm wrote off large sums he still owed.

Chief executive Grant Gelink said: "To the best of my knowledge Niehaus didn't owe Deloitte any money when he left, but I don't know if money was written off. I wasn't CEO at the time."

Niehaus denied owing the company money, adding: "I don't recall ever claiming money from Nedbank because of a stolen card."

On the Sun City helicopter flight he said he had addressed a conference at Kwa Maritane and had to be in Johannesburg an hour later "for the launch of the strategic communications division. The CEO questioned me months later about this expense and accepted my explanation."

He said he had borrowed money only from one Deloitte partner and had "paid it back in full".

Niehaus's financial troubles deepened when he divorced his wife and co-accused in his terrorism trail, Jansie, and married Linda Thango.

Four sources who worked closely with him after 2002 said Thango, a former non-executive director of African Media Entertainment and management consultant, was central to his extravagant lifestyle.

"His wife wanted all the best toys: holidays, jewels, clothes, shoes and shopping, shopping, shopping. Carl got sucked into that lifestyle, loved it and lived way beyond his means," said one of his former ANC bosses.

Others said he had always been attracted to the trappings of wealth, but that Jansie had kept a tight rein on the family finances. Niehaus himself insists that he must take responsibility.

He said: "I never said no [to Linda]. I thought this is the way you keep love – you buy it. I should have been firm and said: 'No more. We can't live like this.' I didn't and I fell into the devastation of debt."

After his departure from Deloitte, Niehaus was "rescued", as one government official put it, in 2004 by a job in the presidency working on celebrations planned for a "decade of democracy".

A top presidency official who oversaw his work said: "We terminated his contract early because he didn't complete the work he was meant to do. He turned out to be inefficient. He himself felt he had to leave – there was no fight."

The official added: "He took his wife to Durban and used the presidency's money to pay for the hotel. We told him that's unauthorised expenditure and you need to pay it back now." Niehaus denies his contract was terminated prematurely, adding that he does not remember the Durban trip.

"I worked there and finished my contract. I was paid a R24 000 advance, which I paid back to Frank Chikane.

"I suppose it's not impossible that I went to Durban during that time, because my wife's mother lived there," he said. After leaving the presidency in mid-2004 Niehaus was appointed Rhema Church chief executive and spokesperson.

He admitted to being asked to leave Rhema after working there for four years "because of a disagreement about the size of my loan with the church, among other things".

Rhema continues to insist that he left amicably and there were no financial irregularities.

"[Church leader] Ray McCauley organised a staff loan for me. They bought me a car and agreed to pay a large amount to [the seller of the Prinzen Gracht house].

"The financial officer and I increased this loan a number of times and Ray was very unhappy because it was not done with his knowledge. I resigned," Niehaus said.

Niehaus also confirmed using Rhema's travel agent to book a holiday in Zanzibar. While employed by the church he bought himself a Porsche and a C-Class Mercedes-Benz.

Rhema gave Niehaus six months to repay R700 000. Mashatile's offer to him to head Geda was, therefore, a lifesaver – which he admits abusing.

On the fraudulent letter in which he forged the signatures of senior Gauteng government officials, he said: "Pierre Swart managed a company called Blue Label, which offered to lend me the money to repay the Rhema debt. I was absolutely desperate, because if I didn't repay it I would've had to sell the townhouse in my wife's name that I had given as surety.

"But there was a hook. In exchange for the loan they wanted a letter committing various provincial ministries to favouring them when they wanted to rent, sell or lease government buildings in the Johannesburg CBD."

Buildings sold with lease agreements in place are worth much more than empty structures, a developer told the *M&G*.

"I was very desperate but what I did was terrible. After I wrote the letter and handed it over, I immediately knew that I had done the worst thing in my life.

"I went to see Mashatile. I confessed that I'm deeply compromised and he was deeply disappointed. I resigned immediately."

Former Gauteng premier and now Congress of the People leader Mbhazima Shilowa confirmed Mashatile told him that Niehaus was asked to leave over "financial impropriety".

Blue Label has major contracts with Vodacom and Telkom. The company made no comment.

Said Niehaus: "The ANC job is a lifesaver for me and things have gone wrong now in a terrible way. I have to be trustworthy to do my job. I live under no illusions about what this article can do to my life. I wish I could turn back the clock."

Chapter 3

The Caster Semenya Saga

Lucky Sindane
Mail & Guardian

It all started when Caster Semenya shattered the world 800 metres record at the Athletics World Championships in Berlin in August 2009. She filled a longstanding desire for the country's athletics bosses to produce an international star, and hers was an heroic narrative: a young woman from a poor rural background shooting to international stardom.

Immediately questions were raised about her gender. The International Association of Athletics Federations (IAAF) and Athletics South Africa (ASA) became involved in a very public who-knew-what-when spat; the South African government and the ANC got involved with suggestions that she was the victim of racism; and a young woman from rural Limpopo found her sexuality headlined across the world.

While ASA were saying publicly no gender-testing had been done before Berlin, Lucky Sindane's well-placed insider and a raft of internal documents showed the complete opposite – that Semenya had indeed been gender-tested in South Africa before she left for Germany.

While ASA president Leonard Chuene had denied she was tested, the *Mail & Guardian* exposé forced his hand – he called a press conference and admitted the opposite. This only fuelled the uproar as powerful political interests moved to protect him.

Eventually South Africa's Olympics governing body Sascoc took charge, suspended Chuene, the ASA board, Chuene's personal assistant Humile Bogatsu, general manager Molatelo Malehopo and events manager Phiwe Mlangeni-Tsholetsane. In their place came an administrator for the bankrupt organisation and an interim board.

Lucky Sindane worked as a sports reporter at the *Mail & Guardian*, writing regularly about football, cricket, athletics and rugby and has kept a close watch on the 2010 World Cup. He was commended in the 2009 and 2010 Mondi Shanduka Newspaper Awards. In 2010 he moved to the Department of Environmental Affairs.

ASA's Tall Tales

An exchange of e-mails between the doctor of the South African athletics team, Harold Adams, and Athletics South Africa (ASA) boss Leonard Chuene makes it crystal clear that Chuene knew Caster Semenya was gender-tested in South Africa before the World Championships in Berlin last month.

Chuene's denial that he knew of any tests conducted locally before the tournament is one of a string of lies exposed by a *Mail & Guardian* investigation.

The e-mail, which the *M&G* has seen, was sent by Adams to ASA general manager Molatelo Malehopo and copied to Chuene on 5 August. The World Championships began on 15 August.

It reads: "After thinking about the current confidential matter I would suggest that we make the following decisions. 1. We get a gynae opinion and take it to Berlin. 2. We do nothing and I will handle these issues if they come up in Berlin. Please think and get back to me ASAP."

An e-mailed response from Malehopo to Adams, sent on the same day, reads: "I will suggest that you go ahead with the necessary tests that the IAAF might need."

Chuene has repeatedly maintained that no tests were conducted in South Africa before the tournament. He has also denied that ASA authorised and paid for the tests.

Chuene has defended his decision to field the 800-m champion in Berlin, by saying that "no reasons were given to him on why he should withdraw Semenya from the championships".

The *M&G* can reveal that Semenya was tested at the Medforum Medi-Clinic in Pretoria early last month and that she received counselling from ASA board member and psychologist Laraine Lane beforehand.

The tests were conducted by Oscar Shimange, a medical doctor specialising in obstetrics and gynaecology.

Approached for comment, Lane said this week: "I cannot discuss issues regarding my clients. I can't deny or confirm anything; it would be a conflict of interest if I did that. I would like to help you, but I can't."

Chuene has also claimed that Adams, who was commissioned by the International Association of Athletics Federations (IAAF) to oversee Semenya's gender tests in South Africa, is not the official doctor of team South Africa.

In an ASA press release about the final team for the World Championships in Berlin, sent out on 4 August and in possession of the *M&G*, Adams is listed in the team's management as "team doctor".

President Jacob Zuma's personal physician, Adams arrived with Semenya on 9 August in Neubrandenburg, Germany, where team South Africa was based.

A senior official close to ASA said that when team South Africa was in Neubrandenburg, Adams received a call from Medforum Medi-Clinic informing him of Semenya's gender test results, which were "not good". The results can take up to two days to arrive after testing.

The official said Adams then convened a meeting with Chuene, ASA vice-president Kakata Maponyane and the events manager of team South Africa, Phiwe Mlangeni-Tsholetsane. Adams advised them to withdraw Semenya from the competition, but they refused. Adams had also examined sprinters Kagiso Kumbane and Tshegofatso Meshoe, and advised that they should be withdrawn because of injury. The ASA had obliged.

Another official told the *M&G*: "Mlangeni-Tsholetsane said they couldn't withdraw Semenya because they needed a medal at all costs. Chuene didn't even bother to brief the athlete about the developments around the tests and the implications. They destroyed an innocent girl because of a medal."

Efforts to get comment from Adams proved fruitless, as he did not return the *M&G*'s calls.

A senior athletics official who knows Chuene well said: "Chuene has been lying to the nation from the onset. It's time for him and his crew to tell the truth, apologise to the nation and resign."

The official said that before the Berlin championships Adams received an e-mail from the IAAF raising concerns about Semenya's gender.

Adams had responded by sending the e-mail already described to Malehopo and Chuene seeking advice on what action to take. After consulting Chuene, Malehopo responded, authorising gender tests.

"The arrangements were made and Semenya was taken in for tests accompanied by her coach, Michael Seme. There's just no way that they didn't know about the tests," said the senior official.

Contacted for comment, Malehopo denied giving Adams the go-ahead. "That is interesting news to me. If people have evidence, they should bring it forward and we will take it from there but I don't know anything."

He said he knew nothing about his 5 August e-mail to Adams. He also promised to respond to questions to him and Chuene, but neither had done so by the time the *M&G* went to print.

ASA's Maponyane has stood by Chuene, claiming that Adams had given no reason for withdrawing Semenya from the competition. "He only said that he was waiting for the results from South Africa but did not explain further. And that is when we learned that Semenya had undergone gender tests in South Africa. We want to know who authorised those tests to be conducted without our knowledge," he said.

The ASA has called for its own commission of inquiry into the Semenya affair, while Parliament's sports committee has demanded that the athletics body be hauled before the National Assembly. But the senior official who spoke to the *M&G* warned that Chuene's friends "will sit in that commission. Parliament will not help either, because Chuene is politically well connected. What we need is a judicial commission of inquiry, which has to be instituted by [Jacob] Zuma. It should look at the burning issue and athletics in general. ASA leaders should step aside until we get to the bottom of this."

Semenya sold to the highest bidder

Athletics South Africa has fired Caster Semenya's Finnish agent, Jukka Härkönen, and taken over his public relations role, which includes marketing the athlete to the corporate world.

ASA events manager Phiwe Mlangeni-Tsholetsane confirmed that the association has taken over the management of Caster's business affairs. The ASA organised the photographs of the world 800-m champion dressed as a glamour girl in *You* magazine for a fee, while preventing her from speaking to other media organisations.

Neither the magazine nor Mlangeni-Tsholetsane would reveal the fee. Semenya is said to have been paid R20 000.

"We fired Härkönen in Berlin and I will be managing Caster until she gets a local agent to look after her affairs," Mlangeni-Tsholetsane told the *M&G* this week.

She defended the association's decision to terminate the contract of the Finnish agent, who also has men's 800-m world champion Mbulaeni Mulaudzi and Olympic triple-jump silver medallist Khotso Mokoena on his books.

"We have difficulties in dealing with our athletes who are managed from outside, especially by Härkönen," she said.

The ASA official e-mailed the *M&G* a damning letter penned by South Africa's former athletics coach, Angus Pohl, about Härkönen's alleged activities to support the claim that the ASA had acted in Semenya's interests.

In the letter, Pohl blames his fall-out with Mokoena just before the Beijing Olympics on the Finnish agent and implies that his behaviour is exploitative. Härkönen refused to comment.

Ironically, ASA stood by Mokoena in his court battle with Pohl, who quit as Mokoena's coach on the eve of the Beijing Olympics but subsequently demanded between R170 000 and R200 000 after the athlete won silver.

Former ASA coach Wilfred Daniels branded ASA's stance "two-faced". "How can they now want to jump into the same bed with a guy [Pohl] who abandoned the team on the eve of the Olympics and successfully sued their athlete for a large amount of his bonus?" he asked.

Daniels also alleged that ASA officials were exploiting Caster for financial gain.

Another ASA official, who refused to be named, said Semenya's coach, Michael Seme, had been left behind when the South African team travelled to Berlin, while Humile Bogatsu, the personal assistant of ASA president Leonard Chuene, went as the assistant team manager.

"Now Seme has been told to stay away from Caster's business dealings," said the official.

"Phiwe [Mlangeni-Tsholetsane] and Bogatsu have taken over the Caster Semenya brand. I don't know how much *You* magazine paid for that interview but I can confirm that Caster only received R20 000."

Daniels further claimed that invitations for Semenya to appear on the television shows of talk-show queens Oprah Winfrey and Tyra Banks fell through because the ASA demanded an appearance fee.

"Caster was willing to appear on the shows, as she wanted to speak for herself. But the whole thing fell apart when Phiwe demanded money," said Daniels. Efforts to get comment from Mlangeni-Tsholetsane on Daniels's allegations proved fruitless. She did not respond to messages left at the ASA.

The ASA source said the association's officials had been barred from talking to the media on the instructions of a newly hired public relations company, MS&L Worldwide.

The company, the source said, had been brought on board for the purposes of "damage control" in the Semenya saga.

MS&L Worldwide issued its first media statement on Thursday on behalf of the ASA, saying that the association would now focus on protecting Semenya's professional career and allowing her to compete legitimately. – *Phathisani Moyo*.

Who is Harold Adams?

If President Jacob Zuma wants to know the truth about the Caster Semenya saga, he need only ask his doctor.

Athletics South Africa's chief medical officer and team doctor, Harold Adams, is also Zuma's personal doctor. Before that he was former president Thabo Mbeki's doctor, taking the position in 1999.

Adams has been identified as one of the pivotal players in the Semenya mess and possibly the only person who knows the whole truth about when the athlete was tested in South Africa and what happened afterwards.

Adams, from a poor background, is also president of Boland Athletics and works at the military hospital in Wynberg, Cape Town.

A hospital spokesperson told the *Mail & Guardian* this week that he was accompanying the president on "convoy duty". He has kept a low profile since the Semenya story broke.

The IAAF is said to hold him in high esteem, and he is a member of the association's medical committee.

The IAAF said last week that it had been struggling to reach him to find out what the South African test on Semenya had revealed. But media reports this week suggest that the federation has now spoken to him.

Adams is no stranger to controversy. He was reportedly investigated by the military police in 2005, in connection with suspected fraud for medicines that he allegedly signed out of the defence force, among other matters.

No charges were brought against him. This week the military police declined to comment on the investigation. – *Yolandi Groenewald*.

Report Damns Chuene   *23 October*

In a bombshell report the doctor of the South African athletics team, Harold Adams, has accused Athletics South Africa (ASA) boss Leonard Chuene of deliberately politicising and sowing confusion in the Caster Semenya gender test saga.

Adams's confidential report, leaked to the *Mail & Guardian*, suggests that Chuene consulted top-level politicians before deciding, against Adams's advice, to field Semenya in the Athletics World Championships in Berlin in August.

The *M&G* understands that one of these politicians was the controversial ANC head of Parliament's sports committee, Butana Komphela.

In the report Adams asks: "Did Chuene consult with the 'high-powered politicians' to merely get an endorsement and political backing for his pre-conceived plan of getting a medal at all costs?"

He says Chuene told a medical team of the International Association of Athletics Federations (IAAF) that "withdrawing Semenya was not acceptable to top-level South African politicians who are also in government and that if the IAAF insisted on Semenya's withdrawal they would face the wrath of the South African government, because it would not hesitate to take the IAAF to the highest court in the land".

Adams accuses Chuene of "an orgy of lies" and "selfish interest to cover his back at the expense of Semenya's welfare". He describes his decision to let Semenya race in Berlin as "reckless, short-sighted and grossly irresponsible".

Chuene did not reply to the *M&G's* questions this week and Komphela was unavailable.

In Parliament this week Chuene blamed the IAAF and the media for Semenya's woes, saying he had only acted to protect the athlete.

Adams's report indicates that Chuene lied to Parliament by saying that the IAAF had suggested Semenya should fake an injury and withdraw from the race, which he considered "unethical".

The report was sent to the ANC and South Africa's Olympic governing body, Sascoc.

It has come to light in the week that IAAF president Lamine Diack was due to have visited South Africa to discuss Semenya's gender test with her and the government. But Diack announced on Thursday that he had cancelled the trip.

Komphela has declared Diack unwelcome in the country.

Said a senior athletics official: "The report should raise questions about why Komphela has kept quiet all this time. Chuene told him he was going to do something bad and would need the support of politicians when he gets back home. "After Komphela realised that Chuene was in trouble, he spoke to [ANC Youth League leader] Julius Malema to try to squash this whole thing."

The report reveals that when Adams recommended that Semenya be withdrawn from the championships, Chuene initially agreed.

Adam says: "The reason for my advice was that the tests might prove too traumatic for Semenya to handle, especially without the necessary support of family and friends around her.

"The other reason was that being tested at the World Championships would not give her enough time to consult extensively and perhaps arrive at a decision to refuse the testing, if she felt it would infringe on her privacy and personal rights."

Adams alleges that Chuene changed his mind the next day after he consulted ASA deputy president Kakata Maponyane and politicians back home.

The report reads: "The following day Chuene informed me that he had changed his mind about Semenya's withdrawal. He said if we withdrew Semenya, what explanation would we give the politicians back home?

"Chuene then requested me to set up a meeting with the IAAF's medical team. I asked him why he did not discuss the matter with the president of the IAAF and agree with him on how to take the process forward, because this was such a delicate matter.

"Chuene said talking to the president of the IAAF would be his last option. He first wanted to politicise the whole thing and to cause confusion within the IAAF medical team."

Chuene has defended his decision to field the 800-m champion in Berlin by saying that "no reasons were given to him on why he should withdraw Semenya from the championships".

Adams asks: "The question is: why did Chuene suddenly doubt my credibility when I have such credentials behind my name? Did Chuene consult with the 'high-powered politicians' to merely get an endorsement and political backing for his preconceived plan of getting a medal at all costs?"

At Chuene's request, Adams arranged the meeting with the IAAF's medical team, where he said Semenya's withdrawal would be unacceptable to top-level politicians and the South African government. "He told me to keep quiet in that meeting and that he and Maponyane would defend the country's position …"

On Tuesday Chuene told Parliament's sports committee that the IAAF medical team gave him two options during their meeting: the first, that Semenya should fake an injury and withdraw from the race, which Chuene rejected as "unethical", and the second that "she run and finish and the matter can be addressed after the race. Chuene was not comfortable with this option."

But Adams says that the IAAF team made it clear "that Semenya could compete at the World Championships, on condition that she accepted that she would be subjected to the IAAF's gender verification tests in Berlin and that, if any unfair advantage was detected on the part of her, she would be stripped of any medal she might have won at the championships; or that Semenya is withdrawn from the world championships.

"If [the latter] was to be the option exercised, the IAAF was comfortable with ASA handling the matter of the gender verification tests back in South Africa and a report on the said tests sent to the IAAF."

The Democratic Alliance's Donald Lee said Chuene should be "ashamed of the role he has played in this saga. It is disgraceful that he has never been admonished, much less dismissed, for his role in violating the dignity of Caster Semenya. He needs to be held accountable and needs to step down as the head of ASA."

Last month the *M&G* exposed Chuene's trail of lies, including his claim that no gender tests had been conducted on Semenya in South Africa.

The report says that Chuene asked Adams to be present at his press conferences to confirm this claim to put the matter to rest "once and for all". Adams turned down both requests because he could not endorse a lie.

"I sincerely believe that Chuene's decision to refuse that Semenya be withdrawn was … reckless, short-sighted and grossly irresponsible. Chuene's orgy of lies had absolutely nothing to do with Semenya but all had to do with Chuene's selfish interest to cover his back at the expense of Semenya's welfare," Adams says.

Youth League president Malema continues to give public support to Chuene, and the ANC's Caster Semenya task team also attacked the IAAF this week, saying the gender tests "were not conducted in keeping with their own stated gender verification policies and rules".

It demanded that the IAAF make a public apology.

Sources said Adams was reluctant to present his report to the task team on Tuesday because the ANC had already taken a position.

"The whole thing was well planned; everyone is now blaming the IAAF and this was part of the plan," the senior official said.

Chapter 4

Golden Girl

Debora Patta and Xolisile Moloi
3rd Degree, e.tv

The Caster Semenya story hogged the headlines for days and weeks in August and September. Her success on the field caused the accusations about her gender to fly, and Athletics South Africa (ASA) took the moral high ground and blamed everything on the International Association of Athletics Federations (IAAF).

The IAAF issued a statement saying it had asked ASA to organise a gender test for Caster Semenya before the games.

Leonard Chuene, ASA president, denied any knowledge of the request and made things worse by claiming the IAAF was fabricating this version of events to deflect from the success of an African woman.

It was a huge news story and *3rd Degree* interviewed Chuene for their programme. Before they got to air, the *Mail & Guardian* published its revelations, claiming that Chuene knew about the gender test before the trip to Berlin.

Under attack, Leonard Chuene called a press conference, where he continued to deny any knowledge of the test. Little did he know that presenter Debora Patta had a source, a deep throat, and at the press conference had in her hand the e-mail that would finish his career.

Debora Patta is anchor and executive producer of *3rd Degree*, e.tv's current affairs programme. Her 20-year career in journalism includes on-air presentation and roles in senior editorial management in both radio and television. In 2009 she was named Vodacom Media Woman of the Year.

Xolisile Moloi joined e.tv as a producer on *3rd Degree* in 2007. She started out as a production assistant in the Johannesburg office of US-based National Public Radio and then moved to CNN, as their

Johannesburg bureau field producer. For several years she lived and worked in Austin, Texas.

"Golden Girl" is on the DVD.

Chapter 5

"I Want My F*%#@!! Pardon"

Julian Rademeyer and Felix Dlangamandla
City Press/Rapport

The front-page photograph of Schabir Shaik in a floral shirt and beach shorts leaving his local Spar supermarket caused a storm. Here was the proof for everyone to see that he was violating his parole conditions. In an interview Shaik demanded his "f---ing pardon" and questioned why he should even ask for a pardon.

The release from prison of President Jacob Zuma's friend and former financial adviser in March 2009 had been controversial. He had served just two years and four months of a 15-year sentence for facilitating an arms-deal bribe for Zuma. Now, apparently in the final stages of a terminal illness, he was carried out of prison and into his Durban home on a stretcher.

Within no time there were rumours and claims that he'd been spotted round and about, but the Department of Correctional Services said they would only take action if they had proof that he had broken the terms of his parole.

So Julian Rademeyer and Felix Dlangamandla set out to get the proof. "Our aim was, on the face of it, a simple one: to obtain concrete photographic evidence that he was breaking parole and expose the lie that he was at death's door," says Julian.

It took careful planning, extensive research into his company and property interests, the use of confidential sources and, most importantly, the teamwork of a photographer and reporter working round the clock to keep watch on his movements. It was a story that could only be achieved through legwork and a bit of old-fashioned shoe leather. And it is precisely the sort of journalism now threatened by new legislation.

The two journalists selected predetermined vantage points and, in separate cars, kept watch, waited and noted the comings and goings of different vehicles.

Shaik's own car was well known in the area. But their breakthrough came when they realised he had swapped it for a new BMW X6, which they confirmed was registered in his name. He had switched cars. Now they just had to watch and wait a bit longer.

And then they got their man. Twice they saw Shaik break parole. On the second occasion, they photographed him leaving his local supermarket, and an incensed Shaik pursued Felix with a milk carton.

Two days later, Julian called Shaik. He denied breaking parole and for the next 30 minutes gave vent to his frustrations in an extraordinary, expletive-riddled interview, wisely caught on tape. "It took plenty of time and patience, but their photos and interviews were incontrovertible. They knocked down once and for all the myth that Shaik, the friend and funder of our president, was out of prison for health reasons," the award judges said.

Correctional Services now had their proof and launched an inquiry. Shaik was given a formal warning and his free time was curtailed. If he breaks parole again, he could go back to prison.

Julian Rademeyer is a senior reporter with Media24's investigations team. He has been a reporter for the past 16 years and has written and worked for *Beeld*, *Sunday Times*, *Pretoria News*, *The Herald*, Reuters, *Sydney Morning Herald* and the Australian Associated Press (AAP). In 2005 he won the Vodacom Journalist of the Year award in the print news category. In 2010 he and Felix Dlangamandla won the Hard News category in the Mondi Shanduka Awards.

Felix Dlangamandla is a specialist photographer with Foto24, the photographic arm of Media24's various newspaper titles. He previously worked for *Beeld* as a senior photographer and later as chief photographer. He also freelanced for the *Sowetan*. In 2010 he won the Hard News category, with Julian Rademeyer, in the Mondi Shanduka Awards for his photographs of Schabir Shaik. In 2007 he was named SAB Sports Photographer of the Year. He graduated from the Vaal University of Technology in 2000.

"I Want My F*%#@!! Pardon"   20 December

"Terminally ill" fraudster Schabir Shaik violated his parole this week and for the first time since his release on medical parole was caught on camera.

He appears to have made a remarkable recovery in the nine months since he was described as being in the "final stages of a terminal illness" and granted medical parole.

This week he snuck out of his Durban mansion in his new jet-black BMW X6 to visit an upmarket townhouse complex, go shopping and even mustered up enough strength to pursue a *City Press* photographer while shouting: "Jou ma se p--s".

"Why don't you apply your creative skills to find out why am I not getting a f---ing pardon because the longer I stay as a prisoner – other people are equally guilty," he said.

Despite a host of sightings Shaik has managed to avoid being photographed. The Department of Correctional Services has said it would only act if it was provided with a formal complaint and proof that Shaik has broken his parole.

On 3 March this year Shaik was carried into his Innes Road home on a stretcher after serving just two years and four months of a 15-year prison term for corruption and fraud relating to illicit financial dealings with President Jacob Zuma and French arms company Thint. The same day the then minister of correctional services, Ngconde Balfour, said that Shaik was "in the final phase of his terminal condition" and that legislation provided he be paroled to "die a dignified death".

On Tuesday morning, wearing sunglasses, a wide-brimmed hat and accompanied by a woman, Shaik drove to The Essenwoods townhouse complex in Stephen Dlamini Road (formerly Essenwood Road). He returned home that afternoon, pulling into his driveway at 1.24 pm. A *City Press* reporter stopped next to Shaik's BMW, registration ND 554-390, at the intersection of Stephen Dlamini and Springfield roads and could clearly identify him sitting in the driver's seat.

On Wednesday morning he popped into his local Spar in Florida Road. Wearing baggy shorts, sandals, sunglasses and a golf cap perched jauntily on his head, he emerged at 9.27 am with two cartons of milk and some magazines.

He spotted photographer Felix Dlangamandla sitting in a parked car outside the main entrance, lunged towards him and struck the vehicle with a milk carton.

Shaik shouted: "Jou ma se p––s!" Then he quickly crossed the road and sped off around the corner as a security guard looked on aghast.

This week he denied visiting The Essenwoods on Tuesday.

He did admit visiting the Spar – which was where he was photographed on Wednesday – but said he had asked his parole officer for permission to fetch medication at a nearby pharmacy. He claimed to have stopped at Spar to buy milk after getting his medicine, but a *City Press* team that followed him did not see him go anywhere else except the Spar nor did he have a medicine packet in his hands when he left.

He suggested that reporters "following me around" could "possibly get f––––d up".

A Correctional Services spokesman is on record as saying that Shaik's parole conditions allow him to leave home only on Fridays to attend mosque and on Saturdays between 12 pm and 4 pm.

But in answer to questions posed by the DA in Parliament, the Ministry of Correctional Services said Shaik was only allowed to leave his home between 10.30 am and 12.30 pm on Wednesdays for physiotherapy.

Any deviations from his parole conditions must first be approved by correctional services. In May Shaik's brother Yunis told reporters that he was "gravely ill". He said his brother "never leaves the house" and "his condition cannot improve because there was permanent damage to him".

In another interview at the time Yunis said "Schabir's heart is enlarged, his kidneys and brain have been badly affected and he has lost about 50% of his sight. My understanding is that my brother is in what doctors call the 'final stage' of a physical shut-down."

Despite his ailing condition, the database of the Companies and Intellectual Properties Registration Office indicates that Shaik and Durban businessman Raymond Horne managed to register a close corporation, Wethersfield Trading CC, on 25 May this year. Shaik's contribution to the CC is 50%. The exact nature of its business is unclear.

By law, anyone who is convicted of fraud or corruption and sentenced to imprisonment of at least six months without the option of a fine is disqualified from taking part directly or indirectly in managing a CC.

Shaik said Horne was his "security adviser" but claimed to have no knowledge of the CC. "I wonder what that is about. Maybe it has something to do with the lesser assets I have. I might have a partner who is a director of the company to manage whatever assets I have left," he said.

One place Shaik seems to be avoiding is the restaurant Spiga d'Oro, his favourite haunt in Florida Road. But a dish named in his honour, linguine à la Shaik – arrabiata with a hint of chilli – is popular with diners and the occasional Shaik-spotter hoping for a glimpse of the "dead man walking".

Shaik Spits Fire

Oh s--t! Foul-mouthed Schabir lets us have it.

Schabir Shaik wants his "f---ing pardon" and he wants it now.

Breaking his silence for the first time since he was granted medical parole nine months ago, Shaik told *City Press* on Friday that as long as he remains a "prisoner ... other people are equally guilty".

Referring to President Jacob Zuma and French arms company Thint, he questioned "how come people that should have been charged are declared free to walk around and the man at the centre of things is still serving house arrest".

"Why should I even be asking for a pardon? If three people were part of a so-called plot to elicit funds from the French, why are the French free, why is the President free and why is Shaik still sitting as a convict. C'mon!

"Surely these are the kind of questions you should be asking rather than following me around and possibly getting f----d up when you do meet me, because I can take only so much.

"I'm not scared of going to jail. I've survived in jail, my friend, with the heads of 28 and the heads of 26 gangs.

"I'm not scared of going to jail as the DA thinks. Why the f--k doesn't [DA leader Helen] Zille go to jail and see if she can handle a day or that other a--hole James Selfe [the DA's spokesperson on Correctional Services]."

Shaik denies numerous reports of his violating parole.

"I'm allowed to go and collect my pharmaceuticals from the chemist. I'm allowed to go and see the doctor. I'm allowed to go to the bank. All I've got to do is inform my correctional officer, which I have done."

"I've been seen playing golf at the country club and at the July Handicap.

I've never been to a July in my life. I don't even like f---ing racehorses. Then I'm seen running through the bushes at a shopping centre. If you see me running, take a photograph of me. I'm not going to hide. I ran towards your photographer. I'm not going to run through the bushes where black mambas will bite me."

Asked whether he was terminally ill, he said: "I can tell you I'm not the Shaik that used to work 16 hours a day running around cutting huge deals. I can't do that anymore."

He says he suffers from "uncontrollable stress" but "being home, just seeing the greenery, feeling the sun, getting fresh air, having good food; that alone allows recuperation".

"That helps me reduce my stress and, to some extent, my recovery."

Shaik claims he is going blind, yet he still manages to drive around Durban in his BMW X6. He says he has "grade four retinopathy" – where the retinas of his eyes have been damaged as a result of high blood pressure – has kidney and heart problems and consequently "what you have, my brother, is these serious organs sustaining serious damage and they, in turn, are going to terminal failure.

"The eyes are failing, the heart is failing and the kidneys are failing."

In the same breath, he said the Department of Correctional Services had released statistics indicating that "somewhere in the order of 6000 people that were released [on medical grounds] have recovered.

"You don't release a person so they can go home and die."

Asked how he manages to drive, Shaik said: "It is not easy. I don't drive all the time. I have got glasses. I spend a fortune on glasses, they change all the time. My eyes are not improving.

"I'm on goji berries now. Someone told me that with them I'll make a miraculous recovery. I'm f---ing gorging goji berries till I'm sh---ing the things out hoping my eyesight will improve but it isn't."

He said he would not release his medical records for public scrutiny because it is his "constitutional right" to keep them private. "I don't want people getting to know about my medical condition any more than you."

He claims he has been ruined financially and "sustained substantial losses in excess of R200 million".

"My legal fees alone were R28 million … You are talking about a man who once had a balance sheet of assets in excess of R4 billion."

He confirmed that he was doing "small renovations" to his house. The BMW X6, he said, is "not a huge expense".

"It is owned by the bank and I pay the bank each month."

He is writing a book, he said, in which he "wants to tell the truth as I see it".

"South Africa has been hoodwinked about the arms deal."

"President Zuma's legacy must be corrected. I want my son to have his dad's truth."

He said Zuma should "never even have been tried".

"Mbeki made Zuma and me the fall guys … The decision to find me guilty was made before I even stepped into court and they had to find Shaik guilty to get Zuma removed as deputy president.

"It is not easy, my brother. Sometimes you wish you were back in prison, sitting in your cell, locked up at 2.30 am. Now you are out in the real world and the real issues are not being addressed.

"It is depressing, but I must keep my head above water. I can't just sit back and say I want to die now.

"I've got a son who looks forward to being with his dad."

Shaik's miracle recovery

- 2 June 2005: Schabir Shaik is convicted in the Durban High Court on two counts of corruption and one of fraud relating to bribes involving then deputy president Jacob Zuma. Shaik was Zuma's financial adviser and confidant.

- 8 June 2005: Shaik is sentenced to 15 years in prison. After an unsuccessful appeal he starts to serve his sentence on 9 November 2006.

- 3 March 2009: Shaik is paroled on medical grounds after serving two years and four months of his sentence. He arrives home on a stretcher, reportedly suffering from hypertension, high blood pressure, depression and chest pains. Amid a growing outcry, then correctional services minister Ngconde Balfour describes Shaik as being "in the final phase of his terminal condition".

- 20 April 2009: The doctors who recommended that Shaik be released on medical parole are cleared by the Health Professions Council (HPCSA) of allegations that they behaved unethically and unprofessionally. HPCSA registrar Boyce Mkhize tells the media that medical reports "reveal a gravely serious medical condition of

Mr Shaik" and that the reports by doctors were "not exaggerated, misrepresented or falsified".

- 20 May 2009: The DA asks for a parole board review of the decision to grant Shaik medical parole.

- 21 May 2009: Shaik's brother Yunis says his condition is not improving. "His condition cannot improve because there is permanent damage to him," he says.

- 25 May 2009: Shaik and a Durban businessman register a new close corporation, Wethersfield Trading CC.

- 3 August 2009: *Mail & Guardian* reporter Niren Tolsi runs into Shaik at a 24-hour petrol station shortly after midnight. Shaik reportedly tells him: "I am working towards better health."

- 10 August 2009: EThekwini DA councillor Dean MacPherson expresses shock after seeing Shaik in Durban's Musgrave area buying balloons next to the side of the road. The councillor releases a cellphone video of Shaik's car to the media. Shaik is not visible.

- 13 August 2009: Correctional services spokesperson Thami Zondi says Shaik denies driving the car.

- 19 August 2009: Correctional services minister Nosiviwe Mapisa-Nqakula says there will be no review of Shaik's medical parole because she has received no proof that he has gone out in his car.

- 19 October 2009: The presidency confirms for the first time that Shaik applied for a presidential pardon on 24 April last year.

- 22 October 2009: A Durban newspaper reports that Shaik played a round of golf at the Papwa Sewgolum Course in Reservoir Hills and has regularly been seen there.

- 10 December 2009: Mapisa-Nqakula tells Parliament that Shaik denies playing golf that day. She says the department has received no formal complaints alleging that Shaik has violated his parole conditions.

- 15 December 2009: A *City Press* reporter witnesses Shaik breaking his parole conditions.

- 16 December 2009: A *City Press* photographer snaps Shaik coming out of his local grocery store.

Chapter 6

Did Mpshe Plagiarise a Hong Kong Judge?

James Myburgh

www.politicsweb.co.za

On 6 April 2009 the national director of public prosecutions made what he called "the most difficult decision of my life".

"It is with a great regret that I have to say today that in relation to this case I cannot see my way clear to go to court in future." And so saying Mokotedi Mpshe dropped the charges of corruption against the future president of South Africa, Jacob Zuma. Just in the nick of time: the election was planned for 22 April, two weeks later.

A gut feeling about the lengthy statement and its legal reasoning and foreign legal precedent prompted James Myburgh to start running it through his computer, using just one of a vast array of new skills open to journalists in the 21st century – finger power rather than shoe leather. He tried various textual comparisons and keyword searches and up popped the Seagroatt judgment.

There's nothing wrong in quoting someone else's judgment, in fact judges and lawyers around the world do it all the time. But usually they attribute it – as "So-and-so said, in whatever the case, on whatever date, in whatever court".

But none of that appeared in Mpshe's decision and the only conclusion could be plagiarism: simply pretending the words were his own, the sort of thing that would get a first-year university student in any subject into trouble.

The 2002 Hong Kong judgment by Justice Seagroatt was appealed and didn't stand, so perhaps it wasn't the best reasoning to use. Seagroatt, now retired, was tracked down by Gill Moodie and quoted on grubstreet.co.za as saying that it was "sloppy and undisciplined to put the statement forward as emanating from his own reasoning".

As the Taco Kuiper judges put it: "It was too late to change the decision, and it did not stop the minister of justice making the culprit an acting judge in the North West High Court. But Myburgh did expose this decision for the political fix that it was."

James Myburgh is the founder-editor of the South African politics website www.politicsweb.co.za, part of the Moneyweb network. He was a researcher for the Democratic Party in Parliament from 1997 to 2001 before going on to study politics at St Antony's College, Oxford.

Did Mpshe Plagiarise a Hong Kong Judge?

14 April

On Monday last week acting national director of public prosecution Mokotedi Mpshe announced his decision to drop charges against ANC president Jacob Zuma. In his statement setting out the grounds for his decision Mpshe cited various (mainly foreign) legal rulings. He then quoted extracts from damning recordings of various cellphone conversations between former Scorpions boss Leonard McCarthy and others in late 2007. These had been presented by Zuma's lawyers to the National Prosecuting Authority (NPA) in the course of their representations. On the face of it, these seem to suggest that McCarthy had been acting as a kind of Mbeki-ite mole within the prosecuting authority.

Having read these extracts, Mpshe rather eloquently concluded: "It is against this broad principle of abuse of process that the conduct of Mr McCarthy must be seen and tested. The question for close consideration is encapsulated in expressions such as 'so gravely wrong', 'gross neglect of the elementary principles of fairness', 'so unfair and wrong', 'misusing or manipulating the process of the court'. If the conduct can be so categorized, it would be unconscionable for the trial to continue."

Quite predictably Mpshe's announcement was welcomed by the ANC and its alliance partners, and condemned by almost all opposition parties. Debate around the NPA's decision has focused mainly on the McCarthy recordings, their meaning and legality. Less attention has been paid to the legal basis underpinning Mpshe's decision to drop charges. A number of commentators have noted that the decision quotes – but effectively ignores – the recent Supreme Court of Appeal judgment which stated that the motive behind a prosecution is irrelevant.

There was always something odd about the section of Mpshe's statement which went under the heading 'legal considerations'. It starts out adequately enough quoting the South African Constitution and then from the judgment in the case of the *State* v *Yengeni*.

Things start going slightly awry when Mpshe quotes the following from the judgment of *Smyth* v *Ushewekonze and Another* 1998: "Section 18(2) embodies a constitutional value of supreme importance. It must be interpreted therefore in a broad and creative manner so as to include within its scope and ambit not only the impartiality of the decision-making body but the absolute impartiality of the prosecutor himself whose function, as an officer of the court, forms an indispensable part of the judicial process."

This judgment was issued by Gubbay CJ in the Harare High Court. The section referred to is from the old Zimbabwean constitution, not the South African one. But given that Gubbay cites South African precedent – and this judgment is cited by judges in South Africa – this does not seem too problematic.

However, things become properly curious as Mpshe proceeds to cite a string of rulings by the courts of the British Commonwealth. First there's Ormrod LJ's judgment in *R* v *Derby Crown Court, ex parte Brooks* is cited, then Mason CJ in *Jago* v *District Court of New South Wales*, then Lord Lowry in *Connelly* v *DPP* 1964; then Lord Steyn in *R* v *Latif*, then Lord Clyde in *R* v *Martin*, and finally Lord Hope in *R* v *Hui Chi-Ming*.

There are a number of questions that one could ask about this. Are, for instance, these rulings really relevant to Mpshe's decision to drop charges? This is not just because South Africa has its own common law and constitution, but because these judgments all discuss the considerations that *the courts* should weigh up when asked to stay proceedings. One would not know this from Mpshe's decision as most references to "the court" have been excised and replaced with phrases such as the "criminal justice process". However, the really interesting question is, where does this all comes from?

At this point it is useful to divert to a judgment handed down by Justice Conrad Seagroatt of the Hong Kong High Court on 13 December 2002. One section is headed "The abuse of process – the perennial dilemma" and it, rather strikingly, cites all the British Commonwealth judgments that

Mpshe's statement referred to. Even more strikingly, the phrases quoted are almost all the same as well – give or take some self-serving summarising, truncation and rewriting by the NPA.

Most striking of all are Justice Seagroatt's concluding remarks. These seem to presage by some six and a half years – almost to the word – the Mpshe comments quoted above. "*It is against this* evolved statement of *broad principle*" Seagroatt wrote, "that the prosecution's failures and shortcomings with regard to disclosure *must be seen and tested*. Those *for close consideration* are best summed up by *such expressions as 'so gravely wrong', 'gross neglect of the elementary principles of fairness', 'so unfair and wrong', 'misusing or manipulating the process of the court'*. If those failures can properly *be so categorized*, are they such as to make it *unconscionable* that a re-trial should go forward?" (My emphasis)

It is rather remarkable how Mpshe's opinion of McCarthy so closely resembles that of Justice Seagroatt's opinion of the prosecution in his case in Hong Kong. Their conclusions are rather similar as well. Just as Mpshe decided that "an intolerable abuse has occurred which compels a discontinuation of the prosecution", Seagroatt ruled that "the failures constitute an intolerable abuse which compel intervention. Accordingly I order a permanent stay on these proceedings."

Incidentally, the Seagroatt ruling was overturned on appeal. In its judgment the Court of Final Appeal noted that the court must take account "of the public expectation that persons charged with serious criminal offences will be brought to trial unless there is some powerful reason for not doing so".

Below is a table setting out paragraphs of the Mpshe statement against relevant sections of the Seagroatt judgment.

Statement by the NDPP, Mokotedi Mpshe, on the matter *S* v *Zuma and Others*, Pretoria, April 6 2009	Judgment by Conrad Seagroatt in criminal case of *HKSAR and Lee Ming Tee*, Hong Kong High Court, December 13 2002
There are generally two categories of abuse of process: (a) a manipulation or misuse of the criminal justice process so as to deprive the accused of a protection provided by law or to take an unfair advantage over the accused; (b) where, on a balance of probability, the accused has been, or will be, prejudiced in the preparation or conduct of his defence or trial by either a delay or haste on the part of the prosecution which is unjustifiable. (*R* v *Derby Crown Court, ex Parte Brooks* [1985] 80 Cr. App. R 164, per Ormrod LJ)	The Divisional Court in *R* v *Derby Crown Court, ex parte Brooks* 1985. 80 Cr. App. R. 164 (Ormrod LJ) went on to define the categories of abuse of process as either "(a) the prosecution have manipulated or misused the process of the court so as to deprive the defendant of a protection provided by the law or to take unfair advantage of a technicality, or (b) on the balance of probability the defendant has been, or will be, prejudiced in the preparation or conduct of his defence by delay on the part of the prosecution which is unjustifiable
The issue can be formulated as follows: The question is whether a legal or judicial process which is aimed at dispensing justice with impartiality and fairness to both parties and to the community which it serves should permit its processes to be abused and employed in a manner which gives rise to unfairness and/ or injustice. (See *Jago* v *District Court of New South Wales* [1989] 168 CLR 23 at 30, per Mason CJ)	In *Jago* v *District Court of New South Wales* (1989) 168 CLR 23 (at page 30) Mason CJ formulated the issue as follows: "The question is ... whether the court whose function is to dispense justice with impartiality and fairness to both parties and to the community which it serves, should permit its processes to be employed in a manner which gives rise to unfairness."

Prosecutors have an inescapable duty to secure fair and just treatment of those who come or are brought before them.	This was a hark-back to Lord Devlin's speech in *Connelly's* case (at page 1354): "Are the courts to rely on the Executive (in the form of the Crown as prosecutor) to protect their process from abuse? Have they not themselves an inescapable duty to secure fair treatment for those who come or are brought before them?
Abuse of process may occur on its own, either because: (a) it will not be possible to give the accused a fair trial, or (b) it will offend one's sense of justice, integrity and propriety to continue with the trial of the accused in the particular case. Discontinuation is not a disciplinary process undertaken in order to express one's disapproval of abuse of process; it is an expression of one's sense of justice and propriety. (See *Connelly* v *DPP* 1964 AC 1254)	Lord Lowry followed the same line of approach: "Whether the proposed trial will be an unfair trial is not the only test of abuse of process. "I consider that a court has a discretion to stay any criminal proceedings on the ground that to try those proceedings will amount to an abuse of its own process either (1) because it will be impossible (usually by reason of delay) to give the accused a fair trial or (2) because it offends the court's sense of justice and propriety to be asked to try the accused in the circumstances of a particular case. I agree that *prima facie* it is the duty of a court to try a person who is charged before it with an offence which the court has power to try and therefore that the jurisdiction to stay must be exercised carefully and sparingly and only for very compelling reasons.

(cont.)

	The discretion to stay is not a disciplinary jurisdiction and ought not to be exercised in order to express the court's disapproval of official conduct."
The framework within which abuse of process has to be considered was set out in *R* v *Latif* 1996 1 WLR 104. There will always be a tension between two extreme positions in that, if a trial is discontinued, the public perception would be that the criminal justice system condones improper conduct and malpractice by law enforcement agencies – and if a trial is discontinued the criminal justice system will incur the reproach that it is failing to protect the public from serious crime.	The House of Lords in *R* v *Latif* 1996 1 WLR 104 sets out the legal framework in which the issue of abuse of process had to be considered. There was a weakness of the extreme positions in which, if the court always refused to stay such proceedings, the public perception would be that a "court condones criminal conduct and malpractice by law enforcement agencies" – and if it always stayed such proceedings it would "incur the reproach that it is failing to protect the public from serious crime".
An assessment of abuse of process involves a balancing exercise. In *Latif* it was clear that a fair trial was possible. The overriding question, however, was whether the trial ought to be discontinued "on broader considerations of the integrity of the criminal justice system". According to Lord Steyn, criminal proceedings may be discontinued not only where there will be no fair	The court's discretion involves a balancing exercise. In *Latif* it was plain that a fair trial was possible. The question was whether the trial ought to have been stayed "on broader considerations of the integrity of the criminal justice system." Lord Steyn, relying upon the speeches in *R* v *Horseferry Road Magistrates Court*, said:

but also where it would be contrary to the public interest in the integrity of the criminal justice system that a trial should take place. An infinite variety of cases could arise. General guidance as to how the discretion to discontinue should be exercised in particular circumstances will not be useful.

But it is possible to balance the public interest in ensuring that those charged with serious crime should be tried against a compelling public interest which expresses a distaste and outrage for abuse of process by law enforcers who are expected to behave with absolute integrity, impartiality, fairness and justice. Such an approach conveys the view that a fair and just criminal system should not accept the attitude that the end justifies the means.

The approach in *Latif* has been followed consistently. Thus:

"No single formulation will readily cover all cases, but there must be something so gravely wrong as to make it unconscionable that a trial should go forward ..." (*R v Martin* [1998] 1 All ER 193, at 216, per Lord Clyde)

"Something so unfair and wrong that the court should not allow

---

"[They] conclusively establish that proceedings may be stayed in the exercise of the judge's discretion not only where a fair trial is impossible but also where it would be contrary to the public interest in the integrity of the criminal justice system that a trial should take place. An infinite variety of cases could arise. General guidance as to how the discretion should be exercised in particular circumstances will not be useful. But it is possible to say that in a case such as the present the judge must weigh in the balance the public interest in ensuring that those that are charged with grave crimes should be tried, and the competing public interest in not conveying the impression that the court will accept the approach that the end justifies the means."

---

141. The House of Lords maintained their approach in their decision in *R v Martin* 1998 1 All ER 193 ... The decision is important for the consistency of approach and range of terminology adopted to describe the abuse which would justify a stay of proceedings:

"No single formulation will readily cover all cases, but these must be

(cont.)

a prosecutor to proceed with what is in all respects a regular proceeding." (*R* v *Hui Chi-Ming* [1992] 1 AC 34, at 57B, per Lord Hope)

"An abuse may occur through the actings of the prosecution, as by misusing or manipulating the process of the court. But it may also occur independently of any acts or omissions of the prosecution in the conduct of the trial itself." (*Martin* (supra), at 215, per Lord Clyde)

something so gravely wrong as to make it unconscionable that a trial should go forward, such as some fundamental disregard for basic human right or some gross neglect of the elementary principles of fairness." (Lord Clyde at page 216d)

Lord Clyde also adopted what Lord Hope had said in *R* v *Hui Chi-Ming* (1992) 1 AC 34 (at page 57B) on the subject of abuse of process:

"Something so unfair and wrong that the court should not allow a prosecutor to proceed with what is in all respects a regular proceeding."

Lord Clyde added: "An abuse may occur through the actings of the prosecution, as by misusing or manipulating the process of the court. But it may also occur independently of any acts or omissions of the prosecution in the conduct of the trial itself." (page 215 j)

SCA judgment on motive and transcripts quoted by Mpshe	
It is against this broad principle of abuse of process that the conduct of Mr McCarthy must be seen and tested. The question for close consideration is encapsulated in expressions such as "so gravely wrong", "gross neglect of the elementary principles of fairness", "so unfair and wrong", "misusing or manipulating the process of the court". If the conduct can be so categorized, it would be unconscionable for the trial to continue.	It is against this evolved statement of broad principle that the prosecution's failures and shortcomings with regard to disclosure must be seen and tested. Those for close consideration are best summed up by such expressions as "so gravely wrong", "gross neglect of the elementary principles of fairness", "so unfair and wrong", "misusing or manipulating the process of the court". If those failures can properly be so categorized, are they such as to make it unconscionable that a re-trial should go forward?
Using one's sense of justice and propriety as a yardstick by which McCarthy's abuse of the process is measured, an intolerable abuse has occurred which compels a discontinuation of the prosecution.	I find, with respect, the words of Lord Lowry, singularly attractive and apposite as an expression of the guiding force: "the court's sense of justice and propriety". These coupled with Lord Steyn's "integrity of the criminal justice system" help to set the yardstick or criterion by which the abuse complained of is to be measured. In my judgment this is one of those rare cases where the failures constitute an intolerable abuse which compels intervention. Accordingly I order a permanent stay on these proceedings.

Chapter 7

WaBenzi Frenzy

Alex Eliseev
The Star

A good story often starts with a tip-off.

In this case an anonymous caller to *The Star* told a curious tale of a new Mercedes-Benz bought and lost in just 24 hours. The car was temporarily owned by Gauteng MEC Nomantu Nkomo-Ralehoko, whose department bought it for the princely sum of R920 000. And then she lost it, in a hijack.

Within days of the story's publication the minister had resigned.

This was just the beginning.

Confirming the details of this story led to an invaluable source in the motor industry and details of a string of other ministers who were spending a small fortune on their vehicles. These included cars bought by MECs, premiers and their departments in Gauteng, Limpopo, Mpumalanga and the Northern Cape.

Cargate began as a minor political outrage and turned into a major political scandal, with an estimated R42 million spent on posh cars. All, of course, allowed for by the ministerial handbook. This includes such essentials for doing the job as a variety of BMWs, Audis, Land Rovers and Porsches, with extras like special black paint, Bose sound systems, leather seats, sun roofs and alloy wheels.

The story gathered momentum and the Democratic Alliance launched a campaign to formally ask each ministry in South Africa what their leaders were driving. Their findings became a flood of embarrassing revelations about millions of taxpayers' money wasted on wheels.

Top of the government list of big spenders were communications minister Siphiwe Nyanda, who bought a pair of BMWs for R2.4 million (the handbook allows for two) and former finance minister Trevor Manuel with another BMW for R1 million.

It was embarrassing for the government and President Jacob Zuma called on ministers and MECs to stop the exorbitant spending. But the damage was done. Pravin Gordhan slipped into his first budget speech in February 2010 a review of the ministerial handbook and the politicians' high-spending days may be over.

Alex Eliseev is a reporter for *Eyewitness News* at Radio 702. He began his career writing for Caxton's community newspapers, worked for the South African Press Association (SAPA) and the *Sunday Times*, before joining *The Star* in Johannesburg in 2005. In 2008 he won the Hard News category in the Mondi Shanduka Awards and in 2009 was a Mondi Shanduka finalist for the WaBenzi Frenzy series.

MEC in Murky Merc Deal   *2 June*

The purchase – and overnight loss – of a luxury Mercedes-Benz worth almost R1 million has landed Gauteng MEC Nomantu Nkomo-Ralehoko with a lot of explaining to do.

The controversy, which follows that of transport minister S'bu Ndebele and his R1 million Merc, broke at the weekend and centred around a rare ML63 AMG which the MEC for agriculture, conservation and environment insisted on taking home on Friday afternoon.

The story began a few weeks back when Nkomo-Ralehoko's husband, Sydney, allegedly spotted the Mercedes-Benz SUV in the showroom of the Alberton-based Bez Mega Motors.

The car belonged to one of the dealership's directors and cost more than R1 million new. It had a custom number plate – 010 BEZ GP – and stood on display while its owner was away.

Negotiations began and it was agreed that Nkomo-Ralehoko would buy the car for R920 000, the price being reduced because it was secondhand.

Steve Hart, the group's general manager, went to work, and within a week Bez Mega Motors was registered as a government vendor and able to accept electronic payment. In the meantime, the car's ownership was changed and all the paperwork completed.

On Friday, Hart received a request to release the car – sold as an official state vehicle – into Sydney's possession.

He felt uneasy about this and called the department to seek advice.

Soon, a letter arrived from Nkomo-Ralehoko – signed and on an official government letterhead – instructing him to allow Sydney to "collect my car Mercedes-Benz ML63 on my behalf".

After receiving payment, Hart had a colleague follow Sydney to their Tulisa Park, Alberton, home, after which he considered the transaction finished.

Hart had dealt with the newly appointed MEC only once – when the letter was sent. The rest of the time he had dealt with her department.

On Saturday afternoon, Nkomo-Ralehoko, her husband and a police officer stormed into the dealership, announcing that the car had been stolen in a house robbery a few hours earlier.

Nkomo-Ralehoko's spokesman, Tshepo Shawa, said five or six men had attacked Sydney at gunpoint and taken the car. Nkomo-Ralehoko was not at home at the time.

There have been unconfirmed reports that Sydney was attacked in the driveway.

Hart was questioned as to why there was no tracker on the vehicle and whether it was insured.

But Hart explained that his insurance cover did not require a tracker to be installed and that, because the sale was cash, the insurance responsibility lay with the new owner the minute the car was collected.

Shawa confirmed the Mercedes-Benz was "an official vehicle", but would not answer the following questions:

- Why an official vehicle was driven by the MEC's husband.
- Why there was a rush to collect it on a Friday afternoon.
- Why the car was stored at the MEC's house.
- Whether it had been insured in time or whether the money would not be recovered.
- How the car was chosen, and why such a rare and expensive one was bought as an official vehicle.
- And whether the purchase followed government procedure.

Shawa said the case was being investigated by the police.

Some other high-profile cases involving Mercedes-Benzes are:

- In May, minister Ndebele caused an outcry by accepting – and later declining – a gift Mercedes-Benz worth R1.1 million from a government contractor. The Mercedes-Benz S500 was given to him by a company with more than R400 million of contracts with his department.

- In 2003, former ANC chief whip Tony Yengeni was convicted for failing to declare to Parliament a near 50% discount he received on a Mercedes ML320 4x4. Yengeni was sent to jail but served only a small part of his four-year sentence.

MEC Cleared Over Uninsured Stolen Merc
3 June

The luxury R920 000 Mercedes-Benz purchased with taxpayers' money by Gauteng MEC Nomantu Nkomo-Ralehoko was not insured – and a senior official is likely to be charged for misconduct.

However, the Department of Agriculture and Rural Development is adamant that the purchase of the rare white ML63 AMG – stolen from the MEC's house just hours after it left the showroom – was completely above board.

The Star revealed yesterday that the secondhand SUV was bought as an official vehicle and collected from Alberton-based Bez Mega Motors by Nkomo-Ralehoko's husband, Sydney, on Friday.

The following day, at around midday, he was held up at the couple's Tulisa Park, Alberton, home and robbed of the Mercedes.

Department spokesman Sipho Thanjekwayo yesterday said he did not know why the car was not insured. Because of the cash sale, the insurance cover of the dealership fell away as soon as the car was collected. There was also no tracking device installed.

It remains unclear why Nkomo-Ralehoko insisted on collecting the vehicle on Friday, when her bodyguard was escorting her to meetings.

A source within the province said it was likely that a senior official would be disciplined because the car should not have been released until the insurance had been sorted out.

The department added there were no rules against a spouse driving an official car, as long as the department was given notice. This, it is claimed, was done in this case.

Nkomo-Ralehoko had sent an official letter to the dealership authorising Sydney to take possession of and drive the vehicle.

Thanjekwayo said keeping the official car at the MEC's home was "normal" and allowed.

He confirmed that documents were being gathered to assist the police investigation, but that no internal probe was under way to determine whether the purchase was done according to procedures.

"From the knowledge I have, everything was done by the book," he said.

The Star reported that Sydney first spotted the car – which belonged to one of the dealership's directors – two or three weeks ago. After negotiations, the price was set and Bez Mega Motors took a week to get itself registered as a government vendor in order to receive payment.

Asked for the reasons behind the choice of the super-luxury vehicle – worth nearly R1 million – and whether it was not an insult to taxpayers and the poor, Thanjekwayo said: "We're not breaking any rules. We wanted a good-quality car that could be used in rural areas.

"The moral issue is another question. We went according to the rules."

In a press release, the department explained that a member of the executive could, according to the guidelines, buy a car that cost no more than 70% of his or her annual salary.

"The department wishes to state for the record that proper procedure was followed," the statement said.

Mystery over MEC's Merc Deepens, with Insurance Brokers in the Dark   *5 June*

To insure the R920 000 Mercedes-Benz bought by Gauteng MEC Nomantu Nkomo-Ralehoko would have cost almost R83 000 a year – or R7000 a month.

And, it has emerged, the brokers who were asked to arrange insurance for the luxury SUV spent a week trying to get her department to commit to the quotation by sending faxes and e-mails and by calling her directors.

When the ML63 AMG was hijacked from Nkomo-Ralehoko's Alberton home, the insurance brokers didn't even know it had been collected from the dealership a few hours earlier.

The Star has learnt that the process of insuring the secondhand vehicle began as early as 22 May, seven days before it was collected from Bez Mega Motors in Alberton. A company that specialises in brokering insurance for government cars provided an e-mail quotation on that day. All that was needed was confirmation from the Department of Agriculture and Rural Development.

A few days later, a response came from the department asking for the quote to be put onto a letterhead – which was done immediately. The letter was e-mailed and faxed, and follow-up calls were made two days before the MEC ordered the dealership to release the car into the care of her husband Sydney. It is not known why she did this.

One suggestion as to why the insurance deal was never finalised was that the department believed it could secure a better deal – one that would fall within the budget. The other reason, posed by the department's spokesman Sipho Thanjekwayo, could have been that Treasury regulations stipulate that state cars can be covered by the government and not by an insurance company. This would depend on whether the car was registered in the MEC's name or not. Thanjekwayo has been unable to give a definite answer.

Yesterday, he said they had not received any feedback from the police about the investigation into the theft of the Mercedes-Benz. There is also no news of whether any heads will roll for the bungle which saw nearly R1 million of taxpayers' money wasted.

The car, a 2008 model, did not have a tracking device because the insurance policy of the dealership – which expired the moment it was driven off the showroom – didn't require one.

After driving home with an escort from the dealership, Sydney left the Merc at the couple's Tulisa Park home. At noon the following day, a gang of robbers held him up at gunpoint and made off with the vehicle.

The department has denied there was anything "murky or untoward" about the SUV's purchase, and claims that all procedures were followed. Sydney, it has been said, was authorised to drive the vehicle.

Police spokesman Inspector Jerbes de Bruyn said investigations were continuing.

Merc MEC Quits after
25 Days in Office
6 June

Twenty-five days after moving into her office, Gauteng MEC for agriculture and rural development Nomantu Nkomo-Ralehoko has stepped down over the bungled purchase of a R920 000 Mercedes-Benz.

And her chief financial officer (CFO), Mamoorosi Qacha, has been put on immediate suspension.

A criminal case has been opened against Qacha over allegations of fraud within the department, and specifically around the Mercedes-Benz deal.

The bombshell announcement came yesterday and saw Nkomo-Ralehoko admit that she had been misled by senior members of staff.

"I realise that I was inappropriately advised, particularly by the CFO, on this process that led to the release of the vehicle without proper insurance and installation of tracking devices," she said.

Boldly, Nkomo-Ralehoko did not stop at suspending Qacha, but said she had to take full responsibility for an act that, ultimately, wasted nearly R1 million of taxpayers' money.

"I sincerely regret this incident and apologise to the people of Gauteng."

The secondhand ML63 AMG was bought from an Alberton-based dealership and collected by Nkomo-Ralehoko's husband, Sydney, last Friday.

After spending one night at the couple's nearby home, it was stolen at gunpoint from Sydney while his wife was at work.

After the story broke in *The Star* this week, the department issued a press statement to state "categorically that there was nothing murky or untoward about the deal". Yesterday's developments flew in the face of that statement.

"It has come to my attention that [Qacha] did not obtain authority from the head of department in this entire process," Nkomo-Ralehoko said.

"The purchase of the vehicle and its theft raised suspicions, which I think the government and the police must fully investigate."

Qacha, it appears, is also embroiled in separate disciplinary cases involving financial mismanagement within the department.

"The circumstances pertaining to the car purchase and theft have caused serious embarrassment to my family, the Gauteng provincial government and the ANC ... it was never my intention to circumvent any government procedure," Nkomo-Ralehoko said.

She was appointed MEC on 8 May and stepped down from a salary package of more than R1m a year.

The DA, which had initiated an ethics probe into the deal, praised Nkomo-Ralehoko for "doing the right thing".

But it said the department still had serious problems to deal with, such as poor service delivery and staff vacancies.

Members of the National Education, Health and Allied Workers Union yesterday staged a protest outside the department's offices against Qacha's suspension.

There is no indication yet of who will step in as the new MEC, and Nkomo-Ralehoko is expected to continue working within the provincial government.

It's a WaBenzi Frenzy   *12 June*

Leather seats: R41 000; sunroof: R13 600; 21-inch alloy wheels: R16 900; and Bose sound system: R5600. Total cost of extras: R206 230. Being the politician with the coolest ride: priceless.

After the April elections, elected leaders across South Africa are rushing out to buy the most luxurious cars the rule book allows.

Ministers, premiers and MECs have been dubbed the "kings and queens of bling", who – as *The Star*'s investigation shows – have spent tens of millions of rands on the latest Mercedes-Benz, BMW, Audi or Land Rover.

WaBenzi is a colloquial term to describe a government official's luxury vehicle of choice (usually a Mercedes-Benz).

In Limpopo, one of the country's poorest provinces, premier Cassel Mathale has just bought an imperial blue BMW 750i worth R1 055 050.

His MEC for public works, Pandelani Ramagoma, opted for a R800 000 Land Rover, on which the tax alone is close on R100 000.

Pitsi Moloto, the MEC for economic development, environment and tourism, bought an Audi Q7 worth R560 000, which – with the help of 19 extras – landed up costing taxpayers R875 333.

The extras include: air suspension; an electrical folding towbar (worth R8200); privacy glass; tyre pressure monitoring; a parking system; cruise control; DVD-based navigation; S-line exterior package (almost R20 000); a cellphone kit; special headlights; and voice recognition. The "Phantom black" paint job cost an extra R2600.

All the departments refused to be drawn into the ethical debate of whether the purchases amounted to a waste of taxpayer money.

"The cars have been bought for politicians who are leaders of government in line with policy," Limpopo provincial spokesman Mogale Nchabeleng said.

Pushed on the ethics, he said that was a debate right across government.

Combined, the three cars cost R2.7 million.

In Gauteng, former MEC for agriculture and rural development Nomantu Nkomo-Ralehoko spent R920 000 on a secondhand Mercedes-Benz. The vehicle was hijacked a day after it left the showroom floor.

One national ministry is buying a R900 000 Mercedes-Benz S350, with a possibility of a second being bought. Another ministry is spending R600 000 on a top-of-the-range Lexus.

In Mpumalanga, one department has just spent R700 000 on an E350 Merc and more than R350 000 on a Toyota 4x4.

In the Northern Cape, an MEC is gearing up to drive a Mercedes-Benz ML500 worth R550 000.

Free State is acquiring 10 official cars allegedly worth some R10 million.

DA chief whip Ian Davidson has lashed out at the car frenzy. "They are the kings and queens of bling, amassing as much as possible in terms of their allowances to pump their egos," he said.

According to the 2009/10 figures, the government allocates an average of R55 000 to build one RDP house (with an additional R20 000 going towards servicing of land). The extras on Moloto's Audi alone could have built three homes.

The ministerial handbook says MECs and premiers are allowed to buy an official vehicle not exceeding 70% of their annual salary package.

They can purchase a new car once an existing one has been driven for 120 000 km or five years.

PART TWO

The Way We Live Now

Chapter 8

Dying to Live

Thanduxolo Jika
Daily Dispatch

The flood of xenophobic attacks on foreigners in 2008, and a long, and apparently sustained, series of attacks going back several years on Somalis living in the Eastern Cape, led the *Daily Dispatch* to ask the question, Why?

The starting point for this special report was a man called Andile Tunzana, jailed for the murder of two Somalis.

Thanduxolo Jika wanted to get him to talk, but the first problem was getting to talk to him. After many months of trying and after being denied official permission to visit, Jika managed to find his way into the prison and get access to the killer. In a series of prison interviews he learned why the Somalis in particular were being targeted.

That was one side of the story. The next challenge was to understand this story from the point of view of the Somalis themselves. Jika and photographer Theo Jeptha spent weeks living with two Somali shopkeepers in Mdantsane, between East London and King William's Town, where they witnessed first-hand the prejudice of South Africans, the corruption of Home Affairs and the daily battles the Somalis face to survive.

They lived, ate and prayed with these people, hearing and seeing the heartbreaking stories of those who escaped one war for another. "It was during this time I got to feel the fear Somalis were living under," says Jika. "Night-time is their worst time as they fear being attacked." Lock-down was at 7 pm. No matter how hot, the windows could not be left open and there was no release until the following morning.

Andrew Trench, editor of the *Daily Dispatch*, says of the investigation: "We hoped that our journalism would prick the conscience of our society and that South Africans would step back and look at themselves and consider the monsters that we were becoming."

The award judges said: "This was enterprise journalism at its best. The result was not just a riveting front-page series, but excellent online multimedia work which took the story to a national audience and brought home most vividly the prejudices and fear at the centre of the attacks on foreigners."

Thanduxolo Jika, 27, is the assistant news editor at the *Daily Dispatch*. He has worked for the paper for nearly four years and specialises in hard news, investigative reporting and analysis. He has a journalism degree from Rhodes University. He won the print category in the 2009 Vodacom awards for "Dying to Live" and was part of the *Daily Dispatch* team that won the online category for the same story.

"Why I Killed"   *3 March*

Andile Tunzana has the blood of four Somalis on his hands and, as he sits in Mdantsane Prison serving two life sentences, he has finally told why he killed.

"We knew they had a lot of money in their shops and had no guns to fight back," said Tunzana, 26, who is doing hard time for the killing of the Somali refugees around East London.

"We shot those who tried to resist and then looked for money. No one cared for them in the township because they are *grigambas.*"

Tunzana's story confirms how South African government policy predisposes Somali refugees to become victims in a country which they hoped would offer sanctuary.

Since his conviction by the East London High Court in 2006 Tunzana says he has converted to Islam – the religion of his victims – and adopted the name Ismael Junaid.

It was his conversion that led to him agreeing to his jail interviews with the *Daily Dispatch*. We conducted hours of interviews with him as part of a four-month investigation into the killing of Somalis in our community. We lived with Somalis to understand the hatred directed at them; we spoke to police who investigated the cases, and to witnesses, survivors and independent experts.

We were also present when corrupt Home Affairs officials took bribes from refugees desperate to renew their permits.

The picture that has emerged is clear: Somalis become victims of crime because of state policy which provides them with limited legal protection, and does not allow them to live a normal life or have access to institutions like banks. They are left vulnerable to be preyed on by criminals and corrupt officials in communities that reject them.

At the time of the murders in 2005, Tunzana was on the run, having escaped from custody while awaiting trial on another murder charge. He and his accomplices robbed and murdered Mohammed Nasier Omar and Mahamud Abdi Mohammed at their spaza shop in Mzamo Street, Duncan Village, on 5 July 2005.

Earlier, he had shot and wounded Mohammed Ismail in the thigh and Mashafa Muhammed in the jaw at their spaza shop in Mtendeni Street, Duncan Village, and shot and wounded Daniel Dala, a security guard at a Somali-owned shop in Lamont Street in CC Lloyd Township.

Tunzana admitted in his interviews with the *Dispatch* that the Somali spaza shops were easy targets.

"We got information that the *amagrigamba* were not banking their money and, instead, were hiding it in their shops. They were easy to rob because they did not resist much and there was no one to protect them."

Tunzana said they planned their attacks around the Somalis' prayer times; Muslims worship five times a day. The gang knew that while other Somalis went to the mosque to pray, there would be only one shopkeeper, which made robberies easy.

"We knew they were the only ones who had a lot of money and were easy to rob in the township. I did not care much about robbing any other person who looks like me because I know that they might be struggling to survive. The Somalis were just other foreign people with money and no one cared about them."

Tunzana said on the day of their rampage they had told themselves they were going to get rid of Somalis. "Ta Ero [Eric Nanto, his accomplice] said let's kill these things [Somalis] today and get rid of them. They come here to take our women and behave like this is their country," said Tunzana.

They showed no mercy.

Buzani Nkunzana, an eyewitness to the robbery and shooting of Ismail and Muhammed, recalled what happened after Tunzana and his three accomplices stormed the spaza on the afternoon of 5 July 2005.

Nkunzana, an electrician, was with Ismail and Muhammed in their bedroom trying to fix their VCR when they heard a big bang. "I got a shock," he said. "I heard people shouting and demanding money from the Somalis on the other side. I then saw the two Somalis walking backwards to the room and a person was pointing a gun at them."

Nkunzana saw the Somalis gunned down.

One of the robbers fired a shot which hit Muhammed and he immediately fell to the floor.

He thinks they shot him because his lighter skin gave him away as a foreigner.

"I just went on the floor next to one of the Somalis and there was just a pool of blood coming from him. I thought this must be my last day alive. I was scared that I was going to die."

But he escaped their attention.

Afterwards, Nkunzana followed the gang from the house and saw people scattering in the street, some screaming, as Tunzana and his gang strolled down the road.

"They were not even running or trying to hide ... they just walked," Nkunzana said.

Tunzana told the *Dispatch* he could not really remember what happened but acknowledges he shot people.

"I remember at one of the shops the *amagrigamba* tried to shoot me but their guns jammed," he said. "They ran away and I shot at them, but they did not die."

Tunzana said, despite his conversion to Islam, his feelings about his crimes remained ambiguous. At times during the interviews he would claim not to have hated his victims. But then he would refer to them using the derogatory *amagrigamba* term.

At first, he blamed alcohol and evil spirits for attacking the Somalis, but in a later interview he admitted he killed because of greed and because he thought he could get away with it because they were foreigners.

"All we wanted was more money for us and it was easy to get it from their shops and do whatever we wanted. I had also managed to avoid police for a long time so I believed that there was no way we could be arrested because these were just *amagrigamba*."

Tunzana said also his new faith had compelled him to tell the truth: "According to Islam, one must confess all his sins and tell the truth. It was right for me to confess to the killings and for God to forgive me.

"If I had taken up Islam before, I would not have robbed and killed my brothers. I hope for forgiveness now."

But Abdullahi Adbi Sheikh, the brother of one victim, Mahamud Abdi Mohammed, is not convinced that Tunzana has converted and does not think he can. "I am a Muslim," he said, "but after all the pain we went through, how can we be expected to give out our hand to the person who did us wrong?

"For me ... I cannot forgive anybody. God forgives."

Timeline of terror

Somalis living in East London have been victims of brutal robberies and murders for years and, in May last year, xenophobic attacks against foreigners exploded across South Africa.

Those who have survived bear the scars, and those who still run spaza shops in local townships do so in constant fear for their lives.

Some of the high-profile attacks on Somalis in the Eastern Cape since 2005 have included:

25 May 2005: Gunmen attack a Zwelitsha spaza shop, killing Somali Faysael Mohammed and leaving store-owner Abdi Ali-Rage critically wounded after he is shot in the stomach.

8 April 2005: Robbers flee with about R12 000 in cash and groceries worth R17 000 after releasing snakes into a Somali shop to scare the owners.

5 July 2005: Somalis Mahamud Abdi Mohammed and Mohammed Nasier Omar are killed in a brutal attack by armed men on six spaza shops owned by foreigners in Duncan Village. Three Somalis are wounded in the shootings.

28 July 2005: Two Somalis are attacked during an armed robbery in Tyutyu Village outside King William's Town. Spaza shop owner Ahmed Abdirahman, 24, is shot in the chest and dies at the scene.

17 August 2005: Somali spaza shopkeeper Kasi Adid, 26, is murdered at his spaza shop in Sterkstroom, near Queenstown. He dies on the way to hospital.

13 February 2007: Seven Somali shops are burnt down and 20 others looted in Motherwell township, Port Elizabeth.

20 September 2008: Hassan Hardi, 34, is shot and killed at his business premises in Buffalo Flats. Three men armed with guns enter his shop and demand money – he is shot as he tries to run away.

28 September 2008: A Somali mother, Sarah Farah, is knifed 113 times and three children – one of whom was disabled – are butchered at Tambo village near Queenstown.

Bullet Shatters Paralysed Teenager's Dream

Abdullahi Haji Gaan, a 17-year-old Somali teenager, fled his war-torn country early last year as he followed his dream of a new life in South Africa – only to be shot and left paralysed.

His family believes he would have been safer in strife-torn Mogadishu, his homeland's capital.

Gaan is wheelchair-bound after being shot last September by robbers at a spaza shop in Mdantsane's NU11, where he worked.

He was woken up by a commotion when two armed men entered the shop after his colleague opened the door for a bread delivery.

Seeing the two armed men, he tried to flee to his room but was spotted and shot in the back.

The teenager now has a bullet next to his spinal cord which doctors at Cecilia Makiwane Hospital cannot remove as it requires a special operation. Gaan does not have the money to pay for the operation.

He said he spent three months in hospital before being discharged after the doctors told him there was nothing more they could do.

Now, with the help of friends at a Somali-owned lodge, Gaan exercises by holding onto steel bars every day in the hope that his left leg will become strong enough for him to walk again.

When we spoke to him, he was in the middle of his exercises.

Gaan survives through his countrymen's help but he hopes that if he can walk again, he will find work so that he can send money to his mother back in Somalia.

"I ran away from home [Mogadishu] because there were a lot of young people and my friends being killed. I did not know that this kind of a thing could happen to me here in South Africa," said Gaan.

Now he regrets ever setting foot in the country.

"My mother was very angry with me for leaving and now I have to deal with this condition," he said.

"They believe if I had stayed home this would not have happened."

He said his journey to South Africa was an ordeal in itself – he braved heat and starvation and managed to avoid police through Kenya, Tanzania, Malawi, Zambia, Zimbabwe and Mozambique, using buses and sometimes hiding in crates, before arriving in this country.

Gaan finally reached a friend in East London who had given him some money to leave Somalia.

He was given a shop-keeping job at a Somali-owned spaza shop but his life took a cruel and unexpected turn in the robbery.

All he wants now is to be able to walk and work again.

And his friends and countrymen believe he has the will to achieve that before the end of this year.

"I Cannot Explain the Pain"

Somalian cries for his brother with vengeance in his heart

Abdullahi Abdi Sheikh's life was shattered when his younger brother, his only family member in South Africa, was gunned down by multiple murderer Andile Tunzana during an armed robbery in East London's Duncan Village just 20 days after he arrived in the country.

Mahamud Abdi Mohammed was killed, along with Mohammed Nasier Omar, when Tunzana and three accomplices went on a robbery-and-killing spree of Somalis in the area on 5 July 2005.

"I cannot explain the pain and the feeling of losing your brother and someone you grew up with and who ate from the same plate with you," said Abdullahi.

Mahamud, the third-born in a family of nine, had already escaped two near-fatal attacks while working in Somali-owned spaza shops in Port Elizabeth in 2003 and 2004.

"We were very close. I even took him to college to study," said Abdullahi.

His whole family escaped war-torn Somalia in 1991 and then lived in a refugee camp near the remote Kenyan village of Dadaab.

Abdullahi left the camp in 1996 in search of a job in Nairobi, the country's capital city, and managed to find work at a restaurant before Mahamud joined him.

In his continued attempts to support their family he sent Mahamud to study as a motor mechanic at a technical training institute, but life was hard and his brother was unable to find a job.

Then, in 2002, he gave Mahamud money to go to South Africa to find a better life. But in South Africa his struggle continued and he only found work in spaza shops owned by Somalis.

Mahamud eventually started his own spaza shop with money sent from Kenya by Abdullahi, who joined him less than a month before he was killed.

Abdullahi said the whole family's lives had been shattered as his brother had also been the main provider for other members back in Kenya.

He regrets ever encouraging his brother to move to South Africa. "I had to wash his body with my hands to clean off the blood on the left side of his chest where the bullet had pierced through. It was very painful carrying his body to the graveyard."

Abdullahi broke down as he spoke about his difficulty in having to explain to his parents how his brother had died and that he had buried him in a dignified Muslim manner.

"They will never trust me again because they did not see his body."

Abdullahi said he would have preferred vengeance as he could not forgive Tunzana and was not convinced that he had changed and converted to Islam, as the killer had claimed.

"I wish I had power," he said. "I would have shattered all their lives as they shattered mine – an eye for an eye."

Blame the Government, Say Experts

South African government policy is indirectly responsible for Somalis and other migrants becoming victims of crime and prejudice, experts say.

Dr Loren Landau, director of the Forced Migration Studies Programme at Wits University, said criminals focused on Somalis because they were excluded from financial institutions and generally had cash in their shops. Refugees were also unable to access the justice system for protection.

"Police have generally been unable or unwilling to protect Somalis and many other migrants. You can attack them with relative impunity."

Landau said the findings of the *Dispatch* investigation generally reflected what they had found in their research.

"I believe there are also general tensions around issues of integration and the perception that Somalis see themselves as somehow superior."

Landau said while many attacks on Somalis were criminally motivated, there were other factors, too, like greed, resentment, hate and local political power battles.

Wits University's chair of psychology Professor Gillian Finchilescu said the vulnerability of Somalis might be seen as an opportunity to commit crimes against them, but the attackers also believed there would be no retribution or chance of being accountable to the law or being condemned by local communities.

In xenophobic attacks, "the victims are an identifiable group that differs from the majority in some way (with different language, customs, religion). They are vulnerable in the sense that they do not enjoy the rights of the rest of the population, which include protection from the law enforcers, and they have less of a voice or no voice that could influence government officials."

Professor Michael Neocosmos, director of Global Movements Research at Monash South Africa, said Somali-killer Andile Tunzana's comments to the *Dispatch* were consistent with his research on xenophobia. "As Somalis and other foreigners are vilified in society they become easy targets for criminals, as your informants say."

Neocosmos said the government was failing to ensure their safety by delaying issuing residence permits and by treating foreigners as if they come to take and not to provide. "People who come to this country must be seen as providers of jobs, opportunities and knowledge."

SA Human Rights Commission commissioner Dr Zonke Majodina, who has produced a report on the lives of Somali refugees in Johannesburg, said Somalis' day-to-day appeared to be framed by a hostile environment which made them feel unsafe.

For a managed programme of integration to be successful there should be a semi-independent body that coordinates all institutions that provide services to refugees, she added.

Tsotsis Outside, a Crush of Customers Inside ... Now What?

4 March

Our Daily Dispatch *team spent two weeks living with two Somalis in their Mdantsane spaza shop and witnessed the hatred and danger first-hand as their hosts try to find a normal life.*

It is Friday night, minutes before 8 pm, and almost closing time at Sisonke spaza shop in Mdantsane's NU1 where Adam Malow is panicking as the number of customers mushrooms.

He is rushing to serve one customer at a time through the pigeon-hole counter. The little store is so packed it's hard to see past the customers and out of the door. The air is stifling.

But time is ticking and Malow, a 26-year-old Somalian refugee, knows he needs to shut up shop soon. For when the sun goes down, danger rises for Malow and his compatriots. It's time to bunker down behind locked gates for another long and risky night.

Outside Sisonke, a four-roomed house where Malow and his friend Abdirizak Mahdi live and work, a group of young troublemakers is lurking.

"We're going to get you tonight. We're coming back. This is Mdantsane," yells one of the group Malow had tried to chase away earlier.

Since all the light bulbs outside the shop were smashed by unknown people, Malow and Mahdi no longer share guard duty outside to monitor customers coming into the store before closing time.

It was their way of increasing the chances of preventing an attack.

"They are always breaking them [light bulbs], I guess, to make sure that we cannot see what is happening outside at night. It is very dark here," said Malow.

He calls Mahdi, who is preparing their supper, to assist him in the shop as he cannot handle the numbers any longer.

As the customers finally leave with their goods, Malow rushes to the burglar gate while, outside, the troublemakers continue with their threats. He clangs the gate shut, puts on the big padlock and gives it a kick to ensure that it is properly locked.

The kitchen burglar gate and door had already been locked by Mahdi, who has now shifted his attention to counting the day's takings before hiding the money away.

In the kitchen, Malow explains that he does not like it when there are a lot of people inside the shop, especially at night, because he cannot see everything that is happening. It panics him because some people could be pretending that they are there to buy while they might be planning a robbery.

"You do not know who is doing what and you cannot think straight. Others are shouting at you and there are those tsotsis outside who might be sending people to spy for them," Malow said.

Before arriving in Mdantsane, Malow was robbed and his shop looted in Jeffreys Bay.

Now he does not trust anyone he is serving.

Malow survived the hardships of growing up in Kenya's refugee camps for eight tough years after fleeing war-torn Somalia with his mother and siblings. "The heat was unbearable in those plastic huts," he recalled.

Malow lost track of his father during a 1991 escape and does not know whether he is still alive. But the family survived, he continued, on 3 kg of maize or flour, oil and beans from the United Nations, which was expected to last for 15 days.

"It was really difficult for us there because the food would only last for three days. After that, we had to go into town to try and sell vegetables or fruits."

Other challenges face them in Mdantsane.

Earlier that day, while Mahdi was in town, an angry customer stormed into the shop with a bush knife claiming that Malow had robbed his child. It turned out that he thought the Somalian had cheated him out of some of his change.

The knife-wielding man, who lives in the shacks adjacent to the spaza, did not try find out what had happened but threatened to stab Malow if he did not give him the correct change.

Malow was forced to press the panic button and call police to arrest the man. Police arrived, reprimanded the man and told him not to threaten Malow again.

In another incident, a local woman swore at Malow, accusing him of selling her used cellphone airtime. "You *kwerekweres* cheat us. Your prices are always going up. Give me my money back," she demanded. Even when Malow helped her to load the airtime she was still rude.

Mahdi says this is one of the reasons they are scared to even walk in the streets at any time, preferring to drive everywhere they go. "It is not safe here because we do not know who might attack us. I do not know why South Africans hate us … we are also Africans."

Mahdi, 32, a graduate from the International University of Africa in Sudan, where he majored in history and Islamic studies, could not find a teaching job in Somalia.

Now in South Africa, he spends his spare time reading or on the Internet, checking in with friends he made at university and who are now also scattered all over the world.

He also tries regularly to call his wife, who is in Kenya.

What pains him about South Africa is the ignorance of the people, especially the youth, who refer to Somalis as *grigambas* and tell them that they must go back to Zimbabwe. "They have little knowledge about Africa. Many do not even know that there is a country called Somalia; only the older people mostly know about us," he said.

Malow, a football enthusiast, is even scared to go to the NU1 stadium to join a local club for practice sessions.

Instead, he has opted to play with a tennis ball inside the shop when they are not busy.

"There is a guy who asked me to come and play for them, but I am scared that other guys would not accept me – I do not know what to expect," said Malow.

After a dinner of *soor* or *ugali* – a combination of egg, pilchards and fried onion with pap – Mahdi does a routine check to see if every door and burglar gate is locked before their last prayer of the day prior to going to bed.

No one will set foot outside the door until the sun rises and they awake to worship Allah and give thanks for surviving to see another day.

Somalis Speak Out   5 *March*

Abdullahi Mahamed Mahamud, 31

After I crossed five borders in different countries to get here, I thought I would be happy, but I encountered two main problems: Firstly, there is a lack of security and a lack of proper documents. I now carry documents which have to be renewed every one or two months. I have to spend a whole week in Port Elizabeth or sometimes use money to get a permit.

Abdvile Mahamed, 42

We have a lot of problems in South Africa, especially the deliberate killings. My brother, Hasim Mahamed, was killed in Nelspruit in 2000 after his shop was robbed. If someone is killed, there is no immediate arrest and there is no proper punishment for the criminal. I do not have any hope that something will be done about my brother's death.

My cousin was also killed in Port Elizabeth in 2005 and nothing has been done about that.

A Rahman Hussein, 36

I request that something be done to help us [Somalis]. My main concern is security for us, which is very important, but little is done about it by the government, community leaders and the people of South Africa at large. Secondly, I appeal to the government of South Africa to give much [consideration] to the documentation that they give us in order to be licensed to carry firearms and get passports and travel documents.

Abass Muhammed, 25

My message to South Africa is that something must be done about Home Affairs because all people have the same papers regardless of whether they have been here for a day or for years. They treat people badly and give poor service, and we feel that we are being discriminated against because these people don't even know whether they are African or not.

Rahman Maalin Damaa, 33

I hope we can get better security because crime is costing us a lot. Three of my brothers were shot dead on 5 September 2008, and some of the people responsible have been released without even being taken to appear in court. From what I see, the justice system of South Africa needs some amendments in regard to how it handles crime. If something happens to you – for example, if one is being robbed or even killed and the police are called – they respond after two hours.

Mohamed Omar Ali, 21, Mdantsane NU8

My message is that lack of documents like identity documents and obtaining passports is a problem.

Ibrahim Yussuf Maalim, 25, Mdantsane NU8

I would like to say that the government should make it easier for us to get identity documents, travel documents and passports. That's my main concern because we like to travel to our home country to visit and come back.

Mukhtar Abdi Solomon, 40, Mdantsane NU10

I came to South Africa in 2003 but I still can't get an ID. What I have is only refugee status. I applied for an ID three times and I am still waiting. I am a father of five and their mother is staying in Somalia and I cannot visit them. I worry a lot when I call my family and my kids ask me: "Dad, when are you coming? We miss you."

Inside the Corridors of Corruption   *6 March*

Desperate refugees are being forced to pay bribes to corrupt Home Affairs officials to secure documentation which should be given to them for free.

During the *Daily Dispatch*'s investigation into the killings of Somalis we travelled to Port Elizabeth's Refugee Reception Centre with two refugees trying to renew their documents and were present when bribes were paid.

The *Dispatch* reporter did not witness the transaction himself but details were recounted by one of the refugees.

"We had to each give the official inside R400 to get our permits renewed for two years. I know this is corruption, but we did not have a choice, otherwise we would have been here longer," said one of the two men.

Refugee and asylum-seekers' permits are issued without payment in South Africa.

On Tuesday at the centre, the *Dispatch* witnessed how the two men were rudely turned away by one of the officials and escorted out of the premises by a security guard.

"This is not Shoprite – go away," shouted an official sitting in the foyer.

The two were chased by a security guard who said only 250 refugees were to be attended to each day and that the quota had been reached for the day.

The two men were left stranded and desperate after a three-hour drive in a packed taxi from East London, 300 km away.

"These [permits] are expiring today. We have to renew them today. I cannot go back to East London without a new permit," explained the refugee to the security guard.

But the guard would not hear any of it, and told them they should return the following day.

The sad, confused and worried men kept looking at their permits as if a miracle would happen.

They did not understand what the officials were going to be doing for the rest of the day as it was only 1.30 pm and there were few refugees waiting outside.

"I can be arrested with this now. I do not understand why they cannot help us because it is still early and they are not doing anything," said the disappointed man.

The two found accommodation with fellow Somalis in Port Elizabeth's Korsten suburb and awoke the next morning to try again.

A cousin of the pair, hearing of their problems, offered to introduce them to some officials at the refugee office.

On the Wednesday morning the two men and their cousin skipped past the queue and walked straight inside the refugee centre without encountering the problems of the previous day.

The cousin told the security guard they were there to see a certain official. They asked the *Dispatch* not to accompany them.

After a few hours the two came back with broad smiles on their faces and two-year permits in their hands.

"This is supposed to be done for free but they make us pay. There is nothing we can do about it because if we want to be in the country we have to pay," said one of the men.

A Somali refugee who arrived in the country in 2006 but who still holds an asylum-seeker permit said there are "middlemen", or "brokers", inside the refugee centre.

He said the brokers pretend to be interpreters but are actually the link between other refugees and the corrupt officials.

"These are my countrymen and I know what they do exactly but it is difficult for a stranger to understand their dealings. If you do not pay, you end up being in my situation and live with asylum-seeker status. There are people from my country who came here last year but have refugee status, and I do not because I do not have the money," he said.

He had to stay four days in Port Elizabeth awaiting yet another asylum-seeker permit, which was eventually renewed for three months.

Another Somali refugee who had been to the centre recently to renew his wife's permit said he paid an official R200. "I do not waste my time any more … in the queue. I just pay whatever they want because that is how we survive. You can spend days there, because officials turn you away if you do not give them money," he said.

One of two Zimbabwean women waiting outside the centre for a compatriot said she had to return twice in one week. "We have been sleeping here but they just take 24 people and tell us to come back tomorrow."

The refugee centre's head, Sipho Lucas, said the bribes and payments were completely illegal. "Asylum-seeker and refugee permits are completely free, there is no charge. Refugees are vulnerable, so any person who uses them as a means to make money is a criminal," said Lucas.

He promised to take action against the official if the two men came forward and identified him. "We are trying our level best to fight corruption. We will take every measure to deal with corrupt officials," he said.

He referred the *Dispatch* to the department's communications directorate for further comment.

Home Affairs spokesperson Joseph Mohajane promised to respond to the *Dispatch*'s questions from Tuesday, but his replies have not been received.

Refugee Saga: A Story of Hope   *12 March*

You'd have difficulty finding anyone in the Port St Johns area using the words *'amagrigamba'* and *'amakwerekwere'*.

Yet the curse words aimed at refugees and strangers are in common use in Mdantsane, where last week we investigated the plight of the Somali refugees.

Our series "Dying to Live" described the hardships and fear the Somalis endure in the township, where they live as virtual prisoners in their homes.

But since last Friday, the *Dispatch* has spent four days exploring another story: one of hope. It is being played out in Mthumbane Location at the Transkei Wild Coast town where Ethiopian refugees are finding promise in their new land.

"We only hear people that visit from the cities using words such as 'amagrigamba' against foreigners," said Novesi Bangilizwe, who rents out flats to Ethiopians.

"They relate to us how bad foreigners are treated in the townships in the cities. But here we live peacefully with them because they are also human beings who are just trying to earn a living. They are part of our community."

Her brother, Wild Coast lifesaver Sikhanyiso Bangilizwe was attacked and killed in a shark attack nearby in January.

Novesi said the Ethiopians assisted her family with her brother's funeral. Their pastor even arrived from Pretoria and conducted a service.

Mthumbane Community Policing Forum chairperson Bonginkosi Ntinini also told how they take part in community affairs. They donated money to a family that had suffered a bereavement, enabling them to buy a coffin, he said. And it was their community spirit that made them especially welcome.

"They live freely here and walk at whatever time carrying their goods and no one attacks them," he said.

"They also give a hand in the community whenever they are needed because they are Christians and part of us."

The refugees run spaza shops selling bedding and pots throughout Port St Johns and its surrounding villages. They are not threatened or spat upon, unlike the Somalis of Mdantsane, who dare not venture outside after dark.

Take Sunday night in Mthumbane Location as an example. Yalew Tessema's spaza shop buzzed with customers and children playing outside as the full moon shone over them.

He was not bothered about the time as he continued to serve customers behind his open counter, often striking up small talk in broken isiXhosa.

"There is nothing to be scared of in this place," he said. "I can close at whatever time of the night if it is really busy. The people here are friendly. We can even sleep without locking our doors."

The 38-year-old asylum-seeker has been in the country for three years since he fled from Ethiopia because of political conflict. He lost contact with his mother and younger brother between Ethiopia and Eritrea in 1998.

Tessema said he was detained for political reasons, but managed to escape and take the tough journey south, avoiding border police in different countries.

"In South Africa, after getting my papers from Home Affairs, I started working with one of my brothers [countrymen], selling socks, T-shirts and bags on the streets of Johannesburg. I also worked in a spaza shop just to save some money."

The dangerous nature of Johannesburg and the threat from criminals led to him moving to Flagstaff to sell his bedding and pots. And that's how he found his way to Port St Johns. He decided to settle with a spaza shop while his countrymen continued selling bedding and pots to surrounding villages.

Two cars arrived as he closed the shop. They parked in the big yard which is surrounded by bush. The three men got out were compatriots returning from selling and collecting money from their customers in the villages. They had left in the early hours of the morning and been out all day.

We joined them that night, eating bread with *goman* – a combination of cabbage, meat and chakalaka – and, after a good night's sleep, set out with them on a tour of the villages.

Desta Lemboro warned that it was going to be a tough day in the Wild Coast heat and that we should buy food and drink to last for the whole day.

After arriving in Tombo village, Lemboro stopped his bakkie and approached three women, telling them that he was selling blankets, duvets and pots. The friendly women told him they did not have money and were waiting for payday. He tried, unsuccessfully, to persuade them to take the goods on credit.

Lemboro then proceeded to the houses in the village. He stopped nearby as there are no access routes and carried his goods to some of the homes.

At each house he greeted the occupants in his limited isiXhosa. The villagers responded positively but, as the conversation deepened, he got more confused.

Despite the language barrier, there seemed to be some understanding about his business and the methods of payment.

The secret to the story of hope in Mthumbane is built on their being part of the community: people dealing with people, helping each other to survive the daily hardships of life.

"We take them as one of our sons because they also bring help to our families," said one of their customers, Thelma Maguga. "They have nothing to fear while they live with us in Mthumbane."

Chapter 9

Toxic Storm

Yolandi Groenewald
Mail & Guardian

A call of desperation from a fed-up community led Yolandi Groenewald to ask some serious questions about the way hazardous waste is handled in South Africa and the way one company in particular handles the process. But it's not just an environmental story. As with so much in South Africa, the story quickly became a political one.

Thermopower was the company at the centre of the investigation and in particular its plant in Clayville, Olifantsfontein, not far from Johannesburg. The local community had marched and petitioned because of the smell and the breathing difficulties that so many of them experienced, but nothing was being done. The Green Scorpions (the environmental police) were running an investigation. A case against the company for breaking environmental laws was on the court roll – but after three years, no progress.

Yolandi and a colleague started by going from door to door, talking to one person after another with respiratory problems. They talked to community leaders and heard of threats and intimidation. A chance remark led the team to trawl through complex company documents. Was this just a story about a smelly factory or was there some political side to it, hindering the investigation, holding up the court proceedings?

After the story was published, Thermopower was finally brought to court, the Green Scorpions checked compliance with the Air Quality Act and the local Ekurhuleni municipality launched an inquiry into the company's conduct. The smell and emissions? They have improved, say the community.

Yolandi Groenewald has worked for the *Mail & Guardian* for eight years as a reporter on the environment. Her work focuses on climate change, land and agriculture. In 2004 she won a merit award in the South African

Breweries Environmental Journalism awards. In 2009 she was a regional winner in the Vodacom Journalist of the Year for a joint feature on the decline of farmer numbers in the agricultural sector, and again won a merit award from South African Breweries for her work on exposing mining companies prospecting in environmentally sensitive areas.

Waste Company at Centre of Toxic Storm
24 July

Residents of Clayville in Olifantsfontein near Kempton Park are locked in a fierce battle with a nearby hazardous waste-disposal company they say is poisoning them. And they maintain that it has links with the African National Congress (ANC).

The company in question is Thermopower Process Technology, Africa's largest hazardous waste disposer and a client of major companies such as Sasol, Monsanto, BASF, AngloGold Ashanti and Afrox Gas.

Thermopower is under investigation by the government's environmental police, the Green Scorpions. A neighbouring tile factory, Norcross, says it has had to shut down twice because its workers have become ill from emissions.

Norcross and a local landowner commissioned environmental consultants to produce a report on Thermopower. It painted a damning picture of environmental abuse and called for an official investigation.

Clayville residents say a suffocating chemical stench that drifts into their houses from the Thermopower plant, about 500 m away, has made summer nights "a nightmare".

At first the residents thought the smell, which started in about 2005, was from the nearby sewerage plant. Community leader Ishmael Seeta said his night-time quests to trace the source led to Thermopower.

"That's when we realised it's dangerous chemicals we were inhaling," he said. "It must be toxic, judging by the smell and taste. We're scared to death of what it can do to our children and families."

Residents – especially the young and the elderly – suffer from chronic coughs, dry throats and headaches. Asthma is rife in the community. "You can actually feel how the smell impregnates your tongue and inner organs," said Anthony Deal, who works at Norcross. "You can literally taste the pungency."

Goodman Mncina said his wife had developed chronic asthma for the first time after living in Clayville.

Eulinder Ramashidzha, 19, told the *M&G*: "The first time I smelled this horrible smell, it made me ill. I couldn't breathe."

She consulted a doctor, who diagnosed asthma. "In summer, when things are worse, I have to use my asthma pump an average of four times a day," Ramashidzha said.

Residents said that when they suffer common ailments such as colds, they persist for weeks.

Thirteen-year-old Bright Mashimbye had suffered from flu for several weeks. He said in a barely audible voice: "Sometimes when we're playing the smoke comes and we start coughing. We're scared of the smell because it affects our voices."

The community has rallied around Seeta and fellow community leader Kgomotso Modiselle, who led a march to Thermopower last November after struggling to engage with the company.

"The company directors have told us directly we're 'too plain' and that they have Luthuli House [ANC headquarters] on their side. They said 40% of the company is owned by Luthuli House and we should speak to the ANC if we need any information," said Seeta.

Modiselle said Thermopower had befriended local ANC councillors because it believed this "gave them a close relationship with the community".

Green Scorpions raid

Environmental NGO groundWork wrote several letters to the government questioning Thermopower's record, and two years ago a Green Scorpions raid found evidence of pollution after workers blew the whistle.

"The contraventions mainly related to storage of both untreated and treated waste on the site for a period longer than permitted, as well as the facility's failure to dispose of some of the residue as legally required," said Joanne Yawitch, deputy director-general in the Environmental Affairs Department.

The Green Scorpions handed the case over to the National Prosecuting Authority for prosecution. It is understood that Thermopower has dismissed the whistle-blowers.

The company's directors have also filed a complaint of intimidation at the local police station against Modiselle, alleging that he is "threatening" them and the firm.

Modiselle claims Thermopower officials phoned his workplace in an "attempt to get me fired".

Christos Eleftheriades, Thermopower's CEO, admitted filing a complaint against Modiselle. "But I don't want to give him that much credit. I don't want to engage in any conversation about him," he said.

"Nothing grows there"

Former workers told the *M&G* that Thermopower has struggled to dispose of certain chemicals. Fired worker Ephraim Mabila said factory manager Martin Oosthuizen had told him to not burn the substances before 8 pm because Norcross would complain. Mabila was one of the whistle-blowers who prompted the Green Scorpions raid.

"On Good Friday night [in 2007], I was asked to work on a night and they put a hosepipe inside the drain at the back of Thermopower," he said. "Today nothing can grow there."

Eleftheriades said the effluent came from Norcross. "I'm telling you this for the first and last time: this factory has not had effluent emissions. Don't even believe that we generate liquids from there."

The community is also up in arms because Thermopower has applied for a licence to handle medical waste and tendered to manage effluent from Thor Mercury in KwaZulu-Natal. Thor closed in the 1990s after an investigation found its effluent was affecting the health of the Cato Ridge community.

GroundWork activist Rico Euripidou said the Green Scorpions investigation pointed to systemic bad practice at Thermopower affecting the health of workers and local residents.

"It would be irresponsible to allow them to proceed with expansion until the investigation is complete," he said.

"It wasn't us"

Thermopower process engineer Shaan Prithiraj said that when he logged most of the complaints from Norcross, the wind was blowing in the wrong direction for his company to be responsible.

"It couldn't have been us," he said. "And if you look at our monitoring reports, you'll see that we've adhered to our emission licence limits."

Independent consultants hired by Thermopower, Margot Saner and Lorraine Hodge, told the *M&G* that the community had targeted the company because it was easiest to label "your friendly neighbourhood hazardous chemical plant".

They claimed that Thermopower had exceeded the emissions limit once or twice when the tile plant had to shut down, but that this had not happened in recent years. Purple smoke was photographed billowing from Thermopower's smokestack at the time.

"Does anyone in the world not make a mistake?" Eleftheriades asked. "That was four years ago."

He alleged the community had been coached.

"If someone comes and tells children that we're the problem, what would they do or believe?" asked Eleftheriades.

"Some of those people who attend the community gatherings are getting paid to do so. They get T-shirts and food."

He said a bad smell "didn't mean [the substance in question] was dangerous".

The chemical culprits

Workers interviewed by the *M&G* identified palladium chloride and phosphorus trichloride as the main chemicals responsible for the complaints of the Clayville community.

Most are said to come from Sasol's Sasolburg plant. Thermopower issues a certificate to its clients to assure them that the chemicals have been properly and safely disposed of.

Chemical engineers consulted by the *M&G* said the phosphorus chlorides would be the most dangerous, but that palladium chloride could also be dangerous – especially if it was ignited.

Phosphorus trichloride is an important industrial chemical used in herbicides, insecticides, plasticisers, oil additives and flame retardants. It is classified as "very toxic" and "corrosive".

Inhalation of the chemical can be fatal and causes coughing, chest pains, breathing difficulty, nausea and fainting spells. Chronic effects of exposure include kidney and liver damage.

Palladium chloride causes skin irritation and may affect the metabolism if absorbed through the skin. It causes eye irritation and may cause chemical conjunctivitis.

If inhaled it causes respiratory tract and mucous membrane irritation, and if inhaled in large doses it may be carcinogenic.

Political connections

A *Mail & Guardian* investigation has revealed that Alan Norman, a former Absa executive described by some who have dealt with him as "the ANC's banker" has been central to [Thermopower's] efforts to find an empowerment partner. Among those considered was Smuts Ngonyama, when he was head of the ANC presidency under Thabo Mbeki.

Norman set up an empowerment company, Clidet 445. This later became Impepho Management, of which he is sole director and which was intended as a vehicle for the Thermopower empowerment deal.

However, a well-placed insider said Thermopower started getting cold feet early last year after the ANC's Polokwane conference toppled Mbeki and his circle and the empowerment talks were called off this year. Ngonyama has since joined Cope.

Norman confirmed that the deal was no longer on, but said there was interest from other "private individuals".

He denied that Ngonyama had ever been involved, but Ngonyama confirmed that he had shown "initial interest". In addition, community leaders claimed they were shown Thermopower documents signed by him.

The *M&G* has established that Norman is now trying to craft an empowerment deal with ANC local councillors in the Olifantsfontein area.

Norman confirmed that Thermopower had approached eight ANC councillors to assist with a "broad-based BEE deal". The *M&G* is in possession of a letter from local ANC councillors thanking the company profusely for engaging with the community.

The letter was in response to one Thermopower had written to the local branches of the ANC about the problems they had with the community. Councillor Tshilidzi Munyai responded in the letter, writing: "With greatest humility, the zonal executive committee of the ANC appreciate with much gratitude indeed for your company to avail its highest management to engage … Despite short notice your cooperation has been way above and beyond our expectations."

The company's chief executive, Christos Eleftheriades, denied that the company had links with the ANC. "There's no link at all," he said. "We looked for an empowerment company, we tried to set one up. You should go talk to the ANC if you want to find out more. I'm bound by confidentiality."

Who is Alan Norman?

Alan Norman has gained a reputation for arranging secretive BEE deals that are linked with "old" ANC stalwarts such as former ANC spin doctor Ngonyama and former ANC treasurer Mendi Msimang. Many of his ANC connections have now jumped ship to Cope.

Norman came to public attention on the back of the controversial Elephant Consortium. The consortium is thought to have profited to the tune of R2.3 billion from the unbundling of Vodacom.

The name "Clidet" has become signature when he sets up empowerment deals. He first registers a particular shelf company as a Clidet – in the case of Thermopower, Clidet 445. When negotiations have progressed, the name changes; Clidet 445 changed to Impepho Management in February 2007.

Norman is the sole director of Impepho Management and of his company Alcorp Investments.

He usually starts out as the sole director of a Clidet company, only revealing the identity of the true directors of the proposed empowerment company once the deal has been finalised. The supposed shareholders of the company are not necessarily listed as directors.

The *Sunday Times* reported that Msimang and Norman are thought to control more than a million shares in the Elephant Consortium, through shelf companies Clidet 531 and Clidet 532, listed as Elephant shareholders.

The names of the two companies were recently changed to MMTB Investment Holdings and Indoni Investments.

Ngonyama's Elephant shares were also allegedly housed in these Clidet companies.

Norman, Msimang and Thandi Lujabe-Rankoe, South Africa's high commissioner to Mozambique, were listed as directors of MMTB Investment Holdings. Six months later Norman and Lujabe-Rankoe resigned.

All three are also shareholders in and directors of Indoni Investments, the *Sunday Times* reported. Norman owns stakes in the two companies through

Alcorp Investments and is a director of 63 other companies that include Chancellor House Holdings and Impepho Building and Civils.

The *M&G* exposed Chancellor as an "ANC business front" in 2006. ANC treasurer Msimang was closely linked with Chancellor.

Impepho Building and Civils, which lists Ngonyama as its director, owns a 30% share in the Liviero construction group.

Chapter 10

Broken Homes

Gcina Ntsaluba
Daily Dispatch

This was a story generated by the news team at the *Daily Dispatch*, but with an unusual source and history. In 2008 the *Dispatch* had run a fun-filled travel adventure project, exploring the forgotten villages and backwaters of the Eastern Cape.

One thing they had noticed at the time was the thousands of empty state-built homes. How strange, they thought, in a province with such poverty and such housing need. And so the Broken Homes investigation was born.

Gcina Ntsaluba and photographer Theo Jeptha spent several months returning to many of these places to uncover the reasons for these mushrooming ghost towns.

The scale of the collapse of the government's housing programme became clear as Gcina revealed that thousands of the houses simply could not be lived in as they were so badly built, and that housing projects had lagged so far behind that by the time the homes were built, the people they were meant for had left the area.

He revealed a housing backlog of 800 000 homes and noted that huge sums, running into millions of rands, were needed to fix the houses that had been built.

The story went online and into print in July. And the biggest surprise of all was the government's reaction.

"For once we were not attacked and vilified," says *Dispatch* editor Andrew Trench.

On the contrary, a public letter from Chris Vick, spokesman for human settlements minister Tokyo Sexwale, thanked them for their work: "I'd like to put on record our appreciation of the vital role that the *Daily Dispatch* has played in highlighting the plight of the poor, and in particular in exposing problems with housing service delivery. It's no secret within our team that it was your Broken Homes report that first helped us, as newcomers to this portfolio, to understand the scale of the problem in the Eastern Cape."

A public campaign culminated in three major contractors being fired, and legal action is in process against dozens more.

Gcina Ntsaluba is now based in Cape Town where he has joined the investigations unit at the *Mail & Guardian*. He studied journalism at Walter Sisulu University in the Eastern Cape before he became a junior reporter for the African Eye News Service in Nelspruit in 2007. He moved to the *Daily Dispatch* in 2008.

Broken Promises Broken Homes   29 July

Bhisho is spending R360 million to fix nearly 20 000 broken homes in the province while the poor live in flimsy cardboard units and ghost towns emerge from the ruins of disastrous housing projects.

In some areas of the province, communities have deserted formal housing settlements because the homes were so poorly built that they cannot live in them any longer.

The number of homes having to be repaired is more than the total number of 19 662 houses delivered in the 2006/07 financial year.

While the provincial government tries to rein in its backlog of 800 000 RDP homes, a two-month investigation by the *Dispatch* has revealed how:

- Homes were built in areas which people have long since left;
- One project in Seymour became state-sponsored "holiday homes" for people who live in other cities and only return in December;
- Residents in Burgersdorp were moved into cardboard houses when their RDP homes began falling to the ground, and were then asked to clean up the mess themselves;
- One project of 600 homes in Tarkastad has been standing empty, while a waiting list to house people continues to grow;
- Depopulation and inferior construction in places like Venterstad have led to the emergence of ghost towns; and

- A community near Bhisho has been waiting five years for electricity and water because the government refuses to provide the services until it has finished the housing project it started eight years ago.

The biggest victims in the province's housing fiasco are among the most vulnerable in the population. Like two pensioners, Loki Makeleni and Ngqukuse Nonxaza, who have been living in a flimsy cardboard home for seven months while their shoddy RDP house in Burgersdorp is repaired.

"The government doesn't care about people who live here. We're going to die in these houses. I'm just waiting for my coffin right now," said the elderly Makeleni.

To rub salt into their wounds, the local Gariep Municipality wanted the same residents to clear the tons of rubble lining the streets – for nothing.

The problems in Burgersdorp are far from unique – in fact, all but one of eight housing projects visited by the *Dispatch* are being rebuilt.

In many cases inexperienced contractors have been blamed for the problems.

Two weeks ago housing MEC Nombulelo Mabandla vowed to blacklist incompetent builders and recover funds from them where necessary.

But she said her department would never forsake emerging contractors and would do all they could to mentor them in future.

"That is why we have developed a training programme for them, called the Emerging Contractors Development Programme," she said.

Seymour and Venterstad are two examples where RDP homes have been deserted or remain unoccupied because there are no local jobs, or poor workmanship has made the buildings unsafe.

Yet the reverse has happened in Tarkastad, where more than 600 residents are on a waiting list to occupy low-cost homes in a nearby project that is standing empty.

Derek Luyt from the Public Service Accountability Monitor in Grahamstown said the department's Service Delivery Charter and Service Delivery Plans for 2009 and 2010 highlight its pitfalls.

"Staff shortages and lack of sufficient skills have severely hampered the department in the past, and it will not be able to deliver sufficient houses of adequate quality unless it solves its human resources problems," Luyt said.

Democratic Alliance spokesperson Pine Pienaar said the huge backlog, lack of monitoring and under-spending in the department were a direct result of the department's inefficiency to fill critical posts in technical and finance departments.

*Rob Rose receives the 2009
Taco Kuiper Award from
Justice Tom Cloete, of the
Valley Trust, for his expose
of Barry Tannenbaum's
collapsed Ponzi scheme*

Leonard Chuene, President of Athletics South Africa, before he was forced to resign over his handling of the Caster Semenya affair

Tearful Niehaus admits fraud

Pages 2 & 3

The ANC spin doctor:

- Forged signatures of top politicians;
- Booked holidays on government accounts; and
- Was pushed out of top jobs for financial misconduct.

Admits:

- "Most of what you've confronted me with is true ... I've made massive mistakes"
- "I fell into the devastation of debt"

One day Carl Niehaus was the ANC spokesman, the next a self-confessed liar and cheat, deeply in debt and with no choice but to resign his post

City Press

DISTINCTLY AFRICAN

20 December 2009   www.citypress.co.za   R8.00 (incl VAT) NAMIBIA: N$8.50

'I want my f*%#@!! pardon'

■ 'Terminally ill' fraudster caught on camera violating his parole conditions

JOU MA! Schabir Shaik walks out of the Spar in Florida Road in Durban on Reconciliation Day
Pictures: Julian Rademeyer and Felix Dlangamandla

INSIDE

2009: It's a wrap City Pulse

Manto's final interview
Page 13

JULIAN RADEMEYER

"TERMINALLY ill" fraudster Schabir Shaik violated his parole this week and for the first time since his release on medical parole was caught on camera.

He appears to have made a remarkable recovery in the nine months since he was described as being in the "final stages of a terminal illness" and granted medical parole.

This week he snuck out of his Durban mansion in his new jet-black BMW X6 to visit an upmarket townhouse complex, go shopping and even mustered up enough strength to pursue a City Press photographer while shouting: "Jou ma se p***s".

"Why don't you apply your creative skills to find out why am I not getting a f***ing pardon because the longer I stay a prisoner, other people are equally guilty," he said.

Despite a host of sightings Shaik has managed to avoid being photographed. The Department of Correctional Services has said it would only act if it was provided with a formal complaint and proof that Shaik has broken his parole.

On March 3 this year Shaik was carried into his Innes Road home on a stretcher after serving just two years and four months of a 15-year prison term for corruption and fraud relating to illicit financial dealings with President Jacob Zuma and French arms company Thint.

The same day the then minister of correctional services, Ngconde Balfour, said that Shaik was "in the final phase of his terminal condition" and that legislation provided for his parole to "die a dignified death".

On Tuesday morning, wearing sunglasses, a wide-brimmed hat and accompanied by a woman, Shaik drove to The Essenwoods townhouse complex in Stephen Dlamini Road (formerly Essenwood Road). He returned home that afternoon, pulling into his driveway at 1.26pm. A City Press reporter stopped next to Shaik's BMW, registration ND 554-380, at the intersection of Stephen Dlamini and Springfield roads and could clearly identify him sitting in the driver's seat.

On Wednesday morning he popped into his local Spar in Florida Road. Wearing baggy shorts, sandals, sunglasses and a golf cap perched jauntily on his head, he emerged at 8.25am with two cartons of milk and some magazines.

He spotted photographer Felix Dlangamandla sitting in a parked car outside the main entrance, lunged towards him and struck the vehicle with a milk carton.

Then he quickly crossed the road and sped off around the corner as a security guard looked on aghast.

This week he denied visiting The Essenwoods on Tuesday.

He did admit visiting the Spar which was where he was photographed on Wednesday - but said he had asked his parole officer for permission to fetch medication at a nearby pharmacy. He claimed to have stopped at Spar to buy milk after getting his medicine but a City Press team that followed him did not see him go anywhere else except the Spar nor did he have a medicine packet in his hands when he left.

He suggested that reporters "following me around" could "possibly get f***ed up".

A correctional services spokesman is on record as saying that Shaik's parole conditions allow him to leave home only on Fridays to attend mosque and on Saturdays between 12pm and 4pm.

But in answer to questions posed by the DA in Parliament the ministry of correctional services said Shaik was only allowed to leave his home between 10.30am and 12.30pm on Wednesdays for physiotherapy.

Any deviations from his parole conditions must first be approved by correctional services. In May Shaik's brother, Yunis, told reporters that he was "gravely ill". He said his brother "never leaves the house" and "his condition cannot improve because there was permanent damage to him".

In another interview at the time Yunis said "Schabir's heart is enlarged, his kidneys and brain have been badly affected and he has lost about 30% of his sight. My understanding is that my brother is in what doctors call the 'final stage' of a physical shut-down."

Despite his ailing condition, the database of the Companies and Intellectual Properties Registration Office indicates that Shaik and Durban businessman Raymond Horne managed to register a close corporation, Wethersfield Trading CC, on May 25 this year. Shaik's contribution to the CC is 50%. The exact nature of its business is unclear.

By law anyone convicted of fraud or corruption and sentenced to imprisonment of at least six months without the option of a fine is disqualified from taking part directly or indirectly in managing a CC.

Shaik said Horne was his "security adviser" but claimed to have no knowledge of the CC. "I wonder what that is about. Maybe it has something to do with the lesser assets I have. I might have a partner who is a director of the company to manage whatever assets I have left," he said.

One since Shaik seems to be avoiding is the restaurant Spiga d'Oro, his favourite haunt in Florida Road, that a dish named in his honour, Linguine a la Shaik - Arrabiata with a hint of chilli - is popular with diners and the occasional Shaik-spotter hoping for a glimpse of the "dead man walking"

■ **Read more on Page 4**

Read more on Page 4

Spain and Chile set to rule 2010
Page 19

Schabir Shaik, released from prison in the final phase of a terminal condition, pops into his local supermarket

*Moketedi Mpshe, then Acting
National Director of Public
Prosecutions, dropped charges
against President Jacob Zuma
in someone else's words*

Shoot
CONFEDERATIONS CUP
TEAMS PREVIEW
INSIDE TODAY

The Star
with BUSINESSREPORT

SPORT
BAFANA
vs IRAQ
SPECIAL
SEE PAGE 28

2 DAYS TO GO

FRIDAY JUNE 12 2009   Established October 17 1887   R5,00 inc VAT   (R5,30 outside Gauteng)   Annual subscribers: R4,36   www.star.co.za

MECs in multimillion-rand car, leather seats, sunroof splurge

It's a WaBenzi frenzy

ALEX ELISEEV

LEATHER seats: R41 000; sunroof R13 000; 21-inch alloy wheels: R16 900; and Bose sound system: R5 600. Total cost of extras: R266 236. Being the politician with the coolest ride: priceless.

After the April elections, elected leaders across South Africa are rushing out to buy the most luxurious cars the rule book allows.

Ministers, premiers and MECs have been dubbed the "kings and queens of bling", who – as The Star's investigation shows – have spent tens of millions of rands on the latest Mercedes-Benz, BMW, Audi or Land Rover.

WaBenzi is a colloquial term used to describe a government official's expensive vehicle of choice (usually a Mercedes-Benz).

In Limpopo, one of the country's poorest provinces, Premier Cassel Mathale has just bought an "imperial blue" BMW 750i worth R1 055 050. His MEC for Public Works, Pandelani Ramagoma, opted for a R800 000 Land Rover, on which the tax alone is close on R100 000. Pitsi Moloto, the MEC for economic development, environment and tourism, bought an Audi Q7 worth R560 000, which – with the help of some extras – landed up costing taxpayers almost R900 000.

Moloto's Audi 4x4 was bought with 19 extra features, which boosted the price to R875 333.

The extras include: air suspension; an electrical folding towbar (worth R8 200); privacy glass; tyre pressure monitoring; a parking system; cruise control; DVD-based navigation; 3 line exterior package (worth almost R30 000); a cellphone kit; special headlights; and voice recognition. The "Phantom black" paint job cost an extra R2 000.

All the departments refused to be drawn into the ethical debate of whether the purchases amounted to a waste of taxpayer money

"The cars have been bought for politicians who are leaders of government in line with policy," Limpopo provincial spokesman Mogale Nchabeleng said.

R875 333

R920 000

EfficientD

R1 055 050

R800 000

POLITICIAN PERKS: Audi Quattro Q7 – Limpopo MEC Pitsi Moloto; Mercedes-Benz ML 63 – former Gauteng MEC Nomantu Nkomo-Ralehoko; BMW 750i – Limpopo Premier Cassel Mathale; Range Rover – Limpopo MEC Pandelani Ramagoma.

Pushed on the ethics, he said that was a debate right across government. Combined, the three cars cost R2.7 million.

In Gauteng, former MEC for agriculture and rural development Nomantu Nkomo-Ralehoko spent R920 000 on a second-hand Mercedes-Benz. The vehicle was hijacked a day after it left the showroom floor.

One national ministry is busy buying a R900 000 Mercedes-Benz S350, with a possibility of a second being bought. Another ministry is spending R900 000 on a top-of-the-range Lexus.

In Mpumalanga, one department has just spent R700 000 on an E350 Merc and more than R350 000 on a Toyota 4x4.

In the Northern Cape, an MEC is gearing up to drive a Mercedes-Benz ML500 worth

R550 000 and the Free State is acquiring about 10 official cars allegedly worth about R10 million.

DA chief whip Ian Davidson has lashed out at the car frenzy. "They are the kings and queens of bling, amassing as much as possible in terms of their allowances to pump their egos at the expense of others."

According to the 2009/10 figures, government allocates an average of R55 000 to build one RDP house

(with an additional R20 000 going towards servicing of land). The extras on Moloto's Audi alone could have built three homes.

The Ministerial Handbook says MECs and Premiers are allowed to buy an official car not exceeding 70% of their annual salary package. They can purchase a new car once an existing one has been driven for 120 000km or five years.

alex.eliseev@inl.co.za

Stolen Merc surprise

ALEX ELISEEV

POLICE are in the process of confirming whether the R920 000 Mercedes-Benz stolen from former Gauteng MEC Nomantu Nkomo-Ralehoko has been snuck across the Swaziland border.

It has emerged that Interpol is waiting for confirmation that one of the cars seized in the neighbouring country is the luxury ML 63 AMG stolen hours after being driven off the showroom.

Several similar cars have been recovered in Swaziland during a joint operation, Interpol spokeswoman Senior Superintendent Tummi Golding said yesterday.

Golding said that a representative had been sent to identify the car.

She could not say how many cars were awaiting identification, but said she had been informed that the car suspected of being the ex-MEC's is not the only one there.

Asked whether this could be the work of a cross-border crime syndicate, she said it could not be ruled out.

Nkomo-Ralehoko had been pushed to resign over the saga.

Workers lauded on 2010 stadium efforts

ON TARGET: President Jacob Zuma kicks a ball at a ceremony at Cape Town's Green Point stadium yesterday.   PICTURE: SCHALK VAN ZUYDAM / AP

ANÉL LEWIS

"WE HAVE made it, we have made it." This was the triumphant call from President Jacob Zuma as he kicked a soccer ball at Cape Town's Green Point stadium to mark the 360-day World Cup countdown.

Zuma was joined by dignitaries that included Western Cape Premier Helen Zille, Cape Town mayor Dan Plato, Minister of Sport Makhenkesi Stofile, MEC for Sport and Recreation Sakkie Jenner and local organising committee CEO Danny Jordaan in celebrating the city's final stretch before the event kicks off on June 11.

But while he acknowledged the preparations they had done for the

World Cup, it was the construction workers who got most of Zuma's praise.

"It is you, the workers, who make it happen. You have put your strength and sweat (into this) in an amazing way," he said to the hundreds of workers who had gathered in the stands to welcome him.

"The workers here have contributed to making history. Thank you very much for a job well done."

Zuma ignored the calls for a rendition of Umshini Wami, choosing instead to regale the guests and throng of local and international media with a tale about the beauty of Cape Town.

The Green Point Stadium, which is now about 73 percent

complete and on track to being handed over on December 14, was awash yesterday with police and sniffer dogs hours before Zuma arrived. Journalists were searched before they could enter the area, where police were on high alert.

Mike Marsden, 2010 project leader and Cape Town executive director of service delivery and integration, said yesterday security was a key priority for 2010.

"Cape Town will be as safe as any city in Europe," he said.

Marsden said the cost of the stadium was expected to be R4.3 billion when completed. An estimated R3bn was being invested in the inner city by the private sector.

▶ See Page 6

switch
and save
Switch to this SPAR Brand Product, for the same quality as leading brands, at an even better price.

SPAR

SOFT MARGARINE

SAVE R7.00
*SPAR Soft Margarine Tub 1 kg
22.99 each

Good For You

INSIDE YOUR SATURDAY Star	TOMORROW	THE SUNDAY INDEPENDENT

Meet the beautiful South African actress who is wowing British audiences opposite Jude Law in Hamlet

Meet the woman who fell in love with jailed apartheid killer Ferdie Barnard – and married him – and the journalist who decided to write a thriller starring both of them.

Meet the woman who went from

university to stripping, erotic massages, editing an Afrikaans porn magazine and back to journalism before writing her memoirs and starting a cyber war in the process.

Find out why the government's multimillion-rand transport system is doomed to fail, but why internet billionaire Mark Shuttleworth's

ubuntu software could change the world for the better

Win tickets to the Confed Cup pool games, make your dad feel like James Bond, Travel with us to exotic destinations or just make the most of your weekend.

It's all in the Saturday Star on sale tomorrow.

The story of Elsa the lion cub, raised by George and Joy Adamson in Kenya, and returned to the wild was made into an Oscar-winning movie in 1966 and captured the hearts and tears of the world.

This inspired the launch of the

Born Free Foundation, now a global wildlife organisation that rescues captive undercover rescues, threats and rifle-point confrontations are well-known in the Born Free team.

Read this remarkable tale in The Sunday Independent this weekend.

The curious case of the Mercedes-Benz bought and lost by Gauteng MEC Nomantu Nkomo-Ralehoko led to her resignation and an outcry over politicians' bling cars

PRIME RESPONSE
Wiseman Nkuhlu hits back over his axing
page 4

SCHOOL SPORT
Results roundup from the weekend
page 18

MALL MISERY
Top deli closes in shopping centre standoff
page 6

Daily Dispatch

Founded 1872

Your paper. Your community. Your life.

Tuesday March 3, 2009. R4.00 incl. VAT

• SA's most award-winning journalism of 2008 •

'He said let's kill these things (Somalis) today and get rid of them. They come here to take our women and behave like this is their country.'

– Andile Tunzana, jailed for two Somali murders.

'Why I killed'

ANDILE Tunzana has the blood of four Somalis on his hands and, as he sits in Mdantsane Prison serving two life sentences, he has finally told why he killed.

"We knew they had a lot of money in their shops and had no guns to fight back," said Tunzana, 26, who is doing hard time for the killing of Somali refugees around East London.

"We shot those who tried to resist and then looked for money. No one cared for them in the township because they are *grigambas*."

Tunzana's story confirms how South African government policy predisposes Somali refugees to become victims in a country which they hoped would offer sanctuary.

Since his conviction by the East London High Court in 2006 Tunzana says he has converted to Islam – the religion of his victims – and adopted the name Ismael Junaid.

It was his conversion that led to him agreeing to his jail interviews with the Daily Dispatch. We conducted hours of interviews with him as part of a four-month investigation into the killing of Somalis in our community. We lived with Somalis to understand the hatred directed at them; we spoke to police who investigated the cases, and to witnesses, survivors and independent experts.

We were also present when corrupt Home Affairs officials took bribes from refugees desperate to renew their permits.

The picture that has emerged is clear: Somalis become victims of crime because of State policy which provides them with limited legal protection, does not allow them to live a normal life or have access to institutions like banks. They are left vulnerable to be preyed on by criminals and corrupt officials in communities that reject them.

At the time of the murders in 2005, Tunzana was on the run, having escaped from custody while awaiting trial on another murder charge. He and his accomplices robbed and murdered Mohammed Nasier Omar and Mahamud Abdi Mohammed at their spaza shop in Mzamo Street, Duncan Village, on July 5, 2005.

Earlier, he had shot and wounded Mohammed Ismail in a thigh and Mashafa Muhammed in the jaw at their Mtendeni Street, Duncan Village, spaza shop, and shot and wounded Daniel Dala, a security guard at a Somali-owned shop in Lamont Street at CC Lloyd Township.

Tunzana admitted in his interviews with the Dispatch that the Somali spaza shops were easy targets.

"We got information that the *amagrigamba* were not banking their money and, instead, were hiding it in their shops. They were easy to rob because they did not resist much and there was no one to protect them."

Tunzana said they planned their attacks around the Somalis' prayer times; Muslims worship five times a day. The gang knew that while other Somalis went to the mosque to pray there would be only one shopkeeper, which made robberies easy.

"We knew they were the only ones who had a lot of money and were easy to rob in the township. I did not care much about robbing any other person who looks like me because I know that they might be struggling to survive. The Somalis were just other foreign people with money and no one cared about them."

Tunzana said on the day of their rampage they had told themselves they were going to get rid of Somalis. "Ta Ero (Eric Nanto, his accomplice) said let's kill these things (Somalis) today and get rid of them. They come here to take our women and behave like this is their country," said Tunzana.

They showed no mercy.

Buzani Nkunzana, an eye-witness to the robbery and shooting of Ismail and Muhammed, recalled what happened after Tunzana and his three accomplices stormed the spaza on the afternoon of July 5, 2005.

Nkunzana, an electrician, was with Ismail and Mohammed in their bedroom trying to fix their VCR when they heard a big bang. "I got a shock," he said. "I heard people shouting and demanding money from the Somalis on the other side. I then saw the two Somalis walking backwards to the room and a person was pointing a gun at them."

Nkunzana saw the Somalis gunned down.

One of the robbers fired a shot which hit Mohammed and he immediately fell to the floor.

He thinks they shot him because his lighter skin gave him away as a foreigner.

"I just went on the floor next to one of the Somalis and there was just a pool of blood coming from him. I thought this must be my last day alive. I was scared that I was going to die."

But he escaped their attention.

Afterwards, Nkunzana followed the gang from the house and saw people scattering in the street, some screaming, as Tunzana and his gang strolled down the road.

"They were not even running or trying to hide ... they just walked," Nkunzana said.

Tunzana told the Dispatch he could not really remember what happened but acknowledges he shot people.

"I remember at one of the shops the *amagrigamba* tried to shoot me but their guns jammed," he said. "They ran away and I shot at them, but they did not die."

Tunzana said, despite his conversion to Islam, his feelings about his crimes remained ambiguous. At times during the interviews he would claim not to have hated his victims. But then he would refer to them using the derogatory *amagrigamba* term.

At first, he blamed alcohol and evil spirits for attacking the Somalis, but in a later interview he admitted he killed because of greed and because he thought he could get away with it because they were foreigners.

"All we wanted was more money for us and it was easy to get it from their shops and do whatever we wanted. I had also managed to avoid police for a long time so I believed that there was no way we could be arrested because these were just *amagrigamba*."

Tunzana said also his new faith had compelled him to tell the truth: "According to Islam, one must confess all his sins and tell the truth. It was right for me to confess to the killings and for God to forgive me.

"If I had taken up Islam before, I would not have robbed and killed my brothers. I hope for forgiveness now."

But Abdullahi Adbi Sheikh, the brother of one victim, Mahamud Abdi Mohammed, is not convinced that Tunzana has converted and does not think he can "I am a Muslim," he said, "but after all the pain we went through how can we be expected to give out our hand to the person who did us wrong?

"For me ... I cannot forgive anybody. God forgives."

Dying to live
Inside the Somali murders ...

Reporting
Thanduxolo Jika

Pictures
Theo Jeptha

A project made possible thanks to the Taco Kuiper Fund for Investigative Journalism at Wits University

Why the minister said no to us

LAST week on Wednesday the Daily Dispatch requested an interview with the Minister of Home Affairs, Nosiviwe Mapisa-Nqakula, about some of the questions raised in our 'Dying to Live' project.

We particularly wanted to ask the minister about government policy, which many blame for the predicament refugees find themselves in and which, they say, predisposes them to become victims of crime.

The interview was scheduled to take place yesterday but, after looking through questions sent in advance, the minister responded that she felt they related to "operational" matters and should be handled by the director-general's office.

We hope to publish some kind of response from the department in coming days. — *Thanduxolo Jika*

'I cannot explain the pain'

Somalian cries for his brother ... but with vengeance in his heart

see page 11

Coming later this week: We witness first-hand the corruption of the SA refugee permit system

TIMELINE OF TERROR

SOMALIS living in East London have been victims of brutal robberies and murders for years and, in May last year, xenophobic attacks against foreigners exploded across South Africa.

Those who have survived bear the scars, and those who still run spaza shops in local townships do so in constant fear for their lives.

Some of the high-profile attacks on Somalis in the Eastern Cape since 2005 have included:

May 25, 2005: Gunmen attack a Zwelitsha spaza shop, killing Somali Faysael Mohammed and leaving store owner Abdi Ali-Rage critically wounded after he is shot in the stomach.

April 8, 2005: Robbers flee with about R12 000 in cash and groceries worth R17 000 after releasing snakes into a Somali shop to scare the owners.

July 5, 2005: Somalis Mahamud Abdi Mohammed and Mohammed Nasier Omar are killed in a brutal attack by armed men on six spaza shops owned by foreigners in Duncan Village. Three Somalis are wounded in the shootings.

July 28, 2005: Two Somalis are attacked during an armed robbery in Tyutyu Village outside King William's Town. Spaza shop owner Ahmed Abdirahman, 24, is shot in the chest and dies at the scene.

August 17, 2005: Somali spaza shopkeeper Kasi Adid, 26, is murdered at his spaza shop in Sterkstroom, near Queenstown. He dies on the way to hospital.

February 13, 2007: Seven Somali shops are burnt down and 20 others looted in Motherwell township, Port Elizabeth.

September 28, 2008: A Somali mother, Sarah Farah, is knifed 113 times and three children – one of whom was disabled – are butchered at Tambo village near Queenstown.

September 20, 2008: Hassan Hardi, 34, is shot and killed at his business premises in Buffalo Flats. Three men armed with guns enter his shop and demand money – he is shot as he tries to run away.

Exposé that shames us all

By ANDREW TRENCH, Editor

COMMENT

TODAY we publish the first instalment of our *Dying to Live* project, which looks at why Somalis are being slaughtered in our community.

This subject is not widely popular.

Our reporting shows that many South Africans couldn't care less about the refugees in our country. The charitable would prefer they were rather not here at all. The uncharitable kill them.

But we have spent four months trying to understand why these vulnerable people are constantly targeted, abused and attacked.

The truth shames us all and exposes as a lie that grand claim in the preamble to our Constitution which says we "believe that South Africa belongs to all who live in it, united in our diversity".

As you will read in the pages of this newspaper today and in coming days, this is not apparently what we, as a society, believe.

Instead, we behave like dogs snarling at a suburban gate when strangers come to call.

Our series exposes the prejudice and hatred we hold in our hearts against those who are not one of "us".

Government policy is utterly inadequate, the system corrupt, and political leadership on this question is practically non-existent – and why, after all, should politicians care? Refugees can't vote. In fact, they pretty much have no rights at all.

But we believe that a newspaper does not always have to write about issues that are popular. Sometimes we need to write articles that make us stop and think for a moment.

We hope you will read our reports and ask yourself if we can be proud of anything our society stands for when we spit on fellow human beings the way we do.

Last year the world was shocked at the wave of xenophobic violence that swept across South Africa. There is little to stop this from happening again.

To the Somali community which has helped us in our reporting we offer our thanks.

It may be a while before your neighbours say this to you, so we will say it:

Hal kan ku soo dhowaada.

You are welcome here.

Dying to live

For an exclusive multimedia look inside the Somali killings visit our site.

http://blogs.dispatch.co.za/dying/

TIMELINE INTERACTIVE MAP VIDEO DIARY AUDIO PICTURES

Now in every Wednesday's Dispatch

OUT OF THE VAULT
Top EL police dog retires and now works part-time

DISPATCH VOICES
Increase in violent rape is cause for grave concern

SPORTS CHIRP
Bulldogs' fight back in opening game

The killing of Somalis in the Eastern Cape took the Dispatch *team into prison, into Home Affairs and into the Somali community for a series the editor hoped would make his readers stop and think*

Sticking with comedy:
**Michael Naicker
returns to EL / 12**

Daily*Life*
Daily Dispatch, Tuesday, March 3, 2009

Reds heat:
**Bok Smith buckles
in Brisbane / 20**

'I cannot explain the pain'

Somalian cries for his brother with vengeance in his heart

HORRIFIC MEMORIES: 'I had to wash blood from his body,' recalls Abdullahi Abdi Sheikh.

Dying to live
inside the Somali murders

Reporting
Thanduxolo Jika

Pictures
Theo Jeptha

A project made possible thanks to the Taco Kuiper Fund
for Investigative Journalism at Wits University

ABDULLAHI Abdi Sheikh's life was shattered when his younger brother, his only family member in South Africa, was gunned down by multiple murderer Andile Tanzana during an armed robbery in East London's Duncan Village just 28 days after he arrived in the country.

Mahamud Abdi Mohammed was killed, along with Mohammed Nasier Omar, when Tanzana and three accomplices went on a robbery-and-killing spree of Somalis in the area on July 5, 2008.

"I cannot explain the pain and the feeling of losing your brother and someone you grew up with and who ate from the same plate with you," said Abdullahi.

Mahamud, the third born in a family of nine, had already escaped two near-fatal attacks while working in Somali-owned spaza shops in Port Elizabeth in 2003 and 2004.

"We were very close. I even took him to college to study," said Abdullahi.

His whole family escaped war-torn Somalia in 1991 and then lived in a refugee camp near the remote Kenyan village of Dadaab.

Abdullahi left the camp in 1996 in search of a job in Nairobi, the country's capital city, and managed to find work at a restaurant before Mahamud joined him.

In his continued attempts to support their family he sent Mahamud to study as a motor mechanic at a technical training institute, but life was hard and his brother was unable to find a job.

Then, in 2002, he gave Mahamud money to go to South Africa to find a better life. But in SA his struggle continued and he only found work in spaza shops owned by Somalis.

Mahamud eventually started his own spaza shop with money sent from Kenya by Abdullahi, who joined him less than a month before he was killed.

Abdullahi said the whole family's lives had been shattered as his brother had also been the main provider for relatives or members back in Kenya.

He regrets ever encouraging his brother to move to South Africa. "I had to wash his body with my hands to clean off the blood on the left side of his chest where the bullet had pierced through. It was very painful carrying his body to the graveyard."

Abdullahi broke down as he spoke about his difficulty in having to explain to his parents how his brother had died and that he had buried him in a dignified Muslim manner.

"They will never trust me again because they did not see his body."

Abdullahi said he would have preferred vengeance as he could not forgive Tanzana and was not convinced that he had changed and converted to Islam, as the killer had claimed.

"I wish I had power," he said. "I would have shattered all their lives as they shattered mine – an eye for an eye."

Blame the government, say experts

SOUTH African government policy is indirectly responsible for Somalis and other migrants becoming victims of crime and prejudice, experts say.

Dr Loren Landau, director of the Forced Migration Studies Programme at Wits University, said criminals focused on Somalis because they were excluded from financial institutions and generally had cash in their shops. Refugees were also unable to access the justice system for protection.

"Police have generally been unable or unwilling to protect Somalis and many other migrants. You can attack them with relative impunity."

Landau said the findings of the Dispatch investigation generally reflected what they had found in their research.

"I believe there are also general tensions around issues of integration and the perception that Somalis see themselves as somehow superior."

Landau said while many attacks on Somalis were criminally motivated there were other factors, too, like greed, resentment, hate and local political power battles.

Wits University's Chair of Psychology Professor Gillian Finchilescu said the vulnerability of Somalis might be seen as an opportunity to commit crimes against them but the attackers also believed there would be no retribution or chance of being accountable to the law or being condemned by local communities.

In xenophobic attacks, "the victims are an identifiable group that differs from the majority in some way (with different language, customs, religion). They are vulnerable in the sense that they do not enjoy the rights of the rest of the population, including protection from the law enforcers, and they have less of a voice or no voice that could influence government officials."

Professor Michael Neocosmos, Director of Global Movements Research at Monash South Africa, said Somali killer Andile Tanzana's comments to the Dispatch were consistent with his research on xenophobia. "As Somalis and other foreigners are vilified in society they become easy targets for criminals, as your informants say."

Neocosmos said the government was failing to ensure their safety by delaying issuing residence permits and by treating foreigners as if they come to take and not to provide. "People who come to this country must be seen as providers of jobs, opportunities and knowledge."

SA Human Rights Commission commissioner Dr Zonke Majodina, who has produced a report on the lives of Somali refugees in Johannesburg, said Somalis' day-to-day life appeared to be framed by a hostile environment which made them feel unsafe.

For a managed programme of integration to be successful there should be a semi-independent body that co-ordinates all institutions that provide services to refugees, she added.

Bullet shatters paralysed teenager's dream

ABDULLAHI Haji Gaan, a 17-year-old Somali teenager, fled his war-torn country early last year as he followed his dream of a new life in South Africa – only to be shot and left paralysed.

His family believes he would have been safer in strife-torn Mogadishu, his homeland's capital.

Gaan is now wheelchair-bound after being shot last September by robbers at a spaza shop in Mdantsane's NU11, where he worked.

He was woken up by a commotion when two armed men entered the shop after his colleague opened the door for a bread delivery.

Seeing the two armed men he tried to flee to his room but was spotted and shot in the back.

The teenager now has a bullet next to his spinal cord which doctors at Cecilia Makiwane Hospital cannot remove as it requires a special operation. Gaan does not have the money to pay for the operation.

He said he spent three months in hospital before being discharged after the doctors said him there was nothing more they could do.

Now, with the help of friends at a Somali-owned lodge, Gaan exercises by holding onto steel bars every day in the hope that his left leg will become strong enough for him to walk again.

When we spoke to him he was in the middle of his exercises.

Gaan survives through his countryman's help but he hopes that if he can walk again, he will find work so that he can send money to his mother back in Somalia.

"I ran away from home (Mogadishu) because there were a lot of young people and my friends being killed. I did not know that this kind of a thing could happen to me here in South Africa," said Gaan.

Now he regrets ever setting foot in the country.

"My mother was very angry with me for leaving and now I have to deal with this condition," he said.

"They believe if I had stayed home this would not have happened."

He said his journey to South Africa was an ordeal in itself – he braved heat and starvation and managed to avoid police through Kenya, Tanzania, Malawi, Zambia, Zimbabwe and Mozambique, using buses and sometimes hiding in crates, before arriving in this country.

Gaan finally reached a friend in East London who had given him some money to leave Somalia.

He was given a chop-keeping job at a Somali-owned spaza shop but his life took a cruel and unexpected turn in the robbery.

All he wants now is to be able to walk and work again.

And his friends and countrymen believe he has the will to achieve that before the end of this year.

Refugee saga: a story of hope

After the horrors of Mdantsane, a different picture is emerging in the townships near Port St Johns where the welcome mat is out

SHARING FOOD: Somalis Liro, Sismu Sueu, Isokreyber Rangifsuu and Ibuines Luovduu eat together after a hard day's work.

Dying to live
inside the Somali murders

Reporting
Thanduxolo Jika

Pictures
Theo Jeptha

A project made possible thanks to the Taco Kuiper Fund
for Investigative Journalism at Wits University

Dying to live

http://blogs.dispatch.co.za/dying/

Community leader Ismael Seeta who pounded the streets at night to track the smells from the Thermopower plant run by CEO Christos Eleftheriades

FUNNY SPELLS
Adding humour to hypnotism
page 14

WORLD RECORD
SA's van der Burgh storms into final
page 23

GRAN LEARNER
106 year old gran learns to read
page 3

Daily Dispatch
Founded 1872

Your paper. Your community. Your life.

Wednesday July 29, 2009   R4.00 (incl VAT)   ● SA's most award-winning journalism of 2008

Broken promises broken homes

Thousands of EC poor live in despair

GOVERNMENT PLEDGES:

2005:
HOUSING, Local Government and Traditional Affairs MEC Neo Moerane-Mamase promises that an urgent audit of all in-complete projects would be completed within the first six months of the 2005/06 financial year.

2006:
PREMIER Nosimo Balindlela promises to build 25 000 new houses but only 11 971 are finished.

2007:
FORMER President Thabo Mbeki vows to eradicate the bucket toilets used by 330 000

households in the country of which 58 474 are in the Eastern Cape) by the end of 2007.

2008:
FORMER MEC for Housing Thoko Xasa promises to build 36 000 houses during the 2008/2009 financial year.
Only 18 424 are completed by June 2009.

2009:
PRESIDENT Jacob Zuma vows to create 500 000 jobs from June to December 2009 at his first State of the Nation address.
More than 200 000 jobs have already been lost between the last quarter of 2008 and first quarter of 2009.

BHISHO is spending R340 million to fix nearly 20 000 broken homes in the province while the poor live in flimsy cardboard units and ghost towns emerge from the ruins of disastrous housing projects.

In some areas of the province communities have deserted formal housing settlements because the homes were so poorly built they cannot live in them any longer.

The number of homes having to be repaired is more than the total number of 19 662 houses delivered in the 2006/2007 financial year.

While the provincial government tries to rein in its backlog of 800 000 RDP homes, a two-month investigation by the Dispatch has revealed how:

● Homes were built in areas which people have long since left;

● One project in Seymour became State-sponsored "holiday homes" for people who live in other cities and only return in December;

● Residents in Burgersdorp were moved into cardboard houses when their RDP homes began falling to the ground, and were then asked to clean up the mess themselves;

● One project of 600 homes in Tarkastad has been standing empty, while a waiting list to house people continues to grow;

● Depopulation and inferior construction in places like Venterstad has led to the emergence of ghost towns; and

● A community near Bhisho is still waiting after five years for electricity and water because the govern-

ment refuses to provide the services until it has finished the housing project it started eight years ago.

The biggest victims in the province's housing fiasco are among the most vulnerable in the population.

Like two pensioners, Loki Makelemi and Ngqukane Nonzaza, who have been living in a flimsy cardboard home for seven months while their shoddy RDP house in Burgersdorp is repaired.

"The government doesn't care about people who live here. We're going to die in these houses. I'm just waiting for my coffin right now," said the elderly Makelemi.

To rub salt into their wounds, the local Gariep Municipality wanted the same residents to clear the tons of rubble lining the streets – for free.

The problem in Burgersdorp are far from unique – in fact, all but one of eight housing projects visited by the Dispatch are being rebuilt.

In many cases inexperienced contractors have been blamed for the problems.

Two weeks ago Housing MEC Nombulelo Mabandla

vowed to blacklist incompetent builders and recover funds from them where necessary.

But she said her department would never forsake emerging contractors and would do all they could to mentor them in future.

"That is why we have developed a training programme for them, called the Emerging Contractors Devel-

opment Programme," she said.

Seymour and Venterstad are two examples where RDP homes have been deserted or remain unoccupied because there are no local jobs, or poor workmanship has made the buildings unsafe.

Yet the reverse has happened in Tarkastad, where more than 600 residents are on a waiting list to occupy low-

cost homes in a nearby project that is standing empty.

Derek Luyt from the Public Service Accountability Monitor in Grahamstown said the department's Service Delivery Charter and Service Delivery Plans for 2009 and 2010 highlight its pitfalls.

"Staff shortages and lack of sufficient skills have severely hampered the department in the past, and it will not be able

to deliver sufficient houses of adequate quality unless it solves its human resources problems," Luyt said.

Democratic Alliance spokesperson Pine Pienaar said the huge backlog, lack of monitoring and under-spending in the department was a direct result of the department's inefficiency to fill critical posts in technical and finance departments.

KILLER HOME: A mother in Burgersdorp stands next to the wall that fell on her 15-year-old boy's head and killed him when he and two friends were playing in this house. The friends were injured.   Picture: THEO JEPTHA

Man shot dead as three prisoners escape
By EDDIE BOTHA

A PRISONER was shot dead and a policeman injured during a dramatic shootout at the Peddie Magistrate's Court yesterday afternoon during which three awaiting-trial prisoners escaped.

Senior prosecutor Lizeal Mitten, who had to run for cover, said the shooting started soon after the case against the three prisoners had been remanded and they were taken to holding cells next to court B.

Mitten said the three prisoners, who face charges of murder and rape, overpowered an inspector and grabbed his gun and cell keys.

"Then all hell broke loose and about 25 shots were fired." Police and security guards chased the prisoners, who ran into a nearby township.

Mitten said it was then discovered that the police inspector had been shot in the chest. He was rushed to hospital. Later it was found that a prisoner had been shot dead in the cells.

Army to help relieve EC drought
By DERRICK SPIES
Business Reporter

THE army has been called in to help the Eastern Cape battle a crippling drought after the government declared most of the province an official disaster area yesterday.

Strict water restrictions are likely to follow after Minister of Water Affairs Buyelwa Sonjica declared the Alfred Nzo, Amathole, Cacadu, Chris Hani, OR Tambo and Ukhahlamba District municipalities disaster areas at the first day of the Eastern Cape Water Indaba in Jeffrey's Bay yesterday.

"We have a crisis when it comes to water in the Eastern Cape. There is also a lot of water wastage, such as the irrigation of

golf estates using freshly treated water, and we will be looking at regulations to ensure that only recycled water is used (for this)."

Sonjica also committed the national department to provide R140.4 million to assist the provincial government with infrastructure projects and a further R5m to assist municipalities to roll out rainwater collection tanks.

Sonjica said declaring the districts disaster areas meant they would be able to apply for additional funding to supply water to those hardest hit by the drought.

She said the latest drought was evidence of how climate change was affecting the province, and predicted that within the next 20 years the province could be semi-

desert. "Rivers in the eastern part of the Eastern Cape are drying up."

But it was not just the drought that has put water supply in jeopardy.

The indaba heard that failing infrastructure, inadequate maintenance, lack of skills and a drop in the quality of water sources had crippled the water supply in the province.

Sonjica said that of the province's treated water was being lost before it reached households because of failing infrastructure.

Executive mayor of Amathole District municipality, Sakhumzi Somyo, said it would cost the province more than R41.7 billion to address backlogs in water and sanitation.

ODD SPOT

Couple all at sea in town of Carpi

A SWEDISH couple looking for the pristine waters of the Italian island of Capri ended up 650km away in the industrial town of Carpi.

They had misspelled the name on their car's GPS navigation system. A spokesperson for Carpi said they drove into town and asked how to reach Capri's famed Blue Grotto sea cave. "We thought they might mean a restaurant. Capri is an island; they did not even wonder why they didn't take any boat." The pair have finally set off for their planned destination. — Sapa-AP

Spokesman for Human Settlements Minister Tokyo Sexwale put on record "our appreciation of the vital role the Daily Dispatch played in highlighting the plight of the poor"

NEWS	MAGAZINE	REVIEW
SA'S CANCER-CURE PIONEER PAGE 5	12 PAGES OF HARRY POTTER MAGIC	GWEN GILL SAYS SO LONG, AND **THANKS** FOR ALL THE FUN **REVIEW, P16**

AFRICA EDITION

Sunday Times

THE PAPER FOR THE PEOPLE

JULY 26 2009 / R7.00 INC. VAT   www.thetimes.co.za   Botswana P13.95, Dubai AED 25.00, Lesotho R13.95, Namibia N$26.95, Swaziland R13.95, Zimbabwe US$1

EXPOSED: DEADLY TAXI RACKET

DUPED: Taxi owner Phola Katsisi with the Toyota Quantum she bought in 2007, which she has now discovered was illegally converted and should not be on the road
● Read her story on Page 2

● Owners unwittingly buy illegally converted panel vans that endanger thousands

● Car dealers, banks and licensing authorities blame each other for deathtrap fiasco

SPECIAL INVESTIGATION

STEPHAN HOFSTATTER and ROB ROSE

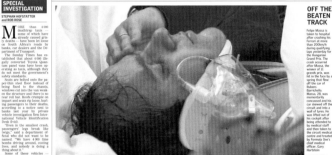

MORE than 4 000 deathtrap taxis — some of which have already caused grisly deaths — have been let loose on South Africa's roads by banks, car dealers and the Department of Transport.

The Sunday Times has established that about 4 000 illegally converted Toyota Quantum panel vans have been operating as taxis, although they do not meet the government's safety standards.

Seats are bolted onto the paper-thin steel floor instead of being fixed to the chassis, windows cut into the van weaken the structure and there is no rear roll bar. Roofs crumple on impact and seats rip loose, hurling passengers to their deaths, according to a notice sent to banks last year by private vehicle investigation firm International Vehicle Identification Desk (Ivid).

"Even in the smallest crash, passengers' legs break like twigs," said a department official who did not want to be named. "We have 4 000 time bombs driving around, costing lives, and nobody is doing a thing about it."

Some of these vehicles — many of which have been involved in serious accidents with high fatalities, including six children on one occasion — were even officially accredited to transport tourists during the recent Fifa Confederations Cup. And they could even be in use during the World Cup next year.

"We will continue to take the risk and work with these taxis, unless we're physically forced to stop," says Michael Venda of the Gauteng Taxi Council.

"We could have transported many tourists to the Confed games with these taxis. We just wouldn't know," said William Thembe, chairman of the Alexandra Taxi Association.

Now minister of transport Sbu Ndebele has vowed to make it a priority to pull these unsafe vehicles off the road.

Branding it a "concern", Ndebele was alarmed that the vehicles had been used to ferry foreigners during the Confederations Cup. He said this must

not be allowed to happen at next year's tournament.

"We don't want to hear of people dying in taxis getting to a match, particularly if we know those vehicles are not suitable."

The illegally converted panel vans are estimated to ferry up to 400 000 passengers a day across South Africa.

The country's banks, the department, roadworthy agencies, Bureau of Standards and car dealers have been blaming each other for indifference, negligence or incompetence.

The Quantums were bought under the government's taxi

recapitalisation scheme and then converted to carry passengers, although the law prohibits this.

● **To Page 2**

SA girds for new strike wave

NASHIRA DAVIDS

SOUTH Africa lost more than half a million working days due to strikes in the first six months of the year — nearly double the number over the same period last year.

Now the country is yet another major strike as municipal workers' strikes are in the pipeline.

About 10 000 Metro plan to down tools under the government's taxi putos are making h SABC, Telkom, and t chemical sectors.

Andrew Levy Employment Publications tracks strike activity around the country. Jackie Kelly, labour analyst for the company, said that by the end of last month more than 500 000 working days had been lost to strike action.

ticipants, she said strikes lasted longer. In total, 12.9 million working days were lost in 2007 and 991 000 days in 2008.

Major strikes this year have hit the road freight industry — involving 60 000 employees — the metro

ployed by municipalities and belonging to both Samwu and the Independent Municipal and Allied Trade Union across the country rejected the latest wage offer of the SA Local Government Association," said the union.

Readers donate 140 000 books

ANGIE Motshekga, the minister of basic education, has pledged her department's support for the Sunday Times's Storybook campaign, by sponsoring 100 000 books.

"Teaching young children to read and creating in them a love of reading will help to lay a solid foundation for their future success," said Motshekga.

"The Sunday Times Storybook campaign is a wonderful initiative to harness the goodwill of every South African towards turning young South Africans into a nation of readers," she added.

The campaign, which was launched in the Sunday Times on July 12, aims to see 2 600 primary schools nationally receive 500 000 Sunday Times Storybooks for their libraries — in five of South Africa's official languages.

The 132-page Story time books contain 10 children's stories, written and illustrated by South African authors and artists.

The stories have been donated by Oxford University Press, Maskew Miller Longman, Macmillan and Cambridge University Press, and readers have already started sending their donations via SMS. Printing company CTP and paper suppliers Mondi Shanduka are both contributing to the project, and Cell C and Virgin Mobile have waived any SMS response revenue.

In the two weeks since the campaign was launched we have received funding for just under 140 000 Storybooks. The Department of Basic Education has donated funding for 100 000 Storybooks and Exclusive Books' social

Phola Katsisi stands beside her illegally converted panel van, cheaper than the real deal but potentially deadly

The man who let the lights go out
– Jacob Maroga, ousted CEO of Eskom

Rough aunties, big hearts
FRIDAY   Page 8

Stoned Cherrie walks the ramp in New York   Page 8

The young and the restless tell us what they want
Pages 23 to 29

Prisons graft: We have proof

Correctional Services took out an advert calling for evidence of dodgy tender deals. We found plenty.

Page 2

IT'S A CORKER
Barack and Michelle Obama have developed a taste for South African bubbly. See page 8

'New' Pikoli's sleazy past
Page 3

Hlophe gives govt the finger
Page 5

Sex and politics – people speak out
Page 19

R17,50 in SA /www.mg.co.za/ SMS "subs" to subscribe or "mg" for news via cellphone www.mg.co.za R1 charge) to 32 368 Zimbabwe / International US$2 / Mozambique / Zambia ZMK11 500 / Kenya Ksh102 / Angola US$7,10 / Botswana P16,28 / Swaziland E16,28 / Malawi MWK 316 / Lesotho M17,50

Bosasa's empire of influence

The company at the centre of South Africa's latest tender-rigging scandal seeks an interdict to stop investigations into its business with government.
Adriaan Basson, Yolandi Groenewald and Glynnis Underhill report

Bosasa's web
and their well-placed circle of friends

Who's connected to whom

- **Gibson Njenje**
  Head of the National Intelligence Agency and Valisango shareholder
- **Mamisa Chabula**
  Former Bosasa chair and friend of the Mbeki family
- **Kevin Wakeford**
  Former chief executive of the SA Chamber of Business and head of the home affairs turnaround team
- **Linda Mti**
  Former prisons boss, head of security for the 2010 World Cup and commander of Valence and Ronnie Watson in Umkhonto we Sizwe
- **Makhenkesi Stofile**
  Minister of sport and brother to rugby administrator Mike Stofile, involved in Eastern Cape rugby with the Watsons for years
- **Buleleo Njenje**
  Wife of Gibson Njenje
- **Nozuko Pikoli**
  Wife of axed NPA boss Vusi Pikoli
- **Siviwe Mapisa**
  Brother of Correctional Services Minister Nosiviwe Mapisa-Nqakula
- **Zola Yeye**
  Former Springbok team manager
- **Titus Mafolo**
  Thabo Mbeki's political adviser
- **Seth Phalatse**
  Former Strategic Fuel Fund chair and husband of Lorato Phalatse, head of Mbeki's presidential office

Gavin Watson, Bosasa's chief executive

*"Valence Watson, Gavin Watson's brother, is the chief executive of Valisango Holdings"

Key connection
- Former Bosasa director
- Consultant to Bosasa
- Struggle links
- Rugby links
- Shareholder or director of Valisango*
- Shareholder of Sondolo IT

The government tenders
- Department of correctional services
- Department of home affairs
- Department of transport
- Department of justice
- Airports Company of South Africa
- Post Office
- Gauteng provincial government
- Eastern Cape provincial government

Graphic: JOHN McCANN
Research: YOLANDI GROENEWALD, ADRIAAN BASSON

Linda Mti   Gibson Njenje   Mike Stofile   Makhenkesi Stofile   Kevin Wakeford

The company at the centre of South Africa's prison corruption scandal is closely connected to powerful individuals on the political landscape, including the country's new spy boss, Gibson Njenje.

A number of them were also close to Thabo Mbeki's presidency.

Bosasa Operations, exposed this week in Parliament for allegedly bribing top prison officials to secure contracts worth more than R1.7-billion, makes a killing from government business. This includes work for the departments of correctional services, justice, home affairs, transport and the provincial governments of Gauteng and the Eastern Cape.

Bosasa's chief executive, Gavin Watson, has close links with the governing ANC through his family's anti-apartheid struggle credentials and his brothers' post-1994 business interests (see graphic).

Njenje is a founding member of Bosasa Operations and was a director of the company before being appointed head of the National Intelligence Agency (NIA) in October.

A number of people benefiting from Bosasa contracts or linked to Watson and his family had links to Mbeki's office, including the ex-president's political adviser, Titus Mafolo, and Mbeki's head of office, Lorato Phalatse, who is married to former Strategic Fuel Fund chairperson Seth Phalatse.

Watson's brother, Valence, is the chief executive of Valisango Holdings, the empowerment partner of controversial mining firm Simmer & Jack. Valence Watson's business partners include Nozuko Pikoli, the wife of axed prosecutions boss Vusi Pikoli, and Siviwe Mapisa, the brother of Correctional Services Minister Nosiviwe Mapisa-Nqakula.

Mapisa-Nqakula told the M&G this

week that she knows Gavin Watson. "Mr Watson is a former CEO of Dyambu Holdings, a company the minister was formerly affiliated to. Mr Watson resigned from Dyambu and went on to form Bosasa. The minister has had no contact with him since then."

According to the minister, she has "no relationship with Bosasa nor has she benefited from the operations of Bosasa". She is "not aware of any relationships members of her family may have" with Bosasa.

The M&G can reveal that Bosasa is seeking to interdict the Special Investigating Unit (SIU) and President Jacob Zuma from continuing its investigation into tender rigging.

In its frantic efforts to halt the SIU's graft probe — which could lead to both civil and criminal charges — Bosasa claims that the SIU leaked sensitive information to the Mail & Guardian that resulted in a "trial by press". Bosasa is referring to a series of M&G exposés of collusion between Bosasa and senior correctional services officials, including former prisons' boss Linda Mti and the department's former chief financial officer, Patrick Gillingham.

Zuma's involvement in the case stems from Mbeki's authorisation, as president, of the SIU probe into Bosasa. The SIU and Zuma are defending the matter.

The Bosasa group has benefited from prison tenders worth more than R3-billion since 2004.

SIU head Willie Hofmeyr shocked Parliament with sordid tales of corruption inside South Africa's prisons, disclosing details about how Bosasa put the likes of Gillingham and Mti firmly in its pocket (See Page 3).

Hofmeyr's briefing also raised uncomfortable questions about why Mapisa-Nqakula has been sitting on the SIU report from at least mid-

September. It is the duty of the minister — Mapisa-Nqakula — or of the acting prisons commissioner, Jenny Schreiner, to launch a civil claim against Bosasa.

Hofmeyr said on Tuesday: "It is a matter that justifies the institution of legal proceedings by the department to recover damages from the company."

Mapisa-Nqakula, who was appointed by Zuma in May to head the prisons department, originally said she had to present the SIU report to Cabinet before releasing it. Her spokesperson, Sonwabo Mbananga, later told the M&G that this release was on hold because of Bosasa's pending legal action against the SIU.

The M&G now has access to the court papers filed by Bosasa against the SIU. Nowhere does it seek to interdict the SIU or Zuma from releasing the final report. Instead the applications focus on the alleged tainting of the probe due to media leaks.

Approached again after Hofmeyr's explosive briefing to Parliament, Mbananga remained adamant: the minister would still not release the report because the SIU has referred it to the National Prosecuting Authority "and therefore the con-

Even after 2007, when it became publicly known that Bosasa was under investigation for tender-rigging, the group continued to secure lucrative contracts from the justice department and the Eastern Cape

tents ... are sub judice".

Bosasa's spokesperson, Papa Leshabane, denied the corruption claims, labelling Hofmeyr's briefing as "speculative, arrived at without hearing Bosasa, are disputed and will be dealt with in the appropriate forum".

Bosasa also disputes the way in which Hofmeyr dealt with the matter at Parliament. According to Leshabane, their attorneys have advised them that Hofmeyr went beyond the powers of the SIU, acted unlawfully and breached Bosasa's constitutional rights.

Although Hofmeyr evidently referred to Bosasa, Mti and Gillingham in his briefing, he didn't name them, citing pending legal action against his unit.

Hofmeyr's presentation this week vindicated the M&G's revelations in February that Bosasa had access to tender documents before they were publicly advertised. Bosasa is demanding R500 000 from the M&G for referring to a "corrupt relationship" between the group and the department of correctional services.

Bosasa's attempt to avoid penalties is two-pronged. First, it is pursuing an application for an interdict preventing the SIU from continuing its investigation until the court has made a final decision.

The application is brought by Bosasa Operations, the company's operations coordinator Angelo Agrizzi, financial coordinator Andries van Tonder, buyer Frans Vorster and Watson. The four men were given notices by the SIU to provide certain documentation during interrogation by the unit.

The applicants claim that the SIU's probe is tainted because of alleged media leaks and the handling of a seizure operation at Bosasa's premises.

In reply the SIU denies leaking

information to the M&G and accuses Bosasa of activating a "data deletion utility" on Bosasa's servers shortly before the SIU arrived.

In the second court action the plaintiffs ask the court for a permanent order against the SIU, "declaring the entire process of the first defendant's (SIU) investigations into the plaintiffs to be fundamentally tainted".

Hofmeyr's presentation brought into sharp focus again Bosasa's astonishing success in winning government tenders. Even after 2007, when it became publicly known that Bosasa was under investigation for tender rigging, the group continued to secure lucrative contracts from the justice department and the Eastern Cape.

The group's most recent tender is a R3,9-billion contract awarded by the Eastern Cape to Phakisa Fleet Solutions, a Bosasa company, to manage the provincial fleet of vehicles.

At the time when the Bosasa group was awarded its first major prisons contract for catering in 2004, the company was owned by Watson's family trust (26%), Bosasa directors Carel Mzele (32,3%) and Joe Gumede (18,3%), and the Bosasa Employees Trust (22,2%).

Between 2004 and 2006 three companies in the group — Bosasa Operations, Sondolo IT and Phezulu Fencing — were awarded six tenders by the prisons department at the value of R1,4-billion.

The SIU's probe focused on four tenders: a catering tender for R70-million over three years; an access control tender at R337-million; a fencing contract for R587-million; and a tender for TV systems in prisons at a cost of R224-million.

Hofmeyr's probe found that in almost all cases Bosasa was involved in the drafting of tender specifications and that procurement policies were severely discounted.

From: Patrick Gillingham [connell@midrand-estates.co.za]
Sent: 22 June 2006 18:36
To: angelo@bossasa.com
Subject: RE: Report 6 June 2006 - VERY CONFIDENTIAL

Hi,
Thanks for the report and it seems if they behaved well during their session.

Regards,

Here's the proof, minister

In the line of fire: big kahuna Ngconde Balfour (above) Patrick Gillingham (below left) and Angelo Agrizzi (below right). Photo: Oupa Nkosi

Last weekend the department of correctional services called for evidence of tender irregularities. Here it is in black and white

Adriaan Basson

On Sunday the department of correctional services placed expensive advertisements in three national newspapers, urging anyone with proof of impropriety in the awarding of prisons' contracts to inform South Africa's law enforcement agencies.

This week we present the proof. Confidential documents and correspondence leaked to the *Mail & Guardian* suggest a highly improper relationship between the department and controversial facilities management group Bosasa.

We can reveal that Bosasa, which has received nearly R3-billion in contracts from Correctional Services Minister Ngconde Balfour's department:

● Had confidential documents leaked to it by the department's former chief financial officer and Balfour confidant Patrick Gillingham;

● Had access to tender documents for major prison projects before they were advertised; and

● Spied on senior correctional services officials during a 2006 workshop.

Bosasa is headed by Eastern Cape businessman Gavin Watson, whose family had close ties with the Eastern Cape ANC during the struggle years, when the Watson brothers became famous for refusing to play rugby for a whites-only Springbok team.

The group also runs the controversial Lindela repatriation camp for home affairs and has large contracts with the post office, Airports Company of South Africa and the departments of justice and transport.

The Special Investigating Unit (SIU) has been probing Bosasa since 2006 and raided its offices in December. Three weeks after the raid the company was re-awarded the massive prisons catering contract it landed in 2004.

The department's advertisements on Sunday were a reaction to the *M&G*'s report last week of alleged irregularities in the awarding of the latest catering deal.

Former prisons commissioner Vernie Petersen suspended Gillingham in September after receiving a preliminary SIU report. Petersen was later transferred to the sports department in what was widely seen as a reprisal for his opposition to Balfour's attempts to extend the 2004 contract.

Balfour also wanted Gillingham to head the tender committee

awarding the new contract, while Petersen insisted that Gillingham not be involved.

2004: a new romance

In 2004 the contract for running prison kitchens was outsourced for the first time. The tender was officially advertised on May 21 in the government's tender bulletin.

But documents show that on May 1 Bosasa employee and co-founder Danny Mansell sent Bosasa's operations coordinator, Angelo Agrizzi, papers containing more than 90% of the bid conditions and specifications.

Three weeks later the correctional services department made available the same document, with the same spelling errors, to the rest of the catering sector. On August 6 Bosasa was awarded the entire contract, worth R239-million a year, for three years.

The department extended Bosasa's contract for another year and expanded it to include more prisons, adding R82-million to the bill. It was the further extension that led to Petersen's clash with Balfour.

In July 2004 the department also gave Bosasa a R1-million tender for nutritional training for prisons' kitchen staff. Again Mansell sent Agrizzi large parts of the tender document, including bid conditions and specifications, on May 12. The tender was advertised on June 4.

2005: you've got mail

The inclusion of CCTV cameras in the catering tender meant that by 2005 Bosasa had a national control centre to monitor the kitchens.

This linked perfectly with its next contract — a R237-million tender for access control and CCTV in 66 prisons. It went to a newly registered company, Sondolo IT, which *Beeld* revealed in 2006 was 40% owned by Bosasa Operations.

Other shareholders included former president Thabo Mbeki's political adviser Titus Mafolo and former Strategic Fuel Fund chair Seth Phalatse.

On December 17 2004 Bosasa's IT coordinator, Johan Helmand, emailed Agrizzi certain tender specifications that were to appear in the official bid document published on February 4 2005.

On April 29 Sondolo IT was awarded the contract.

In 2005 Agrizzi and Gillingham started emailing each other prison

research reports and newspaper clippings. On August 29 Gillingham sent Agrizzi a copy of questions from *City Press*, put to the department about the Bosasa contracts, the leaked documents show.

On December 9 2005 Bosasa landed a R487-million prisons' contract for security fencing through a small Cape Town firm, Phezulu Fencing, it had purchased.

There is double proof that the company had privileged information long before the tender was advertised. Three months earlier, on September 25, Agrizzi emailed Mansell a voluminous document containing bid specifications. "Please verify and check, we can sit tomorrow am," Agrizzi wrote.

On October 3 Agrizzi sent a longer version, headed "Fence Doc Final", to the chief executives of Bekaert Bastion and SA Fence & Gate, Michael Rodenburg and Geoff Greyling respectively, under the subject line: "Fence Doc Final ... Very Confidential ...".

This contained the full bid conditions and specifications published by the department on October 14. Bekaert Bastion supplied cladding material and SA Fence & Gate was contracted to do part of the installation.

This week Greyling "categorically" denied seeing a copy of the bid document before it was published. He said: "It should be recorded that the tender was based on the standard public works/correctional services specification with which we are well acquainted from previous bids.

The prior possession of the tender document by anyone would therefore be of no specific advantage to such person."

Colette Stofberg of Bekaert Bastion (now called Betafence) replied that "years before this contract" Betafence provided technical specifications to the department of public works that were used in this tender.

According to an industry insider the big advantage lies in knowing the quantities required for the tender weeks before your competitors.

On October 10 2005 Agrizzi sent Gillingham a six-page document titled "Equipment Specifications & Guidelines". The same section featured in a tender for a comprehensive tele-

2006: spies in the house

On February 9 Agrizzi sent Gillingham a document, headed "Tender Evaluation Criteria New Waterval", containing comments on bid specifications for a contract for catering services at seven prisons in the Waterval management area, KwaZulu-Natal.

The tender was officially advertised on May 19. Seven days earlier Gillingham sent Agrizzi the confidential evaluation sheet for the Waterval tender with a message: "Hi, Attached please find the reworked evaluation sheet for your comments. You will notice the evaluation sheet for site visits cannot be published and will not form part of this document. Regards, Patrick."

On September 15 Bosasa Operations was awarded the Waterval catering tender, worth R123-million over five years. On April 24 2006 Agrizzi sent Gillingham a letter in which an anonymous writer asks the chairperson of Parliament's correctional services, Dennis Bloem, to "sort out" the attack on the department by "international capitalists" and "activist Afrikaner companies". This week Bloem confirmed receiving such a letter.

On June 21 Agrizzi sent Gillingham a surveillance report of a prisons department security workshop at a Drakensberg hotel in June 2006. The 25-page report makes it clear that the agent was asked to spy on the department's chief deputy commissioner of security, Willem Damons, and his subordinate, Tonie Venter. The report also contains pictures of people and cars at the hotel, as well as the inside of the conference room.

In his message to Gillingham Agrizzi wrote: "I didn't see the reason/need to email you the rest; nothing actually happened." Gillingham replied the next day: "Hi, Thanks for the report and it seems as if they behaved well during their session. Regards."

Bosasa's lawyer, Brian Biebuyck, advised his client not to answer the *M&G*'s questions. He warned the *M&G* to publish "at your peril" and said Bosasa would pursue charges of criminal defamation if defamatory material was printed.

The department's Manelisi Wolela responded that the *M&G*'s questions "are part of a broader brief given to the SIU" and urged the newspaper to

Corruption in the prison kitchens: The Department said 'show us the proof' and the M&G did just that. The story began when Linda Mti was commissioner of the prison service

BANKING
KOSEFF ON INVESTEC'S
LONDON LOSSES **P3**

SUNDAY FEBRUARY 1 2009 · **Sunday Times** · www.thetimes.co.za

Business Times

INTEREST
RATES
Give a little,
guv **P9**

Absa-lute disaster!

Empowerment bigwig Bulelani Ngcuka and golfing legend Ernie Els linked to bank's R1bn black hole

SPECIAL INVESTIGATION

BY STUART THEOBALD

The problem was that the share price fell faster than anyone could sell the shares

A BSA has been hit by losses of about R1 billion after a disaster in its derivatives clearing business.

The banking group was forced to make an announcement to the JSE on Thursday regarding the mess after queries from Business Times. But the announcement did not disclose the full extent of the damage.

A Business Times investigation has traced Absa's exposure and the people involved.

The bank has had to foreclose on single stock futures positions, a type of derivative, in a clutch of small JSE-listed companies after investors defaulted on margin calls through small private client broker Cortex Securities.

These investors include controversial businessman Jac de Beer, who has been the subject of a Scorpions investigation and has had a Department of Trade and Industry (DTI) order issued against him to refrain from "harmful business practices", and Jaco Verster, former CEO of Acer-Bona — a key entity in the debacle.

De Beer is linked to golfer Ernie Els through various developments, and Els himself may be exposed to losses.

Bulelani Ngcuka, former national prosecutions director, also has a large exposure.

Absa's biggest problem is investors in Pinnacle Point — formerly called Acc-Bona, a golfing resort and hotel development company — from whom the bank could have lost R900-million. Further exposures to derivatives in other companies probably top R100-million.

Single stock futures explained

AN INVESTOR — any retail investor can do it — trades with a stock broker to buy or sell single stock futures (SSF) contracts.

An SSF contract says the holder will take delivery of 100 underlying shares at a specified future date at a set price. The contracts are traded on the JSE's derivatives exchange, Safex.

On one side of the trade is the broker and his client. The broker also has an agreement with a clearing bank, which finances the trade and hedges its risk.

The client only puts down a "margin" — a fraction of the total exposure. The bank hedges its risk by buying shares in the market, usually to the full exposure.

The margin is what Safex holds to limit the risk of the price of the shares moving. The client always has to maintain the margin, so if the share price falls, he has to deposit more money with the broker.

An example: a client buys 10 SSF contracts in Anglo American. Each contract is 100 shares, so his total exposure is to 1 000 shares. The counterparty bank takes the trade and buys the 1 000 shares to hedge the risk of delivering the shares at the expiry date of the SSF.

At the time of the deal, the Anglo American share price is R300, so the client has a total exposure of R200 000. The margin requirement, set by Safex, is R3 800 per contract, so the client puts down R38 000 for the deal.

Imagine the next day Anglo's price falls to R180. Now the total underlying exposure is R180 000, a R5 000 loss. The client will be called upon to top up his margin — a "margin call" — to get it back to R38 000. If the client couldn't pay, the position would be closed, the underlying shares sold, and the bank would get back its money.

If, however, the share price increases, say to R220, the total position will be worth R220 000. The client will have made a profit of R20 000.

The amounts would be slightly different in reality, because the bank also charges interest, and various fees are involved.

LEFT HOLDING THE BABY: Outgoing CEO of Transnet Maria Ramos, who takes up her post as CEO of Absa next month, listens to questions during a media conference at the World Economic Forum in Davos, Switzerland, this week, where about 40 world leaders sought to find solutions to the financial crisis. She will have no extra crisis to deal with when she starts the new job ● See Page 9   Picture: VIRGINIA MAYO/AP

YOUR MONEY SECTION HAS MOVED TO THE BACK OF CAREERS

Single stock futures – buying shares without actually paying for them. South Africa's home-grown toxic assets

CONTINUED ON PAGE 4

AN INVESTIGATION SERIES BY
LAVERN DE VRIES & WARDA MEYER

In 1995 Norman Avzal Simons was sent to jail, convicted of the abduction and murder of little Elroy van Rooyen. Residents of greater Cape Town breathed a sigh of relief: the Station Strangler was behind bars. But is he? Simons maintains his innocence to this day.

COLD CASES
STATION STRANGLER
INVESTIGATIONS

FACING FEAR: Identikit images of Station Strangler suspects during the height of the terror on the Cape Flats. Norman Simons bore little resemblance to any of them.

The many faces of the Strangler

Norman Avzal Simons was the prime suspect. The trouble was, the clues just didn't match up

HE HAD long hair. He had short hair. He was tall and slight. He was short and muscular. He had a round face, he had a long face. He was light skinned. He was dark skinned. He had missing teeth. He had no teeth missing. He was a lone presence as insubstantial as a shadow. He was five men on a murderous rampage.

The Station Strangler had as many shapes as fear itself.

By early 1994, after eight years of horror on the Cape Flats, the police and the public alike still had no good idea who the Station Strangler was, how he spoke or what he looked like. Evidence was fragmentary and sometimes inconsistent.

One victim, Jeremy Smith, 12, found in the bush near Weltevrede Road, was missing an ear, apparently severed by the killer.

Another, Neville Samaai, 13, had a hole cut in his trousers with a pair of scissors when the body was found.

Neither detail was repeated at any other crime scene.

Yet all the time the body count was rising. In the first three months of 1994 alone, the decomposed bodies of eleven Strangler victims were dug out of shallow graves, many in bushes, most in desolate dunes, around the length and breadth of Mitchells Plain.

By the time Norman Avzal Simons was arrested in April of that year the Strangler had claimed a total of 22 victims in a cycle of sickening violence against children that started in 1986.

But here is the problem.

If there was only one Station Strangler, it was highly unlikely it was Norman Avzal Simons. He bore little resemblance to most of the identikits. He matched few of the physical descriptions given to police investigators.

Nor was there any similarity between his dress, demeanour or the car he drove – a Mazda – and those connected in evidence with the Strangler.

Moreover, after his arrest – first on the umbrella Station Strangler investigation docket, then subsequently for the murder of Elroy van Rooyen, 10, alone – Simons was scientifically tested against physical evidence collected from the various crime scenes.

Police were trying to link their suspect to at least some of the long series of brutal murders. It was explicitly their intention to garner sufficient evidence to allow them to charge him as the Station Strangler, not for the murder of Elroy van Rooyen alone.

The list of forensic dead-ends includes the following:

● A fingerprint found at the scene where a still unidentified boy, aged about 13 was discovered, near Weltevrede Road, Mitchells Plain. At the same crime scene a scrap of paper was discovered beside the body, reading: "Many more in store". Neither the fingerprint nor the handwriting was that of Simons.

● A second fingerprint was lifted at the scene where the corpse of Neville Samaai, 13, was discovered. This too checked negative against that of Simons.

● Also at the Samaai crime scene a copy of Huisgenoot was found with a crossword puzzle half completed. The handwriting did not match that of Simons.

Tomorrow in Sunday Weekend Argus: Part Three

● Blood and semen were found around the body of Jeremy Smith, 12. They did not match those of Simons.

● Blood and semen samples were found at the scene of the killing of Calvin Spires, 9. They classified serologically as blood type A, but were deposited by a "secretor". Simons is a "non-secretor" and this excludes the possibility of a match.

● A handwritten note, the content of which has not been made public, was discovered near the body of Elino Sprinkle, 11. The handwriting was different from that of Simons.

● A car moving suspiciously in the Weltevrede vicinity where Sprinkle's body was found was reported to police. It was identified as a Volkswagen Jetta and the registration number was given to police. The registration did not connect back to any friend or connection of Simons. Nor did Simons match with eyewitness reports of Strangler sightings:

● The second identified victim of the Strangler, Yusuf Hoffman, 14, who died in 1987, was seen in the company of a man who referred to himself as "John" and wore a gold ring on the middle finger of his left hand. "John" was a tall, coloured male with a light complexion. Simons is of medium height and is dark.

● Samuel Nqaba, 15, victim number six, was last seen getting into an olive-green Valiant station wagon with a tall black man with a long face, aged between 20 and 25, wearing square-shaped dark glasses.

● Denver Ghaza was murdered after getting into the car of a man with a long cut on the left side of his face, stretching from the nose at an angle down the cheek. The man was smoking and bought a beer while in the company of Ghaza. The man was – unusually for the Cape Flats – apparently unable to speak Afrikaans with any fluency. Though Simons is scarred on the face, the scar is a burn, not a cut. He is fluent in Afrikaans.

● Two boys playing with the murdered Sprinkle just before he was abducted, testified to a story that breaks completely with the Strangler pattern. They claim they were approached by five men while on their way to Kapteinsklip railway station.

One of the men was described as being short and having his lower front teeth missing. This man allegedly put a rope around Elino's neck then dragged him into the bushes. This was the last time the boy was seen alive.

In all, as police searched with increasing desperation for evidence and leads in an eight-year investigation, identikit artists compiled more than 10 composite images. All of them gave a markedly different impression of the Strangler's appearance.

But, balanced against all the questions, as Strangler investigator JD Kotze points out, the killings stopped after Simons was arrested.

There were no more bodies found that definitively bore the distinctive "signature" or unambiguously manifested the modus operandi of the Station Strangler. "Serial killers don't change their MOs (modus operandi), they might try to perfect their fantasies, Kotze says, "but they don't change their MOs."

Even so, there may have been more than one Strangler.

UNCLEAR : Forensic dead-ends blocked police from charging Simons with more murders.

The Strangler's MO, as recorded, was relatively variable and relatively unspecific.

Even the murderously sexual drive that is usually definitive of serial killers was not always evident.

Some victims were sodomised, others were not. All that really runs through the sequence is the fact that the dead children were lying face down in the sand, hands bound, and they had been strangled.

The possibility of copycat killers, inspired by the first Strangler, having indulged their own fantasies in imitation cannot be excluded.

Top policeman still sure Simons was serial killer

THE scenery may have changed but former Murder and Robbery detective "JD" Kotze still knows how to find his way around the bushes in Kleinvlei.

A few metres from a graveyard, Kotze points to some sandy dunes. This is the spot where, 15 years ago, the decomposed corpse of 10-year-old Elroy van Rooyen was found.

"The case traumatised a lot of us. Many of our guys were medically boarded for stress afterwards," he says, recalling the Station Strangler murders. "We had to deal with what these people had gone through, the families' hurt."

Kotze, later a Chief Special Investigator with the now-defunct Directorate of Special Operations, recalls that in 1994 then Murder and Robbery chief, Colonel Leonard Knipe put him in charge of investigations into the Station Strangler killings.

"It was a difficult case. We concentrated on the murders of the 90s… there were several dead ends in the first series of murders and a lot of tip-offs in the second spate."

One of the biggest challenges arose from the fact that, when found, the corpses were generally in an advanced state of decomposition.

"There wasn't very much to work with."

That and the lack of reliable witnesses to the sequence of abductions and killings.

"It was like looking for the devil," Kotze says.

The investigating team's break finally came when a police informant fingered a man who frequented psychiatric institutions as possibly being the serial killer.

After following Norman Simons, and observing that it was sometimes only after midnight when he returned to Kenilworth Clinic – where Simons was booked in at the time – the team decided to approach him for questioning.

The team formed the impression Simons had several of the characteristics in a profile put together by psychological profiler Micki Pistorius. In Pistorius's profile it was predicted the killer could be a teacher, a police officer, a minister of religion, or some other figure of authority in the community. She also predicted the killer would himself have been a victim of sexual abuse.

"In many serial killing cases the perpetrators were either molested or abused, or something went wrong in their childhoods… they kill because they want a sense of control and they want to live out their fantasies," says Kotze.

Reflecting on a case which he says he chooses not to think about "because I don't want to relive it", Kotze says he has empathy for Simons. "I knew how he was abused… based on what he said; we followed up leads, and we discovered that he was treated for homosexual-related sexual illnesses. That was never brought into court

CONVINCED: JD Kotze

"I don't know why but the indication I got was that the abuse was ongoing."

Kotze firmly believes Simons really was the Station Strangler. "My opinion and this is only my opinion, is that although there were no facts to convict him, Simons, on the other cases, it is my belief that he was the killer.

"Although Rayno (van Rooyen) didn't identify him on the parade, he did say that he saw the person and he described the man's clothing and the number he had in the line-up. Inherently, children tell the truth. Fouzhia's (Fouzhia Hercules) testimony was also tested in court and it stood up. We were lucky that we had an adult that could identify him."

Of the semen that was found on two of the victims, Kotze maintains Simons's semen was not conclusively ruled out as a match.

And the fact that Simons's handwriting didn't match the note found on one of the victims, also doesn't sway Kotze.

"You'll never find a case where someone is convicted solely based on their handwriting. It's not like a fingerprint, it's not an exact science."

For Kotze the clincher is that the murders stopped after Simons was arrested. That is proof enough for him.

After Simons's arrest, Kotze recalls, he was called out to several crime scenes which detectives suspected might be connected to the Strangler. But none of these convinced Kotze.

"In my experience, serial killers don't change their MOs, they might try to perfect their fantasies though, but they don't change their MOs."

And the Strangler's MO? According to Kotze, he would approach the victim in such a way as to win his trust, then lure him away to some desolate area of sandy dunes near a railway station.

Once there the killer would force the boy to lie face down in the sand – with a sand mound underneath his stomach, so the buttocks were raised.

He would then simultaneously rape and strangle the victim, until the life drained away.

Asked what he would ask Simons if he had the opportunity to speak to him, Kotze says, "I'd appeal to him to come out and tell the truth and admit to what he's done so that the parents of the other children can get closure."

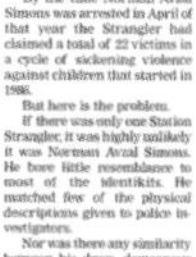

THE COP: Don Engelbrecht

Why city detective ruled out Simons as suspect in string of murders

ONE OF the most seasoned investigators of the Station Strangler murders broke ranks in giving evidence to an inquest at the Mitchells Plain Magistrate's Court in 2008.

The inquest was into the killing of six boys identified as victims.

In the course of its hearings, the court considered whether it could find sufficient evidence to recommend that charges be brought against Norman Avzal Simons – in the end finding that though there was some *prima facie* evidence, there was no reasonable prospect of any successful prosecution.

Before this however, it heard the testimony of Inspector Don Engelbrecht, a police sergeant at the time.

Engelbrecht thought that Norman Simons was not the Station Strangler and, moreover, that he did not kill Elroy van Rooyen.

According to the court transcript, Engelbrecht questioned Simons on April 13, a day after his arrest, after which he ruled Simons out as a suspect based, in part, on the following:

A witnesses in the Elino Sprinkle murder case said a VW Jetta, registration CA 722 331, was seen near the bushes where the boy was found dead. The witness also said he saw a person and heard screaming. After following up the lead, Engelbrecht could find no link between Simons and the Jetta.

Police discovered a handwritten note half a metre away from one of the bodies. The note read: "Many more in store, number 14, station wrangler". The note had a fingerprint but the print found on the note did not match that of Simons. The note, according to Engelbrecht, must have come from the killer because the exact number of murdered boys was 14 – a fact only he would know as media reports had, until then, carried incorrect figures.

In preparation for Simons's case, an officer showed Engelbrecht which places Simons had identified as murder scenes or burial grounds but none of the places that Simons had identified matched any of the murder scenes Engelbrecht knew of and had visited.

Two of the victims had semen traces. The same person left semen on the two boys but the semen didn't match Simons's. Simons never mentioned any of the children in his confession.

"I read the so-called admission, the statement he gave to the magistrate and the pointing out and it didn't change my opinion," Engelbrecht said.

Furthermore, the modus operandi of the killer also largely influenced his opinion: "Few people know what the modus operandi was. And in all the cases where there was testimony from children, the same method was followed.

"And there are more children that are alive that survived an attack – two boys, grown men today, are in their 20s and married. They survived an attack, the same method, basically everything was the same and by chance one of them knew Simons and when I spoke to them, they said 'No, it's not Simons, it's another person'."

At the time of the inquest in July last year, Engelbrecht said that police were still investigating the description offered by the two survivors – that of a black man of medium build who could speak Afrikaans and another language.

Police refused the Weekend Argus access to Engelbrecht.

We were told that we could speak to him in his personal capacity on a range of topics including "his garden, his life" but under no circumstances would we be able to interview him on the investigations into the Stranger murders.

Cold case review: was Norman Stevens the Station Strangler, guilty of 22 murders? Was he guilty of one murder? Or guilty of no murders at all?

Zuma's homestead expanding with state facilities on the side

NATHI OLIFANT

EVEN standing near the multi-million rand construction site at President Jacob Zuma's Nkandla homestead has been forbidden.

Workers are under strict orders not to allow anyone to visit. A man who identified himself as AM Shabalala, the site manager, gave these instructions when the Weekend Argus visited the area at the weekend.

"I will ask you to leave, because we are under very strict orders not to allow any-

one on the site," he said.

Local Inkosi Bhekumuzi Zuma, who was also visiting the site, confirmed that the homestead was being expanded as it was no longer able to accommodate the people who visited the president's home.

He said he was flabbergasted at a report in Friday's Mail & Guardian newspaper that Zuma was tearing taxpayers money by expanding his home.

The newspaper reported that the new houses under construction were allegedly being built to accommodate two of Zuma's wives - Mabhuti Zuma

and MaMkhiza Zuma - currently living there. Construction started a month ago.

The expansion apparently will turn the presidential homestead into a sprawling complex that will include a police station, helicopter pad, military clinic, visitors' centre, parking lot and at least three smaller houses that will serve as staff quarters.

According to another site employee, the construction of the houses adjacent to Zuma's main homestead will cost about R4 million, with the president's family footing the bill.

However, the security medical facilities and the helicopter pad, which are half a kilometre

No government funding will be used for construction

away from the homestead, are being built by the state at a cost of R60m.

On Thursday, the presidency issued a statement denying it had anything to do with the new construction at Zuma's homestead.

"The Zuma family planned before the elections to extend the Nkandla residence, and this is being done at their own cost. No government funding will be used for the construction work," said presidency spokesman Vincent Magwenya.

He confirmed that the state is to undertake construction work outside the perimeter of the Zuma household in line with the security and medical requirements relating to heads

of state. He said security services had to construct accommodation facilities for staff who attended to the president, a helipad to ensure safe landing for the presidential helicopter and a clinic, for medical requirements.

"At the moment, security and medical staff are accommodated in the Zuma household.

"The new measures are designed to separate private from state facilities, family from staff, and to afford the Zuma family the privacy that they are entitled to.

"The demarcation at Nkandla is very clear, and there can be no reason to confuse the private construction work in the Zuma household and the state facilities that will be constructed outside the perimeter."

Many in the community were not aware of the construction of the new facilities, including the clinic.

"Perhaps it is going to be used by government people only," said Maxina Sbezi, a local resident.

The Zuma family refused to comment.

LUXURY LIFE: President Jacob Zuma

'Why were no witnesses interviewed?'

Following Independent Newspapers' investigation into a series of deaths of KwaZulu-Natal taxi operators at the hands of police, the Independent Complaints Directorate has taken over investigations into the February killing of taxi boss Bongani Mkhize and prior police shootings of six of Mkhize's colleagues

BOSS: Bongani Mkhize

SAME STORY: Police claimed Mkhize, and his colleagues in separate incidents, had fired at them. Evidence contradicts this version, say experts.

FRED KOCKOTT

BONGANI MKHIZE, the chairman of the KwaMaphumulo Taxi Association, secured the protection of the High Court in November last year to prevent the Durban Organised Crime unit from "eliminating" him.

Despite the interdict being granted, Mkhize died in a hail of police bullets on Durban's Umgeni Road on February 4.

Police said at the time that Mkhize had been connected to the murder of Nkosi Mbongeleni Zondi, who had died two days previously in a drive-by shooting in Umlazi. They also said Mkhize shot at them in an attempt to evade arrest.

An Independent Newspapers probe revealed that there had possibly been a police cover-up through "non-investigation" of circumstances surrounding Mkhize's death and the earlier deaths of six of his colleagues, all suspected to have been involved in the murder of a top police officer, Superintendent Zethembe Chonco.

It seems that the shootings were investigated independently by different police investigation officers and the dockets then referred to different police prosecutors for the purpose of holding inquests.

The ICD had also publicly declared that its investigations of the killings of all the Chonco murder suspects had cleared the police of any culpability, and had referred the cases back to the police to complete as inquest dockets.

But now the ICD is reviewing all these cases and has recalled all the dockets from the police as part of a broader probe to assess whether the killings were connected.

Refreshed interest in the case follows a meeting of top ICD representatives with a lawyer representing the Mkhize family, Petrus Coetsee, and an independent forensic ballistic expert, Jacobus Steyl, who have publicly expressed concern that the deaths had not been properly investigated.

ICD national spokesman Moses Dlamini confirmed the ICD's decision to review these cases in the light of new evidence that has

PROBE: Police inspect the car in which Nkosi Mbongeleni Zondi was killed in a drive-by shooting in Umlazi last year. Although police said at the time that Mkhize had been 'connected to' the murder, lawyers are now saying it was police who shot Zondi - in the same way Mkhize was killed.

emerged, including preliminary findings of Steyl's ballistic examinations of Mkhize's car, and the police version of these shootings, including claims that Mkhize had opened fire on pursuing police, because all the windows of Mkhize's car had been closed at the time of the shooting.

He said ballistic evidence showed police firing at him from behind, then overtaking, continuing all the while to ride his Lexus with bullets, before final shots were fired into Mkhize's head.

In correspondence to Commissioner Pat Brown, head of detectives in KwaZulu-Natal, and the ICD, Coetsee also highlighted

But Steyl said his preliminary investigations raised doubts about the police version of these shootings, including claims that Mkhize had opened fire on pursuing police, because all the windows of Mkhize's car had been closed at the time of the shooting.

Coetsee said while newspapers quoted eyewitnesses to the killing, no attempt seemed to have been made to contact such witnesses by either police or the ICD.

Mkhize's family also suspects a cover-up.

Coetsee said he was impressed by the responses of the ICD acting provincial head, Leo Jaba, to concerns that he and Steyl had

raised when the team met last week, and the ICD's renewed interest.

Coetsee said the ICD had agreed to forward all these related dockets "at an appropriate stage of these investigations" to the Director of Public Prosecutions (DPP) for a senior representative to study all the dockets as part a broader probe into the killings of Mkhize and his six colleagues.

Steyl confirmed that he had handed over to the ICD ballistic evidence he had recovered in his inspection of a house in Mandeni where Mzumani Johnstone Luthuli (aka Kopolozo) and Nathi Wilson Mthembu, also allegedly Chonco murder suspects, had been killed by police on September 21 last year.

"One 9mm bullet and a 5.56mm bullet from an R4 or R5 rifle

were found on the bloodstained carpet and another 9mm bullet in a cupboard," said Steyl.

He added that while he had yet to get access to the results of the post mortem examinations, his examination of this scene indicated that the two men had possibly been shot in the head by police standing almost directly above them.

"It's encouraging that ICD is taking over and recalling all the other dockets, but it's still a concern that nine months have lapsed since Mkhize's shooting and only now is the ICD starting to look for witnesses," said Coetsee.

Ⓘ NVESTIGATIONS
inl.co.za

Vested interests in KZN taxi industry 'a threat to stability'

FRED KOCKOTT

GOVERNMENT officials' and politicians' vested interests in the taxi industry, and associated violence arising from disputes over routes and permits, has become a serious threat to peace and stability, says KwaZulu-Natal's general manager of public transport, advocate Sonny Chamane.

Chamane said FPicos at all levels, including senior civil servants and policemen at station level, were responsible for many deaths "because of direct or indirect involvement in the taxi industry".

"It is very dangerous, in its present form the taxi industry is a threat to security, and peace and stability," said Chamane.

The murder of Superintendent Zethembe Chonco, and the subsequent police killing of all suspects in the Chonco murder investigation, Chamane said, was a

setback in dealing with the taxi-related conflict in KZN. Chamane said Chonco had been involved in various sensitive investigations, including the theft of 43 guns – among court exhibits at murder cases – from KwaMaphumulo police station.

It was suspected this theft might have been an inside job.

Chamane said Chonco had also made good progress in solving murders related to the conflict between the KwaMaphumulo and Stanger Taxi Associations – "to such an extent that the killing had ended", said Chamane.

"Chonco was arresting people across the spectrum. Now we will never know why he was killed, as the police case is closed, with all the suspects dead."

KwaZulu-Natal violence monitor Mary de Haas, said: "The question will also always arise: Were they really his killers?"

The bullet-riddled, blood-sprayed car in which taxi boss Bongani Mkhize died in Durban, despite a High Court interdict forbidding the police from killing him

Government pledges:

2005

Housing, local government and traditional affairs MEC Neo Moerane-Mamase promises that an urgent audit of all incomplete projects would be completed within the first six months of the 2005/06 financial year.

2006

Premier Nosimo Balindlela promises to build 25 000 new houses but only 11 971 are finished.

2007

President Thabo Mbeki vows to eradicate the bucket toilets used by 230 000 households in the country (of which 58 474 are in the Eastern Cape) by the end of 2007.

2008

MEC for housing Thoko Xasa promises to build 26 000 houses during the 2008/09 financial year.

Only 18 424 are completed by June 2009.

2009

President Jacob Zuma vows to create 500 000 jobs from June to December 2009 in his first State of the Nation address.

More than 200 000 jobs have already been lost between the last quarter of 2008 and first quarter of 2009.

Residents Freeze Waiting for Homes to be Rebuilt
29 July

Residents who were moved out of a poorly built RDP housing project in Burgersdorp and placed in cardboard shelters have been asked to clean the township's rubble-strewn streets – for nothing.

The municipality's call for volunteers to help clear up the mess in Thembisa has been viewed as the ultimate insult by those made homeless after inferior construction forced them out of their low-income homes.

"That is ridiculous.

"How can they expect us to work and not get paid when we are already suffering and don't have houses?" asked Thandiswa Gatyeni, who lives in a cardboard house given to her family by the municipality.

Tons of building material and rubble have been left over from the RDP housing project, whose 929 houses are undergoing repairs at a cost of R12.5 million.

Residents such as Gatyeni claimed that officials from the municipality had fooled them into attending a meeting under the pretence that they were going to get jobs in the clean-up project.

"We all went thinking we were going to get jobs, but when we arrived they told us that there were no jobs.

"It was a lie to get us to go to the meeting.

"They said since we were there, we must volunteer to sweep the streets for free."

Her family was moved out of its original house because it was in such a bad state that the municipality promised to rebuild it from scratch.

But the reconstruction has not yet been finished.

Another resident, Noluvuyo Kolomba, who lives in a cardboard house with six children, said it was insulting to ask unemployed people to work for nothing when there were other people, such as municipal workers, who were paid to do the same job.

"They are taking advantage of the fact that we are desperate for jobs, so they think that we are dumb people who will work for free while others get a salary at the end of the month," said the 38-year-old mother of three, who also looks after three orphans.

She said they were moved out of their house in January and told the reconstruction of their home would take three weeks before they could move back into a better and safer house.

Six months later they are still living in dire poverty, in a cardboard house that is freezing.

"When you wake up, you can see frost on your blanket."

When the *Dispatch* visited the area in mid-July, it looked like a war zone.

The streets were full of leftover construction material and demolished houses.

Gariep's municipal manager and spokesperson, Thembinkosi Mawonga, said there must have been a communication breakdown because the municipality had never promised anyone a job and had been asking for volunteers to help clean the streets.

"There was no mention of money. Even in the council documents there are no financial implications with this project.

"A resolution was taken to use volunteers from schools and other sectors of the community," he said.

Mawonga said the big clean-up had been initiated after complaints were received about illegal dumping sites and other rubbish on the streets.

Housing Department "Won't Repeat Mistakes"

Housing MEC Nombulelo Mabandla has admitted her department has failed to deliver homes adequately to the poor after it under-spent by more than R1bn in the past three years.

She said a total of 60 projects in all eight districts of the province would undergo varying degrees of rectification at a cost of R360 million.

Mabandla said the allocation of houses in places such as Seymour – where an entire housing project was standing empty because people had migrated to larger towns in search of jobs – was due to poor management by housing officials from municipalities responsible for allocating houses to beneficiaries.

"As the department we build houses as per the application by municipalities and we approve projects on the basis that there are identified beneficiaries."

She said in cases where houses had not been occupied, they insisted the municipality concerned find people on waiting lists who could take ownership.

"It is true that in some areas we don't have jobs.

"That is why we have shifted from just building houses to creating integrated human settlements, where we will ensure that jobs also are created," she said.

One example was Ugie, where a housing project had been developed alongside a massive R1.5bn investment by PG Bison in a timber factory.

Mabandla said the poor standard of housing was the main concern of the department.

"Structural defects in these houses are due to shoddy workmanship by our contractors, and more especially from emerging contractors.

"That is why we now have a plan to train our emerging contractors under the Emerging Contractors Development Programme – to make sure this does not happen again," she said.

During her policy and budget speech in June, Mabandla said her department had delivered 18 424 houses during the 2008/09 financial year, an improvement from the previous year's 12 684.

She said the department's total budget of R1.474bn would enable the department to reach its targeted goal of delivering 19 000 houses next year.

Internal problems have plagued the department for years.

This reached the point where Pretoria dispatched a special task team to the province in July last year to provide technical support and assist in accelerating and improving the delivery rate of houses in the province.

Mabandla said her department had plans to avoid repeating the mistakes of the past.

"As from this financial year, we will make sure that our project management capacity is enhanced so that we have project managers and building inspectors all the time at every stage of each project to ensure the quality of the houses," she said.

Progress slow in fixing RDP homes

Things went from bad to worse for two Burgersdorp pensioners, who had been living in a crumbling RDP house – and were then moved into a home made of cardboard.

Loki Makeleni and Ngqukuse Nonxaza have been living in their flimsy shelter in the informal settlement of Thembisa for seven months now, far more than the two months they were told they would have to endure while their house was being patched up.

Conditions are unbearable and the papery walls offer hardly any relief from the devastating winter cold.

"We wake up with aching bodies all the time because we don't sleep properly," said Makeleni.

"This house is too cold. We can freeze and die here any time."

Makeleni said if they left water in a bucket overnight it froze. "And we can't exactly make a fire inside because it will burn the whole house down," said Makeleni.

The couple said the only form of income they received was a monthly pension of R1100.

"It's hard, especially for old people like us who are always sick and need money to go to the clinic," said Makeleni, who has a chest problem and struggles to breathe properly.

She said it seemed they would be living in their cardboard abode for a few more months, considering the slow pace at which their house was being rebuilt.

"They were supposed to have finished five months ago and it does not seem like they will finish any time soon, because they sometimes stop for days."

The temporary house they live in is virtually empty except for a lone cupboard and two single beds.

There is no electricity, running water or a proper toilet.

The floor is made of thick cardboard with visible gaps and the roof has no ceiling, only a zinc slate.

"The government doesn't care about people who live here. We're going to die in these houses. I'm just waiting for my coffin right now," said Makeleni.

Gariep Local Municipality mayor Ncedo Ngoqo said the cardboard houses were a temporary measure to put a roof over people's heads while their houses were renovated.

But he admitted there were problems with the current contractor, who was given the job of fixing the broken homes.

"We are working tirelessly with the contractor to finish these houses as soon as possible.

"The funding has already been approved by the Department of Housing," said Ngoqo.

Teen Killed as RDP Home Collapses on Him

Zoleka Dwili never thought the day would come when she would have to bury her son, let alone her youngest, at the tender age of 13.

While the country was celebrating Youth Day on 16 June, her youngest boy, Sonwabile, died in a freak accident after an RDP house in which he had been playing collapsed on him and two friends in Burgersdorp.

His body was trapped under the rubble of the structure, which was being renovated by a building contractor.

"I thought I was losing my mind. He had said he was going out to play just like he usually did but I had no idea it would be the last time I saw my boy," she said during a *Dispatch* visit to Thembisa, a township in Burgersdorp, three weeks ago.

Speaking from the site of the house where her son had died, Dwili said the contractor had given the family R4700 as compensation for his death.

"The contractor came to see us [the family] shortly after the accident with some people from the municipality and they gave us money which we used for the funeral," she said.

Dwili's sister Nozukile Jantjie, who was the first family member at the scene of the accident, said she remembered it as if it happened yesterday.

"I did not want to believe it. My neighbour told me that he could have been one of the boys injured while playing inside an old house.

"My body just went cold after she told me, but I started walking towards the house where she said the accident happened.

"The closer I got, the more people I saw on the streets. They tried to stop me but I kept walking towards where his body was lying, just to see him."

She said paramedics at the scene told her that her nephew had been killed instantly by a big chunk of a wall that landed on his head.

Jantjie said both her nephew's friends survived the ordeal but sustained head and leg injuries.

Gariep Local Municipality mayor Ncedo Ngoqo said the money was not intended as compensation but rather as financial assistance for the family to give their son a proper burial.

"According to what was reported to me, the subcontractor asked the boys to leave but they did not listen and came back, so nobody knew they were inside when the wall fell down.

"I'm sure it was purely an accident," said Ngoqo.

Failed RDP Project
is Criminals' Hideout *30 July*

An RDP housing project in the small town of Seymour has become a settlement of state-sponsored holiday homes for hundreds of people who have left the area and return only during the holidays.

The few who have stayed behind are living in the grip of poverty, with no jobs or hope of ever securing a regular income.

The fortunes of this town have turned so badly in the past decade that there are only four shops remaining, a far cry from the once-thriving town that boasted banks, petrol stations, furniture shops, a tobacco factory, butcher and supermarket.

The prospects in Seymour are so bleak that teenage girls say child grants offer the only buffer against absolute poverty.

At the heart of the decay is the failed housing project, which is being used as a hideout by criminals who steal building materials like bricks, doors, windows, roofs, sinks and toilet seats from the vacant homes.

Noxolo Jam, who works as a community liaison officer for builders Motheo Contractors, said most of the people who were given RDP houses in Seymour do not live there. Instead they reside in big cities and only come to visit in December.

Some beneficiaries are not even from Seymour originally, and simply took advantage of the fact that government was giving away houses.

"Most of these beneficiaries are not from here, they are from other places like Keiskammahoek, Cathcart and Alice," she said during a visit by the *Daily Dispatch* in June.

"They just came here to collect the keys from us and left. Others put in their relatives."

Jam said almost half of the 461 RDP houses built in District Six, which is what the project has been named, are locked up and standing vacant.

Vandals have made merry with the empty homes and left many in a wrecked state.

A large number of them were so badly built by previous contractors that they had to be rebuilt from scratch.

Resident Luzuko Cwaba, who was born in Seymour 34 years ago, said the main thing driving people away was lack of jobs.

"The only jobs that are available for us here are the odd construction or roadwork projects that come to town once every few years," said the unemployed bricklayer.

He said nearly all the people in Seymour were unemployed and the youth were heading in the same direction.

"There's no life here. If you want money you have to leave and go work in other places. It's that simple," he said.

Buyelwa Canda, 58, and her 68-year-old husband Mzwandile, said rising crime and vandalism were a direct result of the social misery in Seymour, where children are dropping out of school and spending their time in shebeens.

"It's true, there are no jobs here.

"You can ask around, there are so many unemployed people sitting around doing nothing.

"Even young children are sitting in shebeens drinking their lives away because there is no life for them."

The couple said there were only four spaza shops in Seymour, three of which were owned by foreigners.

"If it was not for these people we would starve to death, I'm telling you."

Just up the road from the old couple's house is the home of a family of three sisters aged between 18 and 26, who live on their own and survive on child grant money.

Two of the sisters have babies and the third is still in matric. Their parents, who used to work as farm labourers, died.

"We don't do anything besides sitting around with our children and doing house chores or playing cards," said one of the sisters, Nokubonga Mbara.

Her sister, Doreen Weitz, added that their child support grants were their only income.

Nkonkobe Local Municipality spokesperson Bulelwa Ganyaza said all the RDP housing projects that have been undertaken in Seymour since 1998 have been blocked at some stage owing to bad workmanship and poor use of building material.

She said the first project to get blocked was a R3.4 million development of 232 units in Phase 1, another area in Seymour, which was abandoned by the contractor.

The second project was the R7.3m development of 461 units in District Six by a contractor who also never finished.

"The municipality has applied for funding to fix and complete these projects," said Ganyaza.

Housing Project Paralysed by Dispute

3 August

A dispute over money between the Elundini Local Municipality and a building contractor it had hired to build RDP houses in Maclear has prevented about 250 families from getting homes.

The municipality claims it lost millions of rands when Monde Sontashe of Milani Construction left without finishing the project – which has since been blocked.

Municipal manager Khaya Gashi alleged Sontashe vanished into thin air after partially building only 89 of 250 structures.

He said a forensic report had indicated that irregular procedures to submit claims for payment had been followed, resulting in an additional payment of R353 000 to Sontashe.

When the *Dispatch* contacted him on 24 July, Sontashe denied he had been overpaid by the municipality.

"I told them they can take me to court if they want to because I never signed my own cheques, the municipality signed and approved all my claims.

"The only thing I admit to is not honouring my contract and finishing the project, but that's because the municipality was not paying me, so I left."

Sontashe denied he had only partially built 89 of the 250 houses he had been hired to build.

"The project was nearly halfway when I left in June 2004. I had already completed 102 houses and 12 slabs, for which I was paid R1.7 million."

Sontashe said the project had been valued at about R4.5 million at a subsidy value of R18 000 per house.

"I only received R1.7 million of this money. The rest is still with the municipality," he insisted.

The case was never taken to court and the money paid to Sontashe was never recovered.

When the *Dispatch* visited Maclear in mid-June, the 89 unfinished structures were still standing bare.

Almost all had been vandalised to such an extent that they will have to be rebuilt from scratch.

Residents said the ruins were hiding criminals.

Vuyisile Dyuli of Burgersdorp's Sonwabile township said it was heartbreaking to see the discarded homes being used as hideouts by criminals.

"Tsotsis hide inside them at night or if they see you walking, they catch you and rob you," he said. "If you are a woman, they will rape you most definitely."

Dyuli said since the houses did not belong to anyone, vandalism had become so prevalent that people were building and extending their houses using bricks and other material from the crumbling structures.

"People just take whatever they want," he said.

Long-time Maclear resident and chairperson of the Elundini Chamber of Commerce Pieter Hills said the cost of rebuilding the houses would now be substantially higher.

"Building material prices go up all the time. I estimate that it will cost at least another R5000 to R10 000 per house," he said.

Hills said the longer the municipality took to rectify them, the more vandalism would take place, requiring more work and money to rebuild.

RDP Bungle Leaves
Pensioners Fuming
4 August

Residents of a state housing project in Sweetwaters, near Bhisho, have been waiting for five years for water and electricity from government – and their wait is unlikely to end soon.

At fault is an emerging contracting firm which failed to finish the housing project it started eight years ago.

Until all the work is finished, Buffalo City Municipality says there will be no provision of basic services to those few houses that have been completed.

It's crushing news for people like Noma Matroko, a pensioner from Sweetwaters, who has been waiting for electricity and water to her RDP house for almost five years.

Matroko cooks on a paraffin stove and uses candles to light her home. To stay warm, she collects wood to make a fire, which at least keeps her damp house relatively dry.

"I was one of the first people to move into these houses in this area and I have never had water or electricity," she said. "At my age I have to carry a bucket to fetch water, which is quite a distance for me. I have to stop all the time because I don't have the strength any more."

Matroko has no family to help her: "I have no one left. I live alone because my grandson I was living with was stabbed and killed recently while they were trying to rob someone," she said.

Her neighbour, Vukile Gwaruba, who is a disabled husband and father of two, is in a similar predicament. "The local ward councillor told us he was not going to give us electricity because it's too expensive to put in and he said we would not be able to afford it in any case," Gwaruba claimed.

"He said the government will give us water when it's ready to and we should not rush into things."

Gwaruba said the only source of water available in Sweetwaters is three communal taps put in for the builders during the construction phase.

The rest of the houses do not have taps or electricity.

Sweetwaters ward 42 councillor David Mavuka said water and electricity were being withheld because of an agreement with the Department of Housing to restart the project from scratch.

"It was resolved that those houses must be rebuilt again because they weren't done properly the first time. Only then will we put in these services," he said.

Municipal spokesperson Samkelo Ngwenya confirmed Mavuka's statement and added that Sweetwaters' residents would be supplied with water and electricity when the project is at least up to 80% complete.

"We envisage the project can take up to eight months; currently it's at 25–30%," he said.

Ngwenya said the project was approved in December 2001 to build 559 houses with a subsidy of R25 800 per site.

The contract was awarded to a company which failed to execute the work properly and its contract was terminated in 2006.

Ngwenya said the project has since been taken over by the Department of Housing, which appointed a new contractor to finish the project.

Chapter 11

Hell Hole

Johann Abrahams and Godknows Nare
Special Assignment, SABC 3

Secret filming is always controversial. It can spice up a story. It can make a story. But sometimes it is the only way to tell a story – because the truth is so terrible that people will only believe you when you actually show them what is happening.

A high-ranking prison official, eager to expose the horrific conditions inside Zimbabwe's prisons, approached Godknows Nare. A meeting was arranged in Musina at the border, and, as there was no chance of getting an ordinary camera into the prison, the *Special Assignment* team looked for other ways of getting the crucial video evidence.

They began with a cheap spy camera, a secret camera that beams the pictures instantly to a receiver. This ran for an hour at a time and two prison officials agreed to do the filming.

But it wasn't easy. The camera broke down. The images were shaky. Often the camera was simply pointing in the wrong direction.

They got a better camera, gave some training to the "cameramen" about how to position the body to get the best result, and tried again.

Each week Johann Abrahams and Godknows drove to the border to view hours of material.

As every film-maker knows, the budget will run out and there is always a deadline. So what to do with a lot of shaky, unrelated visuals?

They identified two particular people in the prison and asked their contacts to concentrate on them. And finally, on their last two trips, they saw the evidence with their own eyes – here was the story they could tell.

Their images of starving prisoners were beamed across the world. The International Committee of the Red Cross was granted access and things changed for the better.

There were other repercussions in the prison. Police randomly arrested prison guards whom they suspected but not the people who actually worked on the programme. Some of the detainees were assaulted. *Special Assignment* asked the Zimbabwean Lawyers for Human Rights to assist the detainees and they were later released. The police officers who arrested them were dismissed.

Johann Abrahams is the executive producer of SABC's investigative programme *Special Assignment*. He has a broadcasting and film degree from the University of Kansas in the US, where he also worked as a video journalist. On his return to South Africa in 1994 he joined the Cape Town office of the SABC as a cameraman and then a reporter. He joined *Special Assignment* in 2004 and became executive producer in 2008.

Godknows Nare has freelanced for *Special Assignment* as an investigative journalist and producer since 2006. His first film told another part of the Zimbabwe story – the plight of refugees crossing the Limpopo River. He also works for all major international broadcasters as a fixer, cameraman and investigator.

"Hell Hole" is on the DVD.

Chapter 12

Chicken Run

Susan Puren
Carte Blanche, M-Net

Runner-up in the 2009 Taco Kuiper Award for Investigative Journalism

The story began with a piece of amateur video footage. It showed trays of tiny chirping yellow chicks being dumped into a dry dam. They'd come from a chicken farm in Potchefstroom, in North West province.

It is standard practice to kill day-old male chicks in the egg industry – they can't lay. But there are proper ways of doing this. Dumping them live is not one of them.

The film had been recorded by a former employee. Producer Susan Puren got to hear about it, watched it and knew she had a programme to make.

Starting with the video, she pieced together a story about animal cruelty. The NSPCA got involved and within no time Boskop Layer Chickens was the subject of an unannounced raid, and animal cruelty charges followed.

So far this was a good piece of television – the protestations of the owners that they had never dumped chickens in the dam running on a split screen with the secret film made for riveting entertainment. And it could have ended there.

But there was another story. In the middle of this huge farm is a village where 22 families have been living in squalor for the last 10 years.

They used to be employed, when Boskop was a training centre run by the Department of Manpower. It went bust. Then the farm changed hands, and a once self-sustaining community was reduced to poverty.

Susan was interested in the village and its fate. Internet research produced a link between Boskop and a Dutch company. Trust documents, company records and a business plan were found, and a call to the Dutch embassy opened up a whole can of worms. Millions of rands in grants and aid were involved, all in the name of the people of Boskop. They hadn't seen a cent.

And the man behind all this? Boskop Layer Chickens is owned by Jan Serfontein, the former MEC for agriculture and environment in the North West province.

As the judges said: "*Carte Blanche* took a little story and made it big. What began as a fluffy animal cruelty story, with a dodgy politician thrown in, became a major scandal involving large amounts of provincial and international funding money. Lots of hard slog. Great television."

Susan Puren joined *Carte Blanche*, a weekly current affairs programme on pay television channel MNet, in 2000 and has since then won several awards, including CNN African Journalist of the Year in 2002. She originally worked in print media and radio, until she finally moved to television when she joined the SABC television news team in the 1990s. She specialises in investigative documentaries.

Chicken Run: The Story   *August 2009*

We are unable, for legal reasons, to include a copy of the three programmes that make up 'Chicken Run'. What follows is a descriptive outline of the three films which compose the full story.

Eggs are a big industry. Where once we would all have had a few chickens in our back yard, now most of us buy our eggs by the dozen in a supermarket. The eggs come from huge commercial farms, which in their turn buy their hens from companies that breed hens for laying: companies like Boskop Layer Chickens, which provides some of the 23 million egg-laying hens that South Africa needs each year.

Once the eggs hatch, the company has no use for the male chicks they breed, more than half the crop. So the male chicks are killed.

There are guidelines in place for the mass killing of these perfectly healthy chicks, according to Kevin Lovell, CEO of the South African Poultry Association.

They can be put in a container injected with carbon dioxide – deprived of oxygen, the chicks die quickly.

A faster method is to feed them into a maceration machine – an industrial shredder – with almost instant death guaranteed.

Either way, this is how it should be done.

The dumping of the live chicks in an old dry dam is not recommended, or allowed, by industry rules, yet this is precisely what can be seen on the footage shot by a former employee at the Boskop farm.

Every Thursday, according to a former hatchery worker, about 40 000 live chicks were thrown in the dam. But if Piekie Tale protested about what he was being asked to do, he was told he just didn't want to work.

He wasn't the only unhappy employee. Kobus van Zyl, the former hatchery manager, worked there for two and a half years. He claims the practice of dumping the chicks had been going on for even longer. "This is totally wrong and cruel," he says.

When the *Carte Blanche* team descended on the farm, owner Jan Serfontein and his son Jannie claimed they were gassing them with carbon dioxide, "according to international practice".

They clearly didn't know of the incriminating film footage.

Asked if they throw the unwanted chicks in the dam, they answer clearly: No, never ever, never have.

Presenter Devi Govender was persistent. "Never ever. You're clear about that?"

"I'm clear about that," replied Jannie Serfontein.

The birds were killed using gas, he claimed. Which came from a company called Afrox.

Which is true, the gas does come from a company called Afrox. But when the *Carte Blanche* team turned up at Afrox's offices, it became clear that no gas was being supplied to the Boskop farm. Enquires to supply it had been made, that very morning, for the first time ever, but that was all.

Not working by the rules seems to be routine at Boskop Layer Chickens. According to Kevin Lovell of the South African Poultry Association, all chicken businesses need an environmental impact assessment (EIA).

Jan Serfontein Senior retired in 2009 as the North West province's MEC for agriculture, conservation and environment. This is the department that is the watchdog for the province's environmental laws.

He told the programme that as his was an old business, he didn't actually need an EIA. According to Kevin Lovell, the EIA is a must; not having one is illegal and it could lead to the closure of a business.

Alongside the *Carte Blanche* team at the farm were the NSPCA, alerted to the story and looking for breaches in animal welfare regulations. A fire had swept through the area the previous night, destroying most but not all of the incriminating evidence in the dam. The burnt remains of the tiny chicks were still visible, and Kay Prinsloo, national inspector for the NSPCA, immediately issued a written warning to the Serfonteins not to destroy the 40 000 male chicks in the hatchery at the time.

She returned the next day to oversee the culling of the birds in a macerator, all 40 000 in just four hours.

But that didn't make everything all right with the NSPCA. "This is a very serious matter," said Kay Prinsloo. "We will be opening a case of prosecution, mainly because this is actually blatant cruelty. It's not done through ignorance."

The NSPCA laid nine charges against the business under the Animal Protection Act.

There is another story in Boskop: about people rather than animals.

In 1994, shortly before the first democratic elections, Nelson Mandela was on the campaign trail in Potchefstroom. He visited the Boskop Training Centre, set up in the 1970s by the Department of Manpower to train farm workers.

The children who came to see Mandela that day were from a village near the training centre, home to instructors and their families. In the crowd was Shorty Valiphatwe, born in Boskop village and the third generation of his family to live there. "I was there that day. I was the one who gave Mandela the present."

Not much remains of the Nelson Mandela sports ground in Boskop, and the community centre is locked and fenced off, to keep the villagers out.

The problems began in 1999 when the Boskop Training Centre ran into financial difficulties and the local instructors found themselves without work, without wages and, for that reason, very likely without homes.

The Land Bank stepped in, bought up the village and allowed the residents to remain when the farm itself was put up for sale.

The farm was bought by the Serfonteins' family trust. But the village was not for sale – it is now a tiny island in the middle of 500 hectares of Serfontein land.

At the time of the sale a decade ago, electricity and water supplies to the village were cut off because of the training centre debts.

Shorty Valiphatwe, now the spokesman for the Boskop Land Bank village, says they discussed their problems with Eskom, which was prepared to help. But Jan Serfontein took out the connecting cables (as well as the water pipes, and bulldozed the French drain system). And since then there has been no electricity.

While the Serfontein lawyer, in a written response, told *Carte Blanche* it was "completely untrue that the Serfontein Trust or Boskop Layer Chickens had disconnected sewerage, electrical or water cables to the so-called Land Bank village", Abe Modisane was one of the workers instructed to rip out the electric cables.

"I worked on Jan Serfontein's farm. One day the foreman told us to go to the village and rip out the cables, all the cables."

Once loosened, they used a tractor to pull them out, rolled them up and took them away.

"When Jan says, 'Take out the cables', you take out the cables. All the people from the village were angry but we had to eat and there wasn't any other work."

The villagers now cook on open fires, use an often-dry communal tap for water and have no effective sewerage system.

Not one of them is employed at Boskop Layer Chickens.

Yet, millions of rand have been raised in their name, under the banner of Black Economic Empowerment (BEE).

Jan Serfontein founded the Boskop Community Trust, the address of which was given as the Boskop Land Bank village. Nineteen people were registered as beneficiaries of the trust, but they have nothing to do with the village either.

Then there's Smokey Mountain Trading 262, the business arm of the Boskop Community Trust. In 2005 Jan Serfontein became a director of this BEE company, with two black African co-directors. He resigned on the same day, leaving Murff Mokgwanatsi as a director.

Murff was offered the position while doing construction work on the farm.

"They wanted to start a project, a chicken project, and they wanted me to be a director there," explains Murff.

They wanted him as a director, but in name only. He has never been to a meeting, never seen a bank statement or audit report, never seen any documents intended for directors or beneficiaries. He's not a signatory to company cheques.

When asked why, the lawyer representing the Serfonteins replied in writing: "The directors of Smokey Mountain Trading have always had full access to the company's annual financial statements or bank statements."

Why did the Serfonteins go to all the bother of setting up the trust and the trading company? Because under the banner of BEE millions of rands have been raised in grants and aid, all in the name of the Boskop Land Bank village.

The village's name was used specifically in a business plan written by the Small Business Advisory Bureau of the University of the North West in Potchefstroom.

The plan was used for an agreement between the farm and Hendrix Poultry breeders in the Netherlands, to import a new breed of layer chicken. It was supposed to be an empowerment deal, for the people of the village.

The plan was also used to get money from the South African government, via the Department of Agriculture in the North West province. Paul Mogotlhe, deputy director of the department, explained: "The plan was to empower black people around that area so that they can become shareholders in an economic development project, but also to provide them with employment opportunities."

Large sums of money changed hands: R3.2 million was allocated and spent in 2006, and another R2.5 million in 2007, according to Paul Mogotlhe.

The Dutch government gave around R5 million and a batch of chickens to start the business, empowering, so they believed, a group of emerging farmers running an independent business.

"They used me to get money from the government," says Murff Mokgwanatsi. And he couldn't do anything to stop them. "I was fighting alone. Other beneficiaries, everyone, were too afraid to help."

The village has never seen a penny or any benefit, says Shorty Valiphatwe. "If there was something, the place would have been better, with running water, electricity and maybe the school would be a better school."

How is it possible that neither the South African nor the Dutch government has ever communicated with the supposed beneficiaries of the trust, the directors of the trading company, or the people of the village?

Both governments are now trying to find out.

PART THREE

Bad Business

Chapter 13

Death-trap Taxis

Stephan Hofstatter and Rob Rose
Sunday Times

Twelve million South Africans travel by taxi every day – to and from work, to and from the shops. They are the most used form of transport.

Yet thousands of taxis are no better than speeding death traps, illegal conversions of vans to unsafe passenger vehicles. While a real taxi has roll bars and seats secured to the chassis, these illegal vehicles have seats bolted onto the thin steel floor. The result? A series of fatal accidents in which the seats fly off and people are killed.

The story began with an investigation into how the government planned to finance an ambitious scheme to replace the old taxis with new vehicles, under its recapitalisation programme – the sort of business reporting that Stephan Hofstatter and Rob Rose are known for. But it soon turned into a nightmare investigation of death and injury on South Africa's roads.

Toyota had warned in a letter way back in 2005 of the grisly prospect of "death or injury" from illegal conversions.

Thanks partly to inside information from a whistle-blower – Absa's former head of taxi finance, Hennie de Beer – Hofstatter and Rose were able to get hold of a raft of documents confirming that the banks ignored the warnings, fearing the financial implications of acknowledging millions in "toxic taxi debt".

A letter from the Department of Transport to a body representing all the banks in February 2008 alerted them to the fact they were financing vehicles that were non-compliant and they would be held accountable. Yet the banks largely shrugged off the problem, aware that any write-off of the estimated R600m in toxic taxi debt would be devastating to their investors.

However, as the investigation developed, interviews with insiders, bank officials, government sources and insurance companies, as well as confidential government documents, revealed that the problem was far larger than believed: more than 4000 illegally converted death traps were on the road.

Worse, many of the drivers of these vehicles were unaware that they'd been sold a dud and, unable to survive without the taxi income, said they would use these vehicles during the 2010 World Cup. The first story caused transport minister S'bu Ndebele to publicly vow to pull the illegal vehicles off the roads.

The revelations sparked parliamentary hearings, promises from government that the problem would be addressed, and extensive debates about how such an important public priority as taxi recapitalisation could be so badly botched.

While it would be good to say the revelations put an end to the problem, this isn't so. Government continues to struggle to implement the directive to pull unsafe vehicles from the roads, facing defiant taxi drivers and officials willing to look the other way for a few rands. A number of horror crashes have claimed more lives since the first *Sunday Times* story – raising questions about the country's commitment to deal decisively with public safety.

Stephen Hofstatter joined the *Sunday Times* investigations team in 2009 and was named Mondi Shanduka newspaper journalist of the year. Previously he was contributing editor and columnist at *Business Day*, a regular contributor to *Noseweek* and the *Sunday Times*, and has written for several local and international publications, including *Der Tagespiegel* in Berlin and *Africa Report* in Paris. He co-authored photographer Jürgen Schadeberg's book *Voices from the Land* and contributed to his most recent book, *Tales from Jozi*.

Rob Rose joined the *Sunday Times'* investigations team in 2009 and is the winner of the 2009 Taco Kuiper Award for Investigative Journalism. In 2010 he was also named Financial Journalist of the Year in the Sanlam Awards, won the overall award in the Citadel financial journalism awards, and was named Telkom business journalist of the year. He has a law degree but lasted only two weeks as an articled clerk before swapping law for journalism. He joined *Business Day* in 2002, before moving to *Financial Mail* magazine.

Exposed: Deadly Taxi Racket

26 July

More than 4000 death-trap taxis – some of which have already caused grisly deaths – have been let loose on South Africa's roads by banks, car dealers and the Department of Transport.

The *Sunday Times* has established that about 4000 illegally converted Toyota Quantum panel vans have been operating as taxis, although they do not meet the government's safety standards.

Seats are bolted onto the paper-thin steel floor instead of being fixed to the chassis, windows cut into the van weaken the structure, and there is no rear roll bar. Roofs crumple on impact and seats rip loose, hurling passengers to their deaths, according to a notice sent to banks last year by private vehicle investigation firm International Vehicle Identification Desk (Ivid).

"Even in the smallest crash, passengers' legs break like twigs," said a department official who did not want to be named. "We have 4000 time bombs driving around, costing lives, and nobody is doing a thing about it."

Some of these vehicles – many of which have been involved in serious accidents with high fatalities, including six children on one occasion – were even officially accredited to transport tourists during the recent Fifa Confederations Cup. And they could even be in use during the World Cup next year.

"We will continue to take the risk and work with these taxis, unless we're physically forced to stop," says Michael Yende of the Gauteng Taxi Council.

"We could have transported many tourists to the Confed games with these taxis. We just wouldn't know," said William Thembe, chairman of the Alexandra Taxi Association.

Now minister of transport S'bu Ndebele has vowed to make it a priority to pull these unsafe vehicles off the road.

Branding it a "concern", Ndebele was alarmed that the vehicles had been used to ferry foreigners during the Confederations Cup. He said this must not be allowed to happen at next year's tournament.

"We don't want to hear of people dying in taxis getting to a match, particularly if we know those vehicles are not suitable."

The illegally converted panel vans are estimated to ferry up to 400 000 passengers a day across South Africa.

The country's banks, the department, roadworthy agencies, SA Bureau of Standards (SABS) and car dealers have been blaming each other for indifference, negligence or incompetence.

The Quantums were bought under the government's taxi recapitalisation programme, which aimed to improve the safety of the 180 000 taxis carrying 12 million people every day.

The banks, including Absa, Nedbank, Standard Bank and Wesbank, as well as vehicle industry credit provider SA Taxi Finance, have financed 973 converted Quantums used as taxis since August 2007, which is when regulations came into force designating these vehicles "illegal", according to an analysis of the government's vehicle database, eNatis.

The rest were either paid for in cash or financed by the banks before August 2007. According to eNatis, there were more than 4000 of these converted Toyota Quantum panel vans operating as taxis on SA's roads.

The banks have admitted to the *Sunday Times* that they had more than 700 of these vehicles on their books, at an estimated finance value of R140 million.

SA Taxi Finance said it had 584 on its books, Wesbank and Absa "less than 50", Standard Bank 40, and Nedbank only 3. Toyota Financial Services has not quantified its exposure.

Taxi owners were lured by dealers into buying Quantum panel vans from 2005 because they are up to R30 000 cheaper and had more seats than the Toyota Quantum Sesfikile, the vehicle legally mandated to operate as a taxi.

The problem was flagged in a 2005 memo from Toyota, which said illegal conversions must not happen because it placed passengers at risk of "death or injury" and the company "in a situation where the client could sue us".

Toyota last week launched another investigation into illegal conversions of panel vans after fresh allegations surfaced of dealers supplying vans for conversion, Toyota spokesman Ferdi de Vos confirmed this week.

Absa has now decided to treat every deal as fraudulent. "We will either go after the customer, the dealer or the person who converted that taxi," said the bank's head of vehicle finance, Marcel de Klerk.

But a letter sent in February 2008 by the department's Kuben Pillay to the taxi financing committee, which included all the banks, suggests that banks will have to share liability. It says the government was alerted that banks were "financing vehicles that were not compliant with the September 2006 regulations". It warns: "Financiers would be held accountable for financing non-compliant vehicles despite being aware of the requirements."

Alarmingly, authorities have done little more than pass the buck. Though some vehicles have been pulled off the roads by police, there appears to be little concerted effort to do this.

Documents in the *Sunday Times*'s possession show the issue was repeatedly raised by the department's vehicle technical committee, with the regulatory arm of the SABS coming under fire for failing to conduct regular inspection of companies licensed to modify vehicles, as they are required to do by law.

Roadworthy centres, which provided certificates of fitness to these vehicles, were also blamed.

Insiders in the department said illegal conversions had been on the committee's agenda at every quarterly meeting for more than two years, including last week.

"Everybody is trying to blame everyone else," said an official who attended the meeting but did not want to be named. "No one wants to take responsibility."

Bafana Mkwebane, the deputy director-general of transport who chairs the committee, declined to confirm this. "No official will talk to the media about this," he said.

Yende blamed the banks for the problem. "The banks require a taxi permit, so they knew they were financing taxis. We have fallen into a trap because the banks didn't raise any objections to financing these vehicles. The banks just look to see if you are creditworthy. They just want sales," he said.

James Chapman, who runs Santaco Trading – essentially the business arm of the SA National Taxi Council – agreed: "Banks may have been negligent to have allowed these vehicles to end up on their books."

But SA Taxi Finance CEO Martin Bezuidenhout laid the blame squarely on the government. "We as financiers saw documents that were legitimate, and these vehicles were registered by the government as taxis. It's unacceptable that their systems didn't identify these vehicles." Bezuidenhout said he was first informed in October 2008 that SA Taxi Finance had financed these vehicles "and we immediately stopped financing new vehicles that fell into this category".

Wesbank head of sales and marketing Chris de Kock said: "We expect the regulatory authorities [to] inspect the vehicle before a taxi operating permit is issued, or before it is registered as a taxi."

Absa's De Klerk said the VIN number – a registration number on the government system – clearly showed that a vehicle was a panel van, so Absa would not have financed these vans as taxis.

Johann de Beer, head of taxi finance at Nedbank, confirmed that the VIN number clearly showed which vehicles were Toyota panel vans. He said banks did not have too many options once they had financed these vehicles, other than "trying to rectify it".

"If these vehicles slip through, sure, I suppose we're responsible. Can [the authorities] do something to us? Probably they can, because the responsibility is on us to ensure the vehicles we finance are authorised and legal," he said.

Standard Bank's Patrice de Marigny said: "These vehicles came to us through the franchise dealer network", adding that those responsible for converting the vehicles illegally "should be in jail".

Lee Dutton, who heads Ivid, agreed that the primary culprits are the conversion shops and dealers. "These are the guys who knew that what they were doing was illegal, but who knew they could make a quick buck by converting these vehicles and selling them as taxis," he said.

But with everyone disclaiming responsibility, passengers involved in accidents may find themselves unable to claim from insurance.

Insurance company Clarendon provides insurance for about 65 000 taxis – about 80% of the insured taxi market. But CEO Louis Fivaz said when a converted panel van was involved in an accident "we might not pay out" for either the vehicle or passenger liability.

Fivaz said this was especially if the "conversion to an illegal vehicle contributes to the loss".

Meanwhile, the department was investigating and promised to take action "against all concerned", said spokesman Sam Monareng.

The SABS was also investigating van converter companies and would suspend any found doing so illegally, he added.

Responding to reports that the vehicles had been used during the Confederations Cup, local organising committee spokesman Jermaine Craig said: "It's unclear the extent to which these vehicles were used during the Fifa Confederations Cup, but we have raised the issue with the relevant government transport departments."

Illegally Converted Taxis Could Ruin Their Owners

Phola Katsisi is a single mother who lives in Pimville, Soweto.

She supports two families – her two daughters at home, and her mother and caregiver in faraway Zeerust – from the money she earns ferrying commuters in her minibus taxi to and from Johannesburg's oldest township, Alexandra.

When Katsisi, 45, was scouting around for a reasonably priced minibus two years ago, she tried a dealership in De Deur, 25 km south of Johannesburg.

Friends in the taxi industry had told her there were bargains to be had. At the time, government's recapitalisation programme was in full swing, with dilapidated Toyota Hi-Ace vehicles to be replaced by fancy new minibuses, which typically cost more than R200 000.

Months earlier, in August 2007, new safety regulations that applied to all vehicles operating as minibus taxis came into force. They required taxis to be fitted with seat-belts and rollover bars to prevent passengers' skulls being crushed during an accident.

When the dealer asked Katsisi if she wanted a 14-seat Toyota Quantum for R255 000, or a 16-seater model parked in the showroom for R228 000, it was an obvious choice. After paying a R60 000 deposit, she took the necessary documents to the offices of SA Taxi Finance in Johannesburg, and a week later collected her taxi.

Next she took it for a roadworthy, receiving an official licence disc authorising her to carry 15 passengers plus a driver, and authorisation from the Transport Department's licence board to ply her trade. Last month Katsisi was lucky to be among 3000 taxi owners accredited by the Gauteng Transport Department to ferry Fifa Confederations Cup spectators between Johannesburg and Pretoria, getting paid R1400 a day for her efforts.

Things were looking up.

So it came as a nasty shock when Katsisi discovered this month her taxi was on the road illegally. She only found out after fellow Alex Taxi Association members, with the same vehicles, started being pulled off the road by metro police.

"I took this to the government to get a roadworthy and a permit, and they approved it," she says. "How can they say now that it's not legal?"

It turned out her dealer could offer bargain prices because he'd illegally converted a much cheaper Toyota Quantum panel van into a death-trap minibus, with seats bolted onto a paper-thin body rather than the chassis, and no rollover bar.

Now she faces the prospect of losing everything as the government slowly starts cracking down on the illegal conversions by pulling them off the road.

Transport minister S'bu Ndebele confirmed as much this week when he told the *Sunday Times* that "there's no time that you can say to the police that we're allowing unroadworthy vehicles because we have a grand plan. That's not our approach".

But Katsisi isn't alone.

James Chapman, who runs Santaco Trading – essentially the business arm of the SA National Taxi Council (Santaco) – knows of dozens of Santaco members who are in the same predicament.

"What upsets me is that the taxi owners are now the ones taking the flak. But in most cases, they were simply presented with a vehicle they were told was cheaper," he says.

At each level the system failed. Despite warnings from Toyota, as far back as 2005, that converting Quantum panel vans was illegal and dangerous, dealers bought these vehicles from converters and sold them to unsuspecting taxi owners.

Then the regulatory arm of the SA Bureau of Standards didn't raise any red flags and didn't check on the converters who were turning panel vans into taxis. Neither did the government, whose roadworthy agencies duly handed over a certificate of fitness for these vehicles to be used as taxis, and whose eNatis system registered the panel vans as taxis.

Then the banks, which many people expect to be prudent enough to check that they're not financing an illegal vehicle, simply registered the vehicles.

So where does this leave the taxi owners?

SA Taxi Finance CEO Martin Bezuidenhout says the risk can be mitigated.

"These vehicles still have a value, and they need to be taken off the roads. But they can even be converted so they can be used as taxis again." But to do this will cost between R15 000 and R40 000 per vehicle – and with no one owning up to the problem, it seems unlikely a willing funder will step forward.

And it will be the taxi owners, like Katsisi, caught up in a network of events beyond their control, whose businesses stand to be destroyed by this collective botch-up.

"My 5-year-old is in a crèche and 17-year-old daughter goes to school at Bryanston High and I pay over R8000 in monthly instalments," she says. "It will ruin me if I can't use my taxi."

Taken for a Ride over Toxic Taxi Debt
2 August

South African banks held emergency meetings this week after it emerged that they had financed death-trap taxis, leaving them exposed to toxic taxi debt estimated at more than R600 million.

An analysis of the government's eNatis system identified 973 Toyota Quantum panel vans, illegally converted into taxis, which had been financed by the banks after August 2007, when new safety regulations were passed.

However, Lee Dutton, head of the International Vehicle Identification Desk, estimated that there are more than 4000 Quantums on the roads that have been converted into taxis. All are unsafe under current regulations because they do not have rollover bars, and seats are not properly secured to the chassis, which has led to many fatalities already.

Dutton estimated that about 3000 of those vehicles have been financed by SA's banks. Because many banks provided finance of about R200 000 per vehicle, this represents potential bad debt of R600 million.

The minister of transport, S'bu Ndebele, confirmed on Friday that "all unsafe and unroadworthy vehicles will be removed from the roads" – ratcheting up the pressure on banks to identify and deal with illegal vehicles on their books.

But the banks' exposure could be far higher than just for the illegal Toyota Quantums. An eNatis analysis last year "red-flagged" 6802 panel vans of all descriptions – including Ivecos and Mercedes Sprinter vans – that had been converted into taxis since August 2007.

Assuming all of them were financed by the banks at R200 000 each, these vehicles represent an initial exposure of more than R1.3 billion. Experts estimate that up to 40% of the 6802 vehicles may contravene safety rules.

While part of this debt has been repaid to the banks, some taxi associations say they intend to approach the National Credit Regulator to have the initial sales reversed entirely.

Hennie de Beer, the former head of taxi finance at Absa, has assembled a legal team to recover losses incurred by taxi owners who choose — or are forced – to stop transporting passengers in their illegal Quantums.

"We want the taxi owner to be put in the position he was before," he says. "At the very least this means the bank will have to refund their deposits plus instalments to date, plus daily loss of income. The longer banks take to react to this very serious problem, the more it will cost them."

But SA Taxi Finance chief executive Martin Bezuidenhout said: "We don't believe they will have any success in proving that. And the problem of those taxis' safety features can be remedied."

This week, the financiers all proposed different solutions.

SA Taxi Finance, which has 584 of the converted Toyota Quantum panel vans on its books, said it would spend R20 million to make the vehicles "structurally compliant" and return them to the roads. Bezuidenhout says he will provide 100 vehicles to taxi owners to use while their vehicles are being "converted".

But this involves "converting" illegal taxis once again – something which is expressly forbidden by law. Government has confirmed that there are no manufacturers, importers or builders in SA currently approved to convert a Quantum panel van into a commercial taxi.

Dutton agrees this is not a viable solution. "You can't simply fix this, because it would be another illegal conversion. You need government to pass a special regulation specifically to fix the Toyota Quantum issue, allowing these vehicles to be altered to become safe," he says.

Marcel de Klerk, Absa's head of vehicle finance, says his bank is still deciding what action to take on 28 illegally converted panel vans financed by Absa. "We've got three or four actions we can take, because we want to get out of those 28 [contracts] – even if we have to take that taxi, sell it for whatever we can get, and [finance] another taxi for that customer," he says.

KwaZulu-Natal's Department of Transport has already opened criminal cases against an Umgeni-based company that converted panel vans into taxis.

It gets worse. This week *Business Times* established that many taxis were financed using false operating permits, or short-term charter permits. This is a risk because taxi owners, and banks who lent them money, face sudden losses because the vehicles can be pulled off the road at any time. The taxi owners are also fuelling taxi violence as established operators fight for turf with illegal newcomers.

Last year 100 000 "face value documents", which can be used to print false licence disks, were stolen from Alberton's licensing department. Dutton estimates that nearly one million have been stolen in recent years and are in circulation.

"When we became aware of this, we got a list of the numbers of these stolen documents from the Department of Transport. When a bank gets a finance application, it checks if the document it has was part of the stolen batch," he said.

Short-term charter permits allow taxis to operate only on a specified route and for a specified time (typically a few weeks). But banks typically finance taxis over 48–60 months, so the charter permit does not provide proof that the taxi operator will be able to service the debt over that time.

Nedbank's Johann de Beer describes this as "very risky". "You'd be careful not to lend based on that. You need a viable route for the duration of the [financing] contract to ensure the taxi owner can repay you," he said.

Hennie de Beer said charter permits represented a nasty chunk of bad debt for banks.

"An investigation in January by the Cape Town permit board showed that between 3000 and 4000 charter permits were issued in the last quarter of 2008. And we have proof that a lot of these permits were used to obtain taxi finance," he said.

None of the banks admitted they had financed vehicles using invalid permits. But *Business Times* is in possession of an affidavit from one taxi driver, Ayanda Tulumani, who says he was sold an illegal permit for R1500 by a vehicle dealership, which he never got. SA Taxi Finance then financed a R250 000 taxi for him.

Other documents in our possession show that finance was granted based on charter permits. A temporary operating licence granted to Vuyani Nziweni in April demonstrates that Toyotas were financed using a "temporary operating licence" that was meant to apply only from 9 April to 22 April.

A debt counsellor's analysis seen by *Business Times* of 500 clients shows 48 had their taxis financed without valid permits.

With Ndebele now focusing on pulling unsafe or illegal taxis off the roads, banks could face bigger write-offs than they thought.

Nedbank, for one, acknowledges the risk. "Could there be toxic taxi debt? I suppose there could, if the [taxi industry] isn't able to pay its accounts," said Johann de Beer.

This risk will increase if taxi owners cannot generate income because their vehicles have been pulled off the road.

Taxi Financier in the Dock Over Extra Fees
16 August

SA Taxi Finance, the country's biggest independent taxi financier, is in the dock for breaking the National Credit Act in lending deals it struck with 18 000 taxi owners.

This will come as a nasty surprise to blue-chip firms – including Standard Bank, Old Mutual, Sanlam, Investec and Futuregrowth – which invested R4 billion in the business through its opaque financing arm, SA Taxi Securitisation.

Jan Augustyn, head of investigations at the National Credit Regulator (NCR), told *Business Times* that the regulator has forced SA Taxi to change the way it does business.

The first problem was that SA Taxi charged a "vehicle sourcing fee" to borrowers. Not only was there no provision in the Credit Act for this, but no taxi owners interviewed by *Business Times* were aware they were paying this fee. The fee was typically R4500 including VAT, on which interest was charged for 48 to 60 months.

Augustyn said this was a "breach of the National Credit Act, in our opinion", and ordered that the fee be reversed for all 18 000 clients. "However, SA Taxi Securitisation did not levy permissible charges – like an initiation fee or monthly service fee – on their contracts, so we agreed they can add these on, then offset these fees against the sourcing fee," he said.

But this raises questions about whether the regulator is being too soft, giving SA Taxi licence to levy service fees retrospectively.

"We're not giving them licence to do that," said Augustyn. "They have to send letters to all their clients, and ask them to consent to this. If they don't agree, the clients can follow the normal route of going to court, but from our point of view, this is a sensible compromise."

The upshot, according to SA Taxi CEO Martin Bezuidenhout, is that it will refund each client about R1400 – costing it R25 million.

But Hennie de Beer, Absa's former head of taxi finance whose complaint sparked the probe, said even if fees are levied retrospectively, the difference is nearer R50 million.

Bezuidenhout said his company "disagreed with the regulator about this complex legal issue, but decided not to challenge it".

The regulator found other problems too – starting with the identity of the lender.

While most taxi owners believed they were borrowing from SA Taxi Finance, it was actually SA Taxi Securitisation that advanced the loan. SA Taxi Finance is the "broker" that markets SA Taxi Securitisation's business.

Augustyn ordered SA Taxi to send letters to all clients clarifying this, as "consumers need to know who they're dealing with".

The NCR is still investigating whether SA Taxi benefited from "commissions" paid by insurance companies to push business their way – something it denies.

Said Augustyn: "We have asked for a full audit to be performed on all loan agreements by independent auditors to see whether SA Taxi Securitisation did get commissions or fees that they weren't entitled to, or that clients weren't told about." The auditors must report back to the NCR before the end of the year.

Futuregrowth invested R950 million in SA Taxi Securitisation and fund manager Jason Lightfoot said last year that his company "believes that no regulations have been transgressed".

Does the new NCR finding mean Futuregrowth did not ask the right questions? "Not at all," said Lightfoot, adding that "regulations were never clear" about a vehicle sourcing fee, and it was "never prohibited".

The ruling comes at a tough time for SA Taxi. A *Sunday Times* investigation last month showed that SA Taxi financed 584 illegally converted Toyota Quantum panel vans that Toyota said were unsafe. Financiers are still thrashing out a solution.

Yet SA Taxi, 90% owned by unlisted Transaction Capital, operates behind an opaque façade. Though it has a R4 billion debtors' book, it remains a private company – unlike all banks and most lenders.

This means SA Taxi's accounts are not available to the public, so it is impossible for an outsider to verify claims about its financial health. Nor does the public have insight into how much the likes of Sanlam or Investec have invested.

Mark Lamberti, chair of SA Taxi and founder of Massmart, said the public has no need to know details of SA Taxi's bad debts or profit, as this is Transaction Capital's concern. "I'm not sure how any of [those details] would be helpful to clients ... and some debenture holders prefer their investments not to be disclosed," he said.

Lamberti said SA Taxi is regulated by the Banks Act, monitored by the Financial Services Board and rated by Moody's. "While the absence of [public] information may engender caution or, worse still, suspicion, it should not engender condemnation," he said.

But the Moody's rating is a "private rating", which means the public cannot get access to ratings reports. "It was expedient to do a private rating at the time," said Bezuidenhout. "It's not as if we've got anything to hide."

The issue of transparency assumed greater importance after more than 110 complaints were lodged with the NCR, claiming SA Taxi extended credit "recklessly".

De Beer, the ex-Absa banker, said several SA Taxi contracts he had seen inflated potential revenue and underestimated typical expenses. "I challenge Augustyn and Bezuidenhout to prove me wrong on an open TV debate."

Yet Augustyn said he found no evidence of reckless lending. This is an important break for SA Taxi Finance; if reckless lending was found, a court could set aside the original deals.

Complaints in *Business Times*'s possession accuse SA Taxi of a litany of Credit Act violations, including hidden costs, contracts not being explained and a failure to properly assess a borrower's ability to repay.

"The contract was never explained to me. I was told to sign if I want the van," said Thethelakhe Ntakane of Philippi in the Western Cape in a sworn statement.

Papa Mkencele of Khayelitsha borrowed R200 000 to buy a taxi, but is now "struggling with my payments". He added: "I was never asked to complete my monthly expenses – only a taxi route calculator."

Debt counsellor Derry Burge, who has lodged numerous complaints with the NCR, said: "The general feeling among debt counsellors is that the regulator is a toothless dog."

Augustyn denied the NCR treads too softly, claiming "different criteria" apply to SA Taxi than to a bank providing "consumption" loans. "They provide credit to a market that would otherwise struggle to obtain finance."

Lamberti said SA Taxi does not use the same "affordability criteria" it would for someone buying a car, but rather looks at how much someone can earn by operating a taxi business. "We do not see SA Taxi as a vehicle finance business, we see it as an SMME finance business. Hence the differences of interpretation around the Credit Act, which was crafted for consumers, not businesses," he said.

Bezuidenhout is adamant that SA Taxi has not cut corners. "We are running a properly controlled business that justifies our market share and Moody's rating."

Government "Failing to Act Against Taxis" *23 August*

Minister of transport S'bu Ndebele has been accused of ignoring warnings about unsafe taxis after a horror smash in the Free State this month claimed three lives.

The *Sunday Times* revealed last month that more than 4000 Toyota panel vans had been illegally converted into taxis, despite warnings from Toyota that it placed passengers at risk of "death or injury".

Now, the *Sunday Times* has verified that the taxi involved in a crash on 6 August was an illegally converted Quantum panel van – nearly a month after Ndebele vowed to pull these unsafe vehicles off the road.

Grootvlei police inspector Thami Tshabalala confirmed that the accident near Heidelberg resulted in three deaths and a number of gruesome injuries.

"The vehicle overturned, and those people that died were thrown out of the vehicle and died instantly," Tshabalala said.

The crash victims were all members of the extended Sangweni family, who were on their way to a wedding in Newcastle.

"Three of my aunts had broken legs, including the one getting married, two were seriously injured and are still in hospital, and three died, including my father," said Tami Mthembu.

"It's terrible – we nearly lost our whole family."

In keeping with traditional custom, the wedding went ahead without the bride, he said.

"She started her marriage with both legs in plaster casts."

Mthembu said his father, who owned the taxi, had believed his vehicle was legal and safe because the Department of Transport had issued him with a roadworthy certificate and taxi operating permit. "He bought what he thought was an approved passenger carrier from a dealership – no one ever told him it was converted from a panel van," said Mthembu.

In yet another slip-up from government, the illegally converted panel van had been licensed to carry 16 passengers – two more than the maximum 14 allowed in genuine Quantum Sesfikile taxis.

Asked if he felt responsible for the deaths in the Free State, Ndebele – who was in Angola with President Jacob Zuma – referred all queries to the deputy director-general of public transport, George Mahlalela.

Mahlalela rejected suggestions that the government should bear responsibility.

"I can tell you that government is acting. If by any chance these guys are not picked up in roadblocks, it's really unfortunate, but we are enforcing [the directive]," he said.

But traffic officials said this week they were still waiting for instructions from the transport department.

"We have heard nothing from our bosses to take these things off the road," said one who did not want to be named.

"They are dangerous and killing people. If they're wearing seat-belts they'll go through the window, seat and all. But without a directive we can't act."

Chapter 14

Cipro at Centre of SA's Fraud Pandemic

James Myburgh
www.politicsweb.co.za

This story began with a report on a massive fraud against the South African Revenue Service (Sars). Prominent South African companies were being cloned on the Companies and Intellectual Property Registration Office (Cipro) database. That wasn't the only problem: directors were being illegally deregistered and replaced with individuals using false IDs, and near-duplicates of companies were being registered, again illegally.

James Myburgh started to analyse the company records. A number of firms told him how frauds had been perpetrated against them, yet when they had reported illegal duplications and deregistrations, Cipro had been extremely slow to do anything.

By following these threads Myburgh was eventually able to put together a list of over a hundred of the duplicate companies. As he contacted the real companies concerned, it became clear that this was a list of frauds past and present, and some yet to happen.

Most of the companies duplicated in 2007 and 2008 reported having been hit by fraudsters. Some said they had lost hundreds of thousands of rands as cheques had been intercepted in the post and deposited in bank accounts set up in the names of the counterfeit companies.

The 2009 duplications were only just having an impact. Myburgh alerted the SA Guide Dogs Association that it had a duplicate registered in the name of the SA Guide Dogs Association Breeders. The Association was unaware of the clone but had just lost a batch of donor cheques.

Following publication, Cipro quickly acted to close the loophole that allowed these counterfeit companies to be registered on the system. In a PR offensive, five employees were suspended, and the Hawks were brought in to investigate.

The banks were alerted that accounts set up in the names of these duplicates were almost certainly intended for fraudulent purposes. The account of the SA Guide Dogs Association Breeders was frozen and at least some money was restored to its rightful beneficiaries.

James Myburgh is the founder editor of the South African politics website www.politicsweb.co.za, part of the Moneyweb network. He was a researcher for the Democratic Party in Parliament from 1997 to 2001 before going on to study politics at St Antony's College, Oxford.

Cipro at Centre of SA's Fraud Pandemic
7 August

South Africa is currently in the midst of a fraud pandemic. At its centre is the Companies and Intellectual Property Registration Office (Cipro). Over the past two years corrupt officials at Cipro, acting with seeming impunity, have facilitated hundreds if not thousands of scams which have hit the South African Revenue Service (Sars), a number of prominent companies, and hundreds of smaller private businesses.

Two weeks ago we reported how in 2008 duplicates of Sun Microsystems South Africa and SBC International Management Services were fraudulently registered as companies on Cipro. Bank accounts were set up in these counterfeit companies' names. R51m in tax refunds from Sars, due to the legitimate companies, was then diverted into the counterfeits' accounts.

An investigation has revealed that this Cipro-based scam was just the tip of the tip of the iceberg. Counterfeit companies are being fraudulently registered through Cipro, on an ongoing daily basis, to facilitate cheque and other forms of fraud. No proper due diligence is being done. Over the past two years the directors of several prominent companies have also been fraudulently deregistered, and new directors inserted. Again, the intention is to facilitate fraud of one kind or another.

Counterfeit companies

One of the most prevalent scams involves the registration of duplicate or counterfeit companies. These are companies with almost the same name as the real company. For instance, Avusa Media is a well-known media company. In terms of proper procedure Cipro is not allowed to register companies with a similar name. However, in October 2008, officials at Cipro fraudulently approved the reservation of the name Avusa Media (Gauteng), and shortly afterwards a company of that name was established. Its sole director is one 'PM Masondo' of Leyds Street, Pretoria.

Once the company has been registered the fraudsters – who operate using stolen identities – then attempt to establish bank accounts in the name of the counterfeit company. If the bank officials are honest and alert, the real company will be contacted and the fraud nipped in the bud. But all too often an account is successfully set up. This is then used to facilitate fraud against the legitimate company, its clients and suppliers, and innocent third parties.

Clients are sometimes contacted and informed that the banking details of the real company have been changed (to that of the counterfeit.) 'Overpayments' may be made using the counterfeit company's cheques to the legitimate company's suppliers and the fraudsters will ask for a refund.

In many cases cheques are intercepted at the South African Post Office. Companies with similar names to the recipients of the cheque are then fraudulently registered through Cipro. Bank accounts are established in that company's name, the cheques are cashed, and the money removed. Usually, the counterfeit company uses the same name with a word (such as Gauteng) or a number (usually 01) added to the end. If need be, the fraudster can simply add the "01" to the named beneficiary on the stolen cheque, and it can then be deposited into their account.

In order to give an indication of the extent of the problem we are publishing a list of 114 duplicate companies alongside the real businesses and organisations they are trying to impersonate. We have very strong grounds for believing that almost all were established fraudulently, with the intention of perpetrating fraud. We have contacted a sample of the real companies listed. Not a single one had approved the duplicate. Some were unaware of their counterfeit version. A large proportion had been targeted successfully or unsuccessfully by fraudsters using the counterfeit company's identity.

Given our time constraints we were only able to contact a small number of the legitimate companies. However, the following confirmed they had been targeted: Schindler's Lifts, SA Guide Dogs Association, Giants Canning, Trident Steel, Johannesburg Tractor Spares, G & L Agencies, Marlboro Crane Hire, Hypersave Supermarket, Space Television, Colletts Pharmacy, The Media Shop, and AfriSave Cash & Carry.

Hijacked companies

Between 2007 and 2009 a series of well-known South African companies have had their legitimate directors deregistered on the Cipro system. New directors were inserted, probably using stolen identities. In 2007 one 'Michael Thembinkosi Mahlaba' – in reality a tractor-driver living and working near Howick, KwaZulu-Natal – was inserted as the director of Hellermann Tyton, Renold Crofts and Macsteel Tube & Pipe. Other companies affected by this type of fraud include Cashbuild (South Africa), The Lion Match Company, Trident Steel, Fleet Street Publications, Tedelex, and Gardena (SA).

Most of these frauds were carried out using the electronic lodgement of the CM29 (details of directors) form. Due to weaknesses in the system, agents accessing the Cipro database could change the names of directors of any company at will. This was done from 'outside' but it did require insider knowledge. Despite being notified of the problem as early as October 2007, Cipro only acted in February this year. E-lodgements of the CM29 form were temporarily suspended on 25 February 2009 by then acting CEO Renier du Toit. However, this did not stop the problem completely. On 8 April 2009 someone inside Cipro deregistered the two legitimate directors of BLSA Industries (the company which manufactures PoolBrite). One 'Ndumiso Terran[ce] Mzazi' was inserted as the sole director instead.

All but two of the companies contacted said they were unaware of any consequent fraud. However, one did say that an individual, claiming to be the new owner, tried to open a bank account in the company's name. He had various company documents, correspondence with the firm's attorneys, and a certificate issued by Cipro stating that he was the sole director of the company. A first effort in Johannesburg failed after the company was alerted by the branch concerned. But he later succeeded in opening an account in a small town, and the fraudsters used the good name and reputation of the company to conduct various cheque and credit card frauds.

Some companies have been hit both by hijacking and counterfeiting scams. As noted above, Macsteel had directors in a subsidiary deregistered. In July 2008 a counterfeit company called Macsteeli Trading was established for purposes unknown. Trident Steel meanwhile has been subjected to a sustained assault by fraudsters employing, inter alia, the following counterfeit companies: Trident Steel 22 (February 2007), Trident Sterling Tube-Manufactures (November 2007), Trident Tube Manufacturer (November 2007), Trident Steel (East) (January 2008), Trident Sterling Tube Manufacturers (Gauteng) (January 2008), Trident Steel Experts Construction and Projects (January 2009.) Trident Steel is a trademark and other companies are not allowed to use those two words in their name. This, and the company's complaints, did not stop Cipro from waving through these names over a two-year period.

Comment

Once the counterfeited (or hijacked) company has been registered and a bank account opened, it becomes very difficult for the police to solve subsequent frauds. The new directors usually use forged or stolen identities. A common practice is for the fraudsters to use stolen identity documents and scan and electronically alter proof of residence documents in order to meet Fica requirements. Unless the fraudsters are caught in the act, or with the false IDs in their possession, it is almost impossible to nail them successfully. Moreover, those caught are usually just runners. They would often rather go to prison for a few years than put their families at risk by fingering the syndicate bosses masterminding the scams (often Pakistanis and Nigerians).

In a written response to a query from Politicsweb, Cipro CEO Keith Sendwe said he was aware of the basic points we raised. The organisation, he said, was "pulling out all stops to prevent fraudulent activities taking place".

In their reply Standard Bank stated: "Although we are aware of the extent of the problem of cheque interception and fraud and of accounts being opened fraudulently and in some cases with similar names to registered entities, we have not confirmed that this is as a result of alleged corruption in Cipro, nor that legitimate details are or have been altered at Cipro. We are not able to comment on allegations which are clearly being made against Cipro."

114 Dodgy Duplicate Companies

Below is a list of 114 duplicate companies along with their genuine counterparts. Notably, charities such as the SA Guide Dogs Association and the SPCA – which receive many donations by cheque through the post – have had companies registered in their name.

We have good reason to suspect that these duplicates are mostly counterfeits – many established for the express purpose of committing fraud. Given the closeness of the names to the originals, none should have been approved by Cipro.

This list is meant to be indicative, not comprehensive. If your company or organisation has recently had cheques disappear at the South African Post Office, or fraudsters have asked your clients to change payment details, check the list below. You can also check for duplicates by using the "name search" function on the left-hand panel on the Cipro home page. We can be contacted at letters@politicsweb.co.za.

Original Company	Number	Duplicate	Number
AA Travel Guides	1989/005108/07	AA Travel Guides – Africa	2008/095825/23
		AA Travel Guides 01	2009/106155/23
Adcock Ingram Housecare	1972/005657/07	Adcock Ingram Housecare 01	2009/057726/23
Afrisave Cash And Carry	1999/023287/07	Afrisave Cash And Carry (Gauteng)	2009/041719/23
Aklin Carbide	1996/000995/07	Aklin Carbide (East)	2008/205930/23
Alrite Engineering	1966/005824/07	Alrite Engineering (No 1)	2008/114907/23

Original Company	Number	Duplicate	Number
Annique Skin Care Products	1997/015403/07	Annique Skin Care Products (Gauteng)	2008/099975/23
Auto Commodities	1995/000521/07	Auto Commodities (Gauteng)	2008/113033/23
Avusa Media	1952/003139/06	Avusa Media (Gauteng)	2008/191868/23
BJ Engineering	1994/010136/23	BJ Engineering (Gauteng)	2008/217791/23
Bassano Collection Africa	2005/077521/23	Bassano Collection Africa 01	2009/057722/23
Bronco Food Supplies	1992/003098/07	Bronco Foods Supplies 01	2009/073521/23
Cabinet Wholesalers	1990/017910/23	Cabinet Wholesalers (No 1)	2008/097152/23
Cadac	1965/003182/07	Cadac (East)	2007/240673/23
Character Linens	2003/109721/23	Character Linens (Gauteng)	2008/167402/23
Chemvet Steel and Fencing	2006/036702/07	Chemvet Steel and Fencing 01	2009/083338/23
Chipkins Catering Supplies	1993/003084/07	Chipkins Catering Supplies (No 1)	2008/119818/23
		Chipkins Catering Supplies (Jhb)	2007/211554/23
Circa Africa	1944/017181/07	Circa Africa 01	2008/192026/23
Citrashine	1962/000135/07	Citrashine (Gauteng)	2008/160778/23
		Citrashine 01	2008/154642/23
Colletts Pharmacy	1966/011576/07	Colletts Pharmacy (01)	2008/242382/23
		Colletts Pharmacy (Gauteng)	2008/245573/23
Computer Com Trading	2006/034009/07	Computer Com Trading (Gauteng)	2009/049370/23
Condra	1966/005322/07	Condra Cranes	2009/073517/23
Controlled Linen Solutions	2003/024332/07	Controlled Linen Solutions (Gauteng)	2008/219512/23

Original Company	Number	Duplicate	Number
Crossmill Chemicals	1994/026593/23	Crossmill Chemicals (Gauteng)	2009/029215/23
Cullen Coal	1997/001134/07	Cullen Coal 01	2009/073530/23
Decor Wallpaper Company	1984/070180/07	Decor Wallpaper Designs	2008/061741/23
		Decor Wallpaper (Gauteng)	2008/000670/23
Designers Architectural and Environmental Design	1993/032402/23	Designers Architectural and Enviromental Design 01	2008/200651/23
Direct Leisure Golf Distributors	2003/001448/07	Direct Leisure Golf Distributors (Africa)	2008/211116/23
Direct Leisure Sports Distributors	2000/005700/07	Direct Leisure Sports Distributors (Gauteng)	2008/092903/23
Distillers Corporation	1963/007327/06	Distillers Corporation (Gauteng)	2008/259869/23
Easy Rx Support	1999/009231/07	Easy Rx Support 01	2009/137334/23
Econo Tissue	2004/030333/23	Econo Tissue (Gauteng)	2008/071518/23
Eigenbau	1981/007380/07	Eigenbau (Gauteng)	2008/172931/23
Eli Lilly (S A)	1957/000371/07	Eli Lilly (Sa) 01	2009/127472/23
Ergosaf Environmental and Occupational Health Services	1988/013912/23	Ergosaf Environmental and Occupational Health Services (Gauteng)	2008/205928/23
		Ergosaf Enviromental and Occupational Health Services 01	2008/253655/23
Fairtex	1991/005367/07	Fairtex (South)	2009/152650/23
Fargo Africa Distribution Services	1996/003585/07	Fargo Africa Distribution Services (Gauteng)	2009/033406/23
Florsheim South Africa	2000/025636/07	Florsheim South Africa 01	2009/111024/23

Original Company	Number	Duplicate	Number
Formax	1994/010304/07	Formax (Gauteng)	2008/197406/23
Fumigation Worx	**2006/114521/23**	**Fumigation Worx 01**	**2009/095730/23**
G and L Agencies	1987/015649/23	G and L Agencies (Gauteng)	2008/224409/23
		G and L Agencies 01	2008/256616/23
GV Donald Africa	**1959/000769/07**	**GV Donald Africa Plumbers**	**2008/074956/23**
Giants Canning	2001/015331/23	Giants Canning (Gauteng)	2009/029213/23
Golden Era Printers and Stationers Bops	**1985/070423/07**	**Golden Era Printers and Stationers Bops (No 1)**	**2008/113029/23**
HDS Furniture Manufacturers	2006/029148/07	HDS Furniture Manufacturers 01	2009/145281/23
Headway Engineering	**1995/010462/23**	**Headway Engineering (South)**	**2009/152653/23**
Hlanganani Protection Services	1996/009314/07	Hlanganani Protection Services 01	2009/062186/23
Hypersave Supermarket	**1990/000611/23**	**Hypersave Supermarkert and Wholesalers (Gauteng)**	**2009/041721/23**
Imperial Cargo	1985/001558/07	Imperial Cargo 01	2009/090777/23
Incledon Dpi	**2002/020359/07**	**Incledon Dpi 01**	**2009/025589/23**
Internatio Mueller Chemicals Distribution South Africa	1962/000158/07	Internatio Mueller Chemicals Distribution South Africa 01	2008/233858/23
		Internatio Mueller Chemicals Distribution South Africa 05	2008/238075/23
JG Train and Company	**1950/039759/07**	**JG Train and Contractors**	**2009/001356/23**
Jetline-E Com Melrose Arch	2003/014093/07	Jetline-E Com Melrose Arch 01	2009/073523/23

Original Company	Number	Duplicate	Number
Johannesburg Tractor Spares	1971/011756/07	Johannesburg Tractor Spares (East)	2008/114908/23
		Johannesburg Tractor Spares (North)	2009/029214/23
		Johannesburg Tractor Spares 01	2008/163659/23
Kalex Marketing	1994/034499/23	Kalex Markerting 01	2009/091051/23
Kone Elevators South Africa	1994/003712/07	Kone Elevators South Africa 22	2009/121295/23
Lake International Technologies	1946/023685/07	Lake International Technologies 01	2009/001969/23
M Naran And Sons Carpets	1995/020814/23	M Naran And Sons Carperts (Gauteng)	2008/179990/23
Mabula Game Reserve	1991/002447/07	Mabula Private Game Reserve 01	2009/090778/23
Mabula Time-Sharing Share Block	1969/005889/06	Mabula Time-Sharing Share Block 01	2009/083337/23
Marlboro Crane Hire	1992/007221/07	Marlboro Crane Hire 01	2009/109209/23
Medal Paint Manufacturers	1982/001195/07	Medal Paint Manufacturers (West)	2007/193549/23
Monsanto South Africa	1968/001485/07	Monsanto S A Sales	2008/224313/23
		Monsanto South Africa 01	2008/235425/23
Nampak Tissue	1999/000544/07	Nampak Tissue (Africa)	2009/057728/23
		Nampak Tissue 01	2009/104049/23
Navada Clothing Manufacturers	1995/003836/07	Navada Clothing Manufacturers 01	2008/259927/23
Pastel Software	1987/004342/07	Pastel Software (Gauteng)	2008/087570/23
Pictorial Press	1959/002909/07	Pictorial Press (Gauteng)	2008/000644/23

Original Company	Number	Duplicate	Number
Pioneer Picture Framers	**1967/013331/07**	**Pioneer Picture Framers 01**	**2009/001971/23**
Plastic Recycling	1992/027295/23	Plastic Recycling 01	2008/188105/23
Playersball Sports Distributors	**2000/019208/07**	**Playersball Sport Distributors – Gauteng**	**2008/092902/23**
Plush Products	1983/010966/07	Plush Products (Gauteng)	2008/208433/23
Qtec Moulding	**2000/026830/07**	**Qtec Moulding-Africa**	**2008/087769/23**
Quality Sugars	1966/006600/07	Quality Sugars (Africa)	2008/211115/23
Rosebank Travel Service	**1963/006454/07**	**Rosebank Travel Service 01**	**2009/091049/23**
Rutherford Joinery	2000/013377/07	Rutherford Johannesburg Joinery	2008/000669/23
SA Guide Dogs Association	**Charity**	**SA Guide-Dogs Association Breeders**	**2009/145280/23**
Sanlic-International	1944/017219/07	Sanlic–International Trading	2008/113032/23
Sato Labelling Systems	**1968/013531/07**	**Sato Labelling System (Africa)**	**2007/198553/23**
Schindler Lifts (SA)	2006/024747/07	Schindler Lifts 01	2009/104044/23
Space Television	**2002/017820/23**	**Space Television (Gauteng)**	**2008/074945/23**
SPCA	Charity	Johannesburg Spca (Gauteng)	2009/033412/23
Splinter Projects	**1995/053317/23**	**Splinter Projects 01**	**2009/073527/23**
Ssem Mthembu Medical	1987/001244/07	Ssem Mthembu Medical (Gauteng)	2007/172114/23
		Ssem Mthembu Medicals (Jhb)	2007/232388/23
Steelite Towbar and Silencer Centre	**1992/003612/23**	**Steelite Towbar and Silencer Centre 01**	**2008/260530/23**

Source: www.cipro.co.za. Although we have done our best to avoid error, please check company details against the Cipro database.

Original Company	Number	Duplicate	Number
Sterling Clothing	1987/004657/07	Sterling Clothing (Gauteng)	2008/172930/23
		Sterling Clothing 01	2008/144964/23
Sterling Clothing Manufacturers	1966/007723/07	Sterling Clothing Manufacturers 01	2008/256650/23
The Cone Shop	**2001/000989/23**	**The Cone Shop (Gauteng)**	**2009/021874/23**
		The Cone Shop 01	**2009/001355/23**
The Document Warehouse	1999/010656/07	The Document Warehouse (1)	2008/197405/23
The Media Shop	**1997/013488/07**	**The Media Shop 01**	**2009/090780/23**
The Workforce Group	1999/006358/07	The Workforce Group (Gauteng)	2008/121061/23
Thebe Medicare	**2002/001567/07**	**Thebe Medicare 01**	**2008/144959/23**
Transpaco Packaging	1970/009248/07	Transpaco Packaging(Gauteng)	2007/197179/23
Trend Pack	**2002/011632/23**	**Trend Pack (Africa)**	**2008/211117/23**
Trident Steel	1972/006101/07	Trident Speciality Steel	2008/000660/23
		Trident Steel (East)	2008/005990/23
		Trident Sterling Tube Manufacturers (Gauteng)	2008/005989/23
		Trident Sterling Tube Manufactures	2007/221233/23
Vent-Sure Agency	**2004/094355/23**	**Vent-Sure Agency 01**	**2009/113624/23**
Verotest	1995/044489/23	Verotest (Gauteng)	2008/255655/23
Wenxing Trading	**2005/012562/23**	**Wenxing Trading 01**	**2008/255654/23**

Chapter 15

Keeping the Lights On

Jan de Lange
Sake24/Fin24.com

This story can be traced back to 2004 when Jan de Lange realised South Africa would face electricity shortages within three or four years.

The crisis finally came in January 2008 – with outages across the country and a total shut-down of the mining industry for eight days, at a cost to the South African economy of R50 billion in lost production. Official sources claimed the problem was the reserve margin, the difference between maximum generation capacity and peak demand. The good practice benchmark for the margin is 15%, and once it fell below this, outages followed.

But was that the real explanation? De Lange's sources were telling him that proper management could have prevented the crisis, and the real problem at Eskom was bad management of coal supply lines and maintenance problems.

A confidential copy of Eskom's Daily System Status Report gave him the detail he needed and he could show that coal stocks were the issue throughout January 2008.

Fast-forward a year or more and the problems have not gone away. On 10 September 2009 a bundle of leaked Eskom documents reached Jan de Lange. The leak included a report commissioned by Eskom and written by international energy expert Susan Olsen in July 2007. In it she warned about the coal stocks and the looming crisis. Put together with the Daily Status Reports, Jan had his story and went to press the next day.

Eskom CEO Jacob Maroga called a press conference and the story took on a life of its own. Maroga resigned, or didn't resign. The chair of the Eskom board did the same, or was pushed. President Zuma was or wasn't involved. And Parliament, which had with excellent timing voted Maroga a huge salary increase just as the crisis began – of 27%, taking him to almost R5 million a year – has had time to rue that decision ever since.

Jan de Lange is a specialist writer on the mining industry and labour affairs for *Sake-Beeld*. In a long career as a journalist he has worked the crime beat, done the night shift, and been a news editor and an investigative reporter. Since 1995 he has worked for *Beeld*'s business section. He was runner-up in the 2009 Sanlam Financial Journalist of the Year award.

Eskom CEO "Ignored" Warnings   *11 September*

Eskom chief executive Jacob Maroga was warned by an international energy expert that the utility was heading for a coal crisis, six months before the power crisis paralysed the country in January last year.

The expert, Susan Olsen, a partner at Wingfield Consultancy, a world-renowned oil and coal research group in Boston, Massachusetts, warned Maroga in a comprehensive report on the deterioration of the energy giant's coal stocks that the parastatal was heading for a crisis.

Kobus Schmidt, a DA member of Parliament, handed over the damning report to Elizabeth Thabethe, the chairperson of the Portfolio Committee on Energy.

Olsen researched the issue for Eskom for two years, but her contract with the parastatal was abruptly cancelled within days of sending the report to Maroga and following an interview with him on the issue.

In it she points out how long-term coal contracts, also known as "cost-plus contracts", made it possible for the country's big mining houses to exploit Eskom while enjoying every possible form of security for healthy returns on their investments.

She warned that Eskom's ageing power stations were unable to work at 100% generating capacity with the cost-plus contracts.

The growing demand for electricity, the coal shortages and coal quality problems did not occur overnight. But Eskom, which should keep its fingers on the pulse and ensure adequate coal stocks, neglected to react accordingly, declares Olsen's report.

Eskom's lack of experience and understanding of coal markets led, says Olsen, to unfavourable and unsustainable contractual conditions.

"Two decades ago already, in the apartheid era, Eskom accepted a stipulation by the mining houses that geological risk would be solely for

Keeping the Lights On 153

Eskom's account.

"In today's world 'geological risk' means nothing more than incomplete, and at worst deceptive, statements regarding [coal] reserves," the report continues.

Olsen sent a report to Maroga on 19 July 2007 and a couple of days later had an interview with him.

She could not be reached for comment on Thursday but, according to an acquaintance who worked with her in South Africa, she had described the interview with Maroga as "a waste of breath".

Unacceptable lows

In its audit on the electricity crisis Nersa says that coal supplies at Eskom's power stations have fallen to unacceptably low levels since August 2007.

The Nersa audit, to date the only official investigation into the cause of the crisis, found that coal shortages and the poor quality of the coal played the crucial role in the electricity crisis crippling the country in January 2008 and bringing the mining industry to a standstill by 25 January.

At the time Nersa reckoned that the crisis had cost the country R50bn-odd in lost production.

Confidential reports on conditions at power stations during the height of the crisis from 25 January to 29 January in 2008 also show that coal problems were responsible for the great majority of power interruptions.

Maroga Fires the Messenger   14 September

Susan Olsen, an internationally renowned energy and coal expert, advised Jacob Maroga, CEO of Eskom, in July 2007 to get rid of his head of generation, Ehud Matya, and head of coal procurement, Rob Lines.

Maroga had Olsen fired instead, but seven months later, after the electricity crisis paralysed the country, he did exactly as Olsen advised him. He fired Lines and moved Matya to another, lesser position until Matya later found other employment.

Maroga also raised the status of the coal division, or primary energy as it is called, by placing it directly under the control of a senior executive chief, Brian Dames.

Olsen couldn't be reached yesterday and over the weekend to explain in her own words what transpired during her meeting with Maroga, but a colleague who worked closely with her said the reason for her interview was to prevent the generation and coal division from collapsing.

"Initially she couldn't get an interview with him and she tried everywhere to find help. Dr Bill Leininger, former chair of Ernst & Young in South Africa, later convinced Maroga to see her.

"Leininger also told Maroga that she is extremely competent and should be taken seriously," said the colleague.

Leininger is presently living in Malaysia from where he runs a successful international consulting firm. He visits South Africa up to six times a year and is highly regarded in the energy and mining industries.

But Olsen's interview with Maroga "didn't last long enough to finish a cup of tea", according to her colleague.

Maroga told a press conference at Megawatt Park on Friday night that he gave Olsen's report to Lines and Matya. That was the sum total of his reaction to the report, he said.

Matya and Lines immediately terminated Olsen's employment.

Olsen predicted in the report that the coal and generation division "will collapse under its own weight" unless a commercially skilled managing director was appointed – exactly as happened six months later.

Early in December, when coal stockpiles at Eskom's fleet of power stations were at critically low levels, the coal procurement division completely stopped buying coal in terms of short-term contracts, Nersa concluded in their audit investigation into the crisis.

Ras Myburgh, CEO of Kumba, was seconded to Eskom by the middle of last year, after a request by Maroga to Anglo American.

Myburgh is presently commercial chief at Eskom's coal division. He was chief of Kumba's former coal division, nowadays Exxaro, and is regarded as an extremely competent manager of commercial coal activities.

Maroga will appear before the parliamentary portfolio committee on energy tomorrow. He will brief the committee on Eskom's annual results.

Why Jacob, Why?

Jacob Maroga, Eskom's chief executive, is friendly, affable and charming.

He radiates a type of fatherly serenity and, what's more, he can think on his feet. Over the past two years he has single-handedly, on numerous occasions, squared up to hostile audiences about the mess at Eskom.

Each time he has persuaded them with charm, presenting clear arguments in which he converts highly technical details into layman's language that even a child could understand.

But when his responses to difficult questions are analysed, it's clear that he always reverts to Eskom's reserve margin, the difference between the power giant's generating capacity and peak demand for electricity.

According to international benchmarks this should be above 15%, but the government's refusal to let Eskom build new power stations has allowed it to drop to under 5%.

The smaller reserve margin really means everything else at Eskom will have to work as efficiently as a Swiss timepiece to avoid problems. Why then did Maroga flatly ignore the clear warning to him by Susan Olsen?

She didn't need the money

Olsen, an affluent, internationally recognised oil and coal consultant in her mid-60s from Boston, Massachusetts, did not liaise directly with Maroga, but knew him and apparently did not doubt he would appreciate the situation when she made an appointment with him in July 2007.

Two years before, Olsen had been appointed by Rob Lines, who then headed Primary Energy, which is just a nicer name for Eskom's coal division, as a consultant for power generation and primary energy. She was recruited by another senior Eskom employee who was working in the US and got to know her there.

Her salary was $30 000 a month – in today's terms nearly R240 000 – which is an indication of how highly she was regarded. "She retired a long time ago. She's rich and doesn't need money. She did it because she wanted to help us," says a colleague who worked with her.

She was appointed in the period following the crisis in the Western Cape, when a large bolt damaged the rotor of one of Koeberg's two turbine generators and, for all practical purposes, destroyed the turbine.

Eskom had to transmit electricity along power lines from Mpumalanga to the Cape, but the transmission lines were in such bad condition that the entire Western Cape was crippled for months.

Despite assurances in Parliament from Alec Erwin, then minister of public enterprises, that there was no threat of an electricity crisis, the power problems in the Western Cape were a first indication to Eskom's management of how the electricity network had deteriorated.

Olsen normally reported to Lines, but they did not get along well. "She discovered problems at the Optimum coal mine, but Lines ignored her complaints," said the colleague.

In the report that she sent to Maroga shortly before her dismissal, she highlighted the so-called "cost-plus" contracts that had mostly been concluded years before and were later converted to fixed-price contracts.

That seemed good to Eskom, but only until the mining houses in time began to export the mine's coal. Then all the inferior-quality coal was delivered to Eskom and the higher-quality coal exported. "Optimum, Grootegeluk and Douglas/Middelburg are examples," the report announces.

Optimum produces about 11.5m tons of coal a year, half of which is delivered to Eskom. The rest is exported.

She sought several people's advice because her concerns about the malpractices were falling on deaf ears. Eventually, through a contact, she got an interview with Maroga.

Olsen's recommendations

From her report of just over six typed pages it is clear she advised Maroga to replace Lines. The following are some extracts:

- The division's "failure to enforce the quality provisions of existing coal supply agreements has resulted in damage to generating plant".

- Majuba Power Station receives coal from more than a dozen sources, very little of which even remotely resembles its design coal.

- "it is only to the credit of Majuba Power Station's operating people that the station remains available despite the widely fluctuating and mostly unknown qualities of coal it receives on any given day. No wonder Scottish Power hired two of Majuba's shifts and moved them en masse [sic] to Scotland."

And in her conclusion:

- "GPE [Generation Primary Energy] lacks leadership, experience, knowledge and direction. It is haemorrhaging talented staff and is left with those who have delivered it to its current condition."

- "Without intervention and an imperative to become a fuel procurement and management department worthy of Eskom's world-class operating plain [*sic*], without appointment of a commercial competent managing director supported temporarily by external exports, I predict that GPE will collapse under its own weight."

But Olsen was not in Maroga's office long enough to have a cup of tea. He passed her report on to Lines and Ehud Matya, the head of electricity generation.

A couple of days later, all the files on her desk had been removed when she arrived in the morning. She had a flat in Johannesburg and a car provided by Eskom, but these were immediately withdrawn. Less than two weeks later she was on a plane back to the US.

Six months later exactly what she had predicted happened.

A confidential daily report on conditions at power stations on the fatal day of 25 January 2008, which was secretly handed to Sake24, shows that 29 generating units produced insufficient power that day. At 14 of them coal problems were the cause. These units can each generate 475 to 575 megawatts of electricity. The inferior-quality coal reduced this to between 30 and 115 megawatts per unit.

Nersa's audit after the events in January 2008, which cost the country R50bn in lost production, showed that coal stocks after August 2007 – a month after Olsen's appointment with Maroga – dropped below acceptable levels.

In December there was an average of 11 days' supply at power stations, but at the beginning of December the coal division simply suspended buying according to the short-term contracts. The reason? Yes, Primary Energy had packed its bags and gone on holiday.

By January the average stockpile was less than one day's consumption.

A month later, however, Maroga did what Olsen had advised him to do: he got rid of Lines and Matya.

Never Again Load Shedding, Promises Eskom Chair

18 October

South Africa will not be punished again with load shedding even when the economy recovers and the demand for electricity increases again, says Bobby Godsell, chair of Eskom.

Godsell disclosed on Friday in an exclusive interview with Sake24 that the board of Eskom is giving serious attention to the report of Susan Olsen, the American energy consultant who warned six months before the electricity crisis last year that Eskom's coal supply lines were about to collapse.

It eventually happened at the beginning of last year and forced Eskom to apply load shedding.

Godsell said the Olsen report should have been placed before the board after it was written in July 2007, but he doesn't know if it was. He only became involved a year later.

"The report is of immense importance and is now serving before the board," he said.

According to him, the main present challenge to Eskom is operating through the winter of 2010 without another electricity crisis, but South Africans will not experience load shedding again as there are other ways of overcoming the small present reserve margin of between 8% and 9%.

"I think load shedding is a stupid idea that we should try to forget. Forced cutbacks of power supply by Eskom are a clear sign of failure by Eskom. You are there to fulfil the needs of your clients. That is your job as a business," he said.

"The system of load shedding was a clumsy, complicated and bureaucratically difficult system. There are much better ways to handle supply threats.

"I know from my days in the mining industry that Eskom often contacted the mines and asked them to reduce consumption by up to 15%. I understand the decision in January last year was taken on advice of the national control centre, but there are better ways. People could have picked up the phone and talked to larger electricity consumers to realise emergency cuts in a different way other than sending off lawyers' letters declaring Eskom can't guarantee a safe supply any longer," said Godsell.

It is, however, clear that hard times are awaiting electricity-intensive industries like aluminium smelters and producers of ferrochrome. Over and above higher tariffs, Eskom will discuss a review of consumer contracts with them.

The rules in the economy have changed. "We can't manage a country and never expect to make investors uncomfortable. The right thing is to engage them and achieve an agreed result," said Godsell.

Zuma "Saved Eskom Boss"   *4 November*

On Friday President Jacob Zuma intervened to prevent Jacob Maroga from being sacked by the Eskom board.

As a consequence, the Eskom board has been embroiled in a fierce dispute with government – led by Barbara Hogan, minister of public enterprises, and her deputy, Enoch Godongwana.

Since the weekend various other members of Cabinet have also become involved. Meanwhile, Eskom is apparently leaderless and the electricity giant's lips are sealed.

Official spokespersons have for days been embarrassed by requests for information, and unable to provide answers.

"It's tremendously disconcerting that the leadership of an organisation that has so much strategic significance for the whole country has been paralysed in this way by intervention from politicians," Sake24's source, a top official and major player in the electricity industry, said on Tuesday.

According to the source, on Thursday evening Eskom's board, following a two-day monthly board meeting, decided that Maroga should vacate his post. He was formally asked to resign, but refused – which implies that he was fired.

The same evening the news that he had to go was leaked to a newspaper, which published it on Friday morning.

Early on Friday morning Zuma came to hear of it. He immediately ordered Hogan to intervene and prevent the dismissal.

"Certain protocols and processes that needed to be followed to terminate Maroga's services had at that point not been finalised. This enabled Hogan to block the process," explained Sake24's source.

A furious squabble has since been raging between the board and government representatives.

From other sources Sake24 determined that on Friday morning Hogan and Godongwana together visited Eskom's head office at Megawatt Park in Sandton.

Hogan and some of her Cabinet colleagues are now attempting to put pressure on the members of Eskom's board to change their decision about Maroga.

There is apparently even talk that the board may be given its marching orders.

On Tuesday Hogan's spokesperson, Ayanda Shezi, declined to comment on the issue.

Themba Maseko, spokesperson for the presidency, said the presidency had no comment.

The main reason for the board's dissatisfaction with Maroga is ostensibly his handling of the report by Susan Olsen. In July 2007, six months before the electricity crisis, Olsen, an American energy consultant, warned Maroga in a comprehensive report that Eskom's coal division "would collapse under its own weight" unless serious steps were taken.

Olsen had worked exclusively for Eskom for two years. Her contract was terminated within days of the 19 July 2007 interview with Maroga, in which she herself had brought the seriousness of the crisis in the coal division to his attention.

Maroga Battle Brewed for Months
6 November

Maroga, until yesterday CEO of Eskom, wanted the power utility to play an active transformation role, whilst the board insisted that Eskom focus on its core function: the generation and transmission of electricity.

That was probably the main driver behind the political meddling leading to Maroga's dismissal being postponed yesterday for a third time – even after it was announced to Eskom staffers.

Facts that emerged recently regarding Maroga's handling of the electricity crisis, especially conditions in the coal division – the main reason for the crisis – were only the last straw.

A report by Susan Olsen, an American energy expert who warned Maroga that the coal division was about to "collapse under its own weight", was made available to the board only after its existence was disclosed in Sake24. It probably also played a role in the final breakdown of Maroga's relationship with the board.

Business people dealing with Eskom on a regular basis have been increasingly upset about the handling of the Maroga saga.

"It is clear that the board is under immense political pressure. Can you imagine the long-term implications of this for Eskom's credibility? This is an organisation that regularly issues and guarantees bonds on the capital market," a senior official of one company said.

Chapter 16

Kitchen Confidential

Adriaan Basson
Mail & Guardian

When Special Investigating Unit (SIU) head Willie Hofmeyr stood up in Parliament in November 2009 and shocked the nation with tales of crude favouritism, bribery and fraud in South Africa's prisons department, it came as sweet vindication for Adriaan Basson.

He had been studying the Bosasa contracts since 2006 and never stopped asking questions, phoning people and collecting documents. In January 2009 the story intensified as the company was awarded yet another multimillion-rand tender for prison catering services.

The department replied with expensive advertisements in two Sunday newspapers urging members of the public with evidence of wrongdoing to come forward.

Little did they know that his meticulous pursuit of the story had finally reaped the ultimate reward – a batch of documents in a brown envelope containing the smoking gun, the proof that Bosasa's chief operating officer and the department's finance chief were colluding with each other.

The story then took a dark turn. An anonymous phone call from a woman who claimed to be sympathetic to his cause turned out to be from a communication strategist who knew a great deal about his personal life. Bosasa had been spying on Basson and he interpreted the phone call as a threat, to himself, his friends and his family.

Undeterred, he kept on digging. His work kept up the pressure on the SIU to finalise its probe. At the end of 2009 its report went to the South African Police Service and the National Prosecuting Authority, which are now completing their criminal case. The Department of Correctional Services has instituted disciplinary action against its finance chief.

Bosasa threatened criminal charges, which it never pursued, but did start a defamation case against Basson and the *Mail & Guardian* in the South

Gauteng High Court, which they are defending.

In a country where reporting on corruption often sinks without trace, this story pushed the authorities to do what they are supposed to do.

Adriaan Basson joined the *Mail & Guardian* as an investigative reporter in 2007. He started his journalism career at *Beeld* in 2003 as a crime and courts reporter and was a founding member of Media24's investigations unit. He was joint winner of the first Taco Kuiper Award for Investigative Journalism; with colleagues from the *Mail & Guardian,* the Mondi Shanduka story of the year award in 2007; and again with colleagues from the *Mail & Guardian* the Taco Kuiper Award for 2008. His Bosasa investigation scooped the 2009 Mondi Shanduka award for investigative journalism.

Kitchen Confidential   *23 January*

Three weeks after being raided by the Special Investigating Unit (SIU), during a massive tender-fraud investigation, controversial facilities management company Bosasa Operations was awarded another multimillion-rand contract by the Department of Correctional Services.

The prisons department has now awarded contracts worth more than R2.5 billion to companies in the Bosasa group in the past five years.

Bosasa's latest treasure is the sought-after catering contract to provide thousands of prisoners in 31 of South Africa's largest prisons with food. The government's tender bulletin specifies that the contract was awarded at "±R279 million" a year for three years. The 31 prisons fall within seven management areas.

Bosasa previously held this contract, which was awarded for the first time in 2004. Before 2004 prison staff and inmates ran the kitchens in correctional facilities.

The *Mail & Guardian* reported in late 2007 on the SIU's investigation into tender rigging in the department, which includes massive tenders awarded to the Bosasa group.

A dispute about the extension of Bosasa's 2004 catering contract also led to the souring of relationships between correctional services minister

Ngconde Balfour and former prisons boss Vernie Petersen, who refused to grant a further extension of Bosasa's contract.

Petersen eventually succeeded in putting the catering contract out to tender, but soon thereafter – in November last year – was removed from his position.

This week a senior member of Parliament's portfolio committee on correctional services told the *M&G*: "It is now clear why Petersen was removed [because of his opposition to an extension of the Bosasa contract]. That was the motive."

The re-awarding of the catering tender to Bosasa this week led to a chorus of disapproval from unsuccessful catering companies, which accused the prisons department of uncompetitive behaviour. Their fury was further stoked by unconfirmed reports that the department's adjudication committee originally awarded two management areas (Johannesburg and Krugersdorp) to two other catering companies and the rest to Bosasa. This recommendation was allegedly changed at a "high level".

Bosasa spokesperson Papa Leshabane said he was unaware of this, "but we would be more than happy to respond to facts". At least three unsuccessful tenderers are seeking legal advice on the matter.

Adding to their suspicion is a letter dated 15 December that was sent to all tenderers on behalf of director-general Xoliswa Sibeko. The *M&G* is in possession of the document, which states: "A possibility exists that the bid, of which particulars appear below, may not be disposed of before expiry of the current validity period."

Companies are then asked whether they are willing to "hold" their bids for a further period of time. Amendments may be made to bids, but the department reserves its right to "ignore your bid".

The *M&G* believes four companies – Bosasa Operations, C3 Catering, Independent Site Services and Ukweza Catering – were shortlisted and requested to present their proposals to the department at the beginning of November. None of the country's major catering firms, including Fedics, the Compass Group and Royal Sechaba, made the cut.

Another oddity in the case is Balfour's presence at the opening of the tender box in late September after he was reappointed minister by President Kgalema Motlanthe.

According to two sources who attended the gathering, Balfour said: "I'm the new minister in this department. I was gone for two days.

I got reappointed. This is my department and I decide what happens in my department."

The *M&G* was reliably told that the SIU executed search and seizure operations at Bosasa's Krugersdorp premises in early December and also raided the Centurion home of the suspended regional commissioner for North West, Mpumalanga and Limpopo, Patrick Gillingham, towards the end of year.

Gillingham is the department's former chief financial officer and is seen as a close ally of Balfour. He was moved to a position of regional commissioner in 2007 after *Beeld* revealed that he was managing the department's annual R9 billion budget with only a matric certificate. Petersen suspended Gillingham in September last year after receiving a preliminary report from the SIU implicating Gillingham as a "key role player" in "serious tender irregularities".

But Petersen was swapped with Sibeko, then director-general of sport, two months later, after Deputy President Baleka Mbete signed a presidential minute giving effect to the change.

Petersen's removal from the prisons department was slammed by NGOs working in the sector and opposition parties which hailed him as a corruption-buster and inspirational leader.

The re-awarding of the catering tender to Bosasa threatens to lead to a massive standoff between Balfour and Parliament's portfolio committee, which, according to committee chair Dennis Bloem (ANC), will discuss the contract "as a matter of urgency".

DA spokesperson on correctional services James Selfe last year released documentation that showed Bosasa was not the lowest bidder for the catering contract in 2004. Royal Sechaba tendered for R205 million a year, while Bosasa got the contract on their bid of R240 million a year.

The department's spokesperson, Manelisi Wolela, defended the tender process, saying it was handled "clinically and appropriately … in terms of the constitutional principles of fairness and competitiveness".

Prisons Graft: Here's the Proof, Minister

On Sunday the Department of Correctional Services placed expensive advertisements in three national newspapers, urging anyone with proof of impropriety in the awarding of prisons' contracts to inform South Africa's law enforcement agencies.

This week we present the proof.

Confidential documents and correspondence leaked to the *Mail & Guardian* suggest a highly improper relationship between the department and controversial facilities management group Bosasa.

We can reveal that Bosasa, which has received nearly R3 billion in contracts from correctional services minister Ngconde Balfour's department:

- Had confidential documents leaked to it by the department's former chief financial officer and Balfour confidant Patrick Gillingham;

- Had access to tender documents for major prison projects before they were advertised; and

- Spied on senior correctional services officials during a 2006 workshop.

Bosasa is headed by Eastern Cape businessman Gavin Watson, whose family had close ties with the Eastern Cape ANC during the struggle years, when the Watson brothers became famous for refusing to play rugby for a whites-only Springbok team.

The group also runs the controversial Lindela repatriation camp for the Department of Home Affairs and has large contracts with the South African Post Office, Airports Company of South Africa and the departments of Justice and Transport.

The Special Investigating Unit (SIU) has been probing Bosasa since 2006 and raided its offices in December. Three weeks after the raid, the company was re-awarded the massive prisons catering contract it landed in 2004.

The department's advertisements on Sunday were a reaction to the *M&G*'s report last week of alleged irregularities in the awarding of the latest catering tender.

Former prisons commissioner Vernie Petersen suspended Gillingham in September after receiving a preliminary SIU report. Petersen was later transferred to the sports department in what was widely seen as a reprisal for his opposition to Balfour's attempts to extend the 2004 contract.

Balfour also wanted Gillingham to head the tender committee awarding the new contract, while Petersen insisted that Gillingham not be involved.

2004: a new romance

In 2004 the contract for running prison kitchens was outsourced for the first time. The tender was officially advertised on 21 May in the government's tender bulletin.

But documents show that on 1 May Bosasa employee and co-founder Danny Mansell sent Bosasa's operations coordinator, Angelo Agrizzi, papers containing more than 90% of the bid conditions and specifications.

Three weeks later the Department of Correctional Services made available the same document, with the same spelling errors, to the rest of the catering sector.

On 6 August Bosasa was awarded the entire contract, worth R239 million a year, for three years.

The department extended Bosasa's contract for another year and expanded it to include more prisons, adding R82 million to the bill. It was the further extension that led to Petersen's clash with Balfour.

In July 2004 the department also gave Bosasa a R1 million tender for nutritional training for prisons' kitchen staff. Again Mansell sent Agrizzi large parts of the tender document, including bid conditions and specifications, on 12 May. The tender was advertised on 4 June.

2005: you've got mail

The inclusion of CCTV cameras in the catering tender meant that by 2005 Bosasa had a national control centre to monitor the kitchens.

This linked perfectly with its next contract – a R237 million tender for access control and CCTV in 66 prisons. It went to a newly registered company, Sondolo IT, which *Beeld* revealed in 2006 was 40% owned by Bosasa Operations.

Other shareholders included former president Thabo Mbeki's political adviser Titus Mafolo and former Strategic Fuel Fund chairperson Seth Phalatse.

On 17 December 2004 Bosasa's IT coordinator, Johan Helmand,

e-mailed Agrizzi certain tender specifications that were to appear in the official bid document published on 4 February 2005.

On 29 April Sondolo IT was awarded the contract. In 2005 Agrizzi and Gillingham started e-mailing each other prison research reports and newspaper clippings. On 29 August Gillingham sent Agrizzi a copy of questions from *City Press*, put to the department about the Bosasa contracts, as the leaked documents show.

On 9 December 2005 Bosasa landed a R487 million prisons' contract for security fencing through a small Cape Town firm, Phezulu Fencing, it had purchased.

There is double proof that the company had privileged information long before the tender was advertised. Three months earlier, on 25 September, Agrizzi e-mailed Mansell a voluminous document containing bid specifications. "Please verify and check, we can sit tomorrow am," Agrizzi wrote.

On 3 October Agrizzi sent a longer version, headed "Fence Doc Final", to the chief executives of Bekaert Bastion and SA Fence & Gate, Michael Rodenburg and Geoff Greyling respectively, under the subject line "Fence Doc Final ... Very Confidential".

This contained the full bid conditions and specifications published by the department on 14 October. Bekaert Bastion supplied cladding material and SA Fence & Gate was contracted to do part of the installation.

This week Greyling "categorically" denied seeing a copy of the bid document before it was published. He said: "It should be recorded that the tender was based on the standard public works/correctional services specification with which we are well acquainted from previous bids. The prior possession of the tender document by anyone would therefore be of no specific advantage to such person."

Colette Stofberg of Bekaert Bastion (now called Betafence) replied that "years before this contract" Betafence provided technical specifications to the Department of Public Works that were used in this tender.

According to an industry insider, the big advantage lies in knowing the quantities required for the tender weeks before your competitors.

On 10 October 2005 Agrizzi sent Gillingham a six-page document titled "Equipment Specifications & Guidelines". The same section was featured in a tender for a comprehensive television system, comprising 6000 TVs for communal cells, published four days later.

On 28 November Agrizzi e-mailed Mansell the confidential evaluation sheet the department used to adjudicate the TV tender, which Sondolo IT won on 17 March 2006.

2006: spies in the house

On 9 February Agrizzi sent Gillingham a document headed "Tender Evaluation Criteria New Waterval", containing comments on bid specifications for a contract for catering services at seven prisons in the Waterval management area, KwaZulu-Natal.

The tender was officially advertised on 19 May. Seven days earlier Gillingham sent Agrizzi the confidential evaluation sheet for the Waterval tender with a message: "Hi, Attached please find the reworked evaluation sheet for your comments. You will notice the evaluation sheet for site visits cannot be published and will not form part of this document. Regards, Patrick."

On 15 September Bosasa Operations was awarded the Waterval catering tender, worth R123 million over five years. On 24 April 2006 Agrizzi sent Gillingham a letter in which an anonymous writer asks the chairperson of Parliament's correctional services portfolio committee, Dennis Bloem, to "sort out" the attack on the department by "international capitalists" and "activist Afrikaner companies". This week Bloem confirmed receiving such a letter.

On 21 June Agrizzi sent Gillingham a surveillance report of a prisons department security workshop at a Drakensberg hotel in June 2006. The 25-page report makes it clear that the agent was asked to spy on the department's chief deputy commissioner of security, Willem Damons, and his subordinate, Tonie Venter. The report also contains pictures of people and cars at the hotel, as well as the inside of the conference room.

In his message to Gillingham, Agrizzi wrote: "I didn't see the reason/ need to e-mail you the rest; nothing actually happened." Gillingham replied the next day: "Hi, Thanks for the report and it seems as if they behaved well during their session. Regards."

Bosasa's lawyer, Brian Biebuyck, advised his client not to answer the *M&G*'s questions. He warned the *M&G* to publish "at your peril" and said Bosasa would pursue charges of criminal defamation if defamatory material was printed.

The department's Manelisi Wolela responded that the *M&G*'s questions "are part of a broader brief given to the SIU" and urged the newspaper to provide the unit with proof of impropriety. Gillingham did not respond to the *M&G*'s queries.

Linda Mti's Bosasa Bonanza   *6 February*

Controversial facilities management group Bosasa lavished flights and luxury hotel stays on former prisons boss Linda Mti – while it landed prisons contracts worth more than R1 billion.

The mutually beneficial relationship between Bosasa and Mti, now head of security for the 2010 Local Organising Committee, is laid bare by travel records in the *Mail & Guardian*'s possession.

They show that Bosasa:

- Sponsored the domestic airfare of Mti and his family members on at least five occasions;
- Paid for Mti's stay at the luxury Hemingways Hotel in East London on at least two occasions; and
- Rented premium cars for Mti when he visited East London at least twice.

Mti received these benefits while prisons commissioner. During the last two years of his tenure the group won contracts from the Correctional Services Department worth more than R1 billion. Mti failed to respond to numerous queries, while Bosasa's lawyer advised the company not to answer the *M&G*'s questions.

Mti left Correctional Services under a cloud of suspicion in 2006 after *Beeld* revealed that Bosasa's company secretary, Tony Perry, had registered a private company for him. He was subsequently appointed head of security for the Fifa World Cup.

Bosasa's travel records show that:

- On 15 June 2005 Mti flew to East London at Bosasa's expense and was put up in the four-star Hemingways Hotel for four nights. The company also paid for his Avis premium rental car. The trip came shortly after Sondolo IT, 40% owned by Bosasa Operations, won a R237 million contract for the supply and installation of access control systems and CCTV at 66 prisons on 29 April 2005.

- On 25 July 2005 Bosasa sponsored the return airfare of Mti's relative, Sehlule Mti, from Johannesburg to Port Elizabeth and back. Three days later Bosasa paid for Mti and then National Intelligence Agency deputy director-general Gibson Njenje to fly from Johannesburg to Port Elizabeth.

- In December 2005 Bosasa company Phezulu Fencing won a R487 million tender to supply and install security fencing at 66 prisons.

- On 3 March 2006 Bosasa sponsored a weekend trip for Mti to East London, where he stayed in the Hemingways hotel's presidential suite. Bosasa's travel agent was instructed to rent a seven-seat Mercedes-Benz Vito for Mti.

Two weeks later, on 17 March 2006, Sondolo IT won a R224 million tender to install TV sets in all prison communal cells.

A day later Bosasa paid for Mti's son, Vukani, to fly from Johannesburg to Cape Town on a return ticket.

Njenje told the *M&G* he was Bosasa's founding non-executive chairman before being headhunted by the NIA. While in the NIA's employ his travels to Port Elizabeth were covered by Bosasa twice – on 10 June and 28 July 2005.

He told the *M&G* he saw no problem with Bosasa paying for his travel while he was a state employee. "I was headhunted into a government position while active as a businessman with various interests. All I needed to do to comply with the employment conditions was to resign as an executive director from the companies," he said.

"My shareholding and all benefits accruing were a matter of declaring and that I did as required. Some of the companies I was a shareholder in had or have relations with Bosasa. My private travel expenses would be one of the benefits that accrued to all the shareholders of the companies I am referring to.

"So, as it were, it was not a matter of Bosasa 'sponsoring' my travels, but an arrangement between companies."

The *M&G* received three calls this week from "concerned Bosasa employees" who said they were afraid the *M&G*'s reporting about their employer would cost them their jobs.

Two threatened to organise a protest march on the *M&G*'s office, accusing the paper of being "racist" and printing "untruths".

"Who will look after my children if I don't have a job anymore?" an employee from the East Rand said.

Bosasa spokesperson Papa Leshabane did not return the *M&G*'s calls on the matter.

Bosasa's Tender Touch *13 February*

The auditor-general wrote a scathing report on facilities management group Bosasa's lucrative contracts with the Correctional Services Department as early as June 2006, the *Mail & Guardian* can reveal.

His spokesperson, Joreta Linde-Ferreira, said the auditor-general remained "uncomfortable, as the level of assurance sought regarding supply chain management was not forthcoming".

The auditor-general's office handed records and other documents to the Special Investigating Unit (SIU), which is probing the Bosasa contracts and which aims to finalise its investigation within two months.

The *M&G* is in possession of a report sent by the auditor-general to former prisons boss Linda Mti after an investigation found the department had not adequately managed the Bosasa contracts.

The probe also found the department set inappropriate payment conditions, committed "fiscal dumping" by making huge payments at the end of the financial year and flouted its own procurement policies.

Ironically, the department's former chief financial officer, Patrick Gillingham, responded on Mti's behalf. The *M&G* revealed two weeks ago that Gillingham handed Bosasa confidential tender documents before they were publicly available. Last week the *M&G* exposed how Bosasa sponsored flights and luxury hotel stays for Mti.

The auditor-general investigated four tenders awarded to Bosasa companies.

It shows he:

- Suspected private suppliers were involved in drafting bid specifications, saying he could not establish "where and how the specifications originated". Gillingham replied to the auditor-general that the department had drawn up the tender specs.

- Could find no proof that the department's IT personnel or the State Information Technology Agency (Sita) were involved in a tender process leading to the April 2005 award of a R237 million contract to Bosasa company Sondolo IT for the supply and installation of access control systems and CCTV in 66 prisons. "This contract has major IT implications," the auditor-general commented. Gillingham replied that the focus of the tender was more on security hardware than computer software.

- Criticised the extension of the contract to include the staffing of control rooms at the 66 prisons to Sondolo. The auditor-general found that the staffing contract, which made Sondolo an extra R56 million a year, exceeded the limit by adding more than 20% to the original contract price. Gillingham replied that by outsourcing, the department saved R2 million a month and that the extension complied with the department's procurement manual.

- Found that "abnormal payment terms" were included in the tender document, whereby 90% of the price was to be paid for equipment after installation and 10% after the installation was successfully commissioned and ran to the department's satisfaction for three months. Gillingham called the terms "reasonable".

- Found that Sondolo IT was not listed on the department's prospective suppliers list. Gillingham replied that any supplier could be used in an open bidding process.

- Complained after visiting 13 prisons that no access control system was fully operational. Gillingham blamed Telkom for the delays.

The report also notes that invoices were not properly certified, that no proper project management was in place to ensure Sondolo delivered, and that the payment for control room staffing was made without an order and solely on

Mti's motivation. The auditor-general also took issue with a R487 million contract landed by Bosasa company Phezulu Fencing for security fencing at 66 prisons on 9 December 2005, particularly querying its prices, which were not comparable with those of other bidders.

The *M&G* further showed that Bosasa had access to the fencing tender document months before it was formally published.

Gillingham responded that the department used public works department estimates, but enhanced these by including surveillance technology and detection systems.

The auditor-general found that the first payment of R56.4 million to Phezulu Fencing was made on 14 December 2005 – five days after the contract was publicly awarded – contravening payment conditions.

According to Gillingham, Phezulu Fencing indicated that it needed to make "substantial manufacturing deposits" with suppliers to ensure delivery deadlines were met.

During inspections in May 2006, the auditor-general's office found that not all fences were erected by 17 March 2006, the contracted date of completion. "By allowing the delivery date to be extended, other bidders may have been unfairly discriminated against," the report remarked.

Gillingham responded that at the compulsory briefing session for prospective bidders, the department indicated it would allow installation to continue beyond 17 March 2006 but would penalise "unnecessary delays".

On a R224 million contract won by Sondolo IT for installation of 6000 television monitors on 10 March 2006, the auditor-general again remarked that he could not determine who wrote the tender specifications. The *M&G* has reported that Bosasa sent Gillingham a section of the tender document before the tender was advertised.

Gillingham responded that the tender document was compiled in consultation with the department's IT staff and the Council for Scientific and Industrial Research.

The report also noted late delivery on the TV tender. Gillingham stated that the majority of equipment was still "bonded in the warehouses of the suppliers". The department this week instructed the SIU to do an urgent audit on the latest tender awarded to Bosasa Operations – a R900 million catering contract in 31 prisons.

"Very Brave for a Young Man" *22 May*

On a Sunday evening in February I was phoned by a woman with a raspy voice who told me she knew where I lived.

The woman, later identified as communication strategist Benedicta Dube, also knew where and what I had studied, where I was born, what my ID number was and she read to me the names of some of my friends and their professions.

During our conversation of almost 18 minutes Dube also threw in lines such as: "You are very brave for a young man" and said she would "kill" me if I told anyone about our conversation.

Her phone call came after I exposed in the *Mail & Guardian* over a period of three weeks the corrupt relationship between facilities management company Bosasa and the Department of Correctional Services.

Dube posed as sympathetic – she warned me Bosasa had commissioned a private investigator to do a report on me and offered to meet me to discuss the "bigger" issues behind the story.

I was sceptical – she spent most of our conversation talking about my personal details "because I want to be sure I'm talking to the right person". My suspicions were confirmed by an inside source, who told me Dube had been briefed on me by Bosasa executives since at least August 2008 (I've been investigating the company since early 2006). A strategy to discredit the *M&G* and me was discussed.

My attempts to secure a meeting with her have proved futile. I am convinced her motives were never to caution, but rather to intimidate.

The *M&G*'s lawyer wrote to Bosasa and Igagu Media (where Dube is "group executive: media and publishing") on 6 May, demanding an immediate return of all my personal information in their possession.

Bosasa's lawyer denied the company had acted in an "unlawful manner as alleged or at all" and said Dube's information "falls within the public domain". Igagu Media did not respond. Dube claims she doesn't recall our conversation and that she doesn't work for Igagu anymore. She accused the *M&G* of "blackmail journalism".

Prisons Fire Fraud Busters

In a major setback for the fight against corruption, the Correctional Services Department has terminated its contract with Willie Hofmeyr's fraud-busting Special Investigating Unit (SIU).

This comes after correctional services minister Nosiviwe Mapisa-Nqakula was lauded this week for her hardline stance on good governance when she suspended prisons boss Xoliswa Sibeko.

Sibeko and the department's acting finance chief, Nandi Mareka, were suspended pending an investigation into the approval of expensive rental houses for Sibeko and Gauteng prisons boss Thozama Mqobi-Balfour.

The true commitment of Mapisa-Nqakula and her department to fighting graft is again called into question by the termination of the contract with the SIU. According to SIU spokesperson Trinesha Naidoo, the department did not renew its contract with the unit when it came to an end on 31 March this year.

The timing of the cancellation of the contract is curious for the following reasons:

- On 1 March, 30 days before the SIU was fired, the department spent thousands of rands on an eight-page supplement in Sunday newspapers flaunting the department's relationship with the SIU;

- The supplement was headlined "Fraud busters" and had a large picture of former correctional services minister Ngconde Balfour on its front page, quoting him as saying: "We promote good governance, openness and accountability";

- In the supplement the department reported that its relationship with the SIU had prevented "fraudulent expenditure" of up to R3.5 billion and that about 500 departmental officials had been disciplined and dismissed;

- The SIU's correctional services team is finalising its biggest and most controversial investigation into tenders worth billions of rands awarded by the prisons department to the ANC-linked facilities management group Bosasa and its affiliates; and

- The SIU was supposed to report back to Parliament's correctional services committee this month about progress on major procurement investigations, including the Bosasa probe.

Department spokesperson Bheki Manzini said this week that Mapisa-Nqakula would "apply her mind" after receiving a report from the SIU on work done during the previous contract, from March 2006 to March 2009. He conceded that the contract with the unit had expired, but said that this did not necessarily mean it would not be renewed after the unit had briefed the minister. The meeting is scheduled for next week.

Manzini denied that the future of the department's relationship with the SIU depended on its report to Mapisa-Nqakula, but could not explain why the contract had not been automatically extended for another three years.

The SIU has been called the government's own forensic audit firm. Headed by Hofmeyr, also a deputy national director of public prosecutions and head of the assets forfeiture unit, it is contracted and funded by state departments to provide investigation services for specific periods of time.

This creates forensic capacity within government, which is often outsourced to private audit firms for exorbitant sums.

The prisons department first signed a contract with the SIU in 2002 after widespread corruption was uncovered by the Jali Commission. When the first contract expired in March 2006, it was renewed for a further three years.

Apart from Correctional Services, the SIU's biggest successes so far have been in the Social Development and Housing departments. Billions of rands have been saved by the detection of social grants fraud and government officials cooking state housing lists. Hundreds of officials have been prosecuted.

"There will be an impact on the SIU's financial position," Naidoo conceded, "but the SIU is confident that it will be able to replace it with other projects." She confirmed that the decision not to renew the contract would not have an effect on investigations initiated under the previous agreement.

This includes the unit's probe of contracts awarded to Bosasa Operations and affiliated companies Sondolo IT and Phezulu Fencing.

An interim executive team has been put in place to assist with the management of SIU operations.

Corruption investigations have no 'effect on tender awards'

Controversial security company Sondolo IT, under investigation for tender-rigging in the Department of Correctional Services, has been awarded another major government contract – this time by the Justice Department.

The contract, for the safeguarding of courts countrywide with electronic security equipment for two years, with an additional three years of maintenance, is worth a cool R600 million.

Sondolo IT is part of the Bosasa group of companies that have been awarded contracts worth billions of rands by government institutions, including the Correctional Services, Home Affairs and Transport departments.

When the contract was awarded in August last year, it was publicly known that the SIU was probing Sondolo's contracts with Correctional Services.

Justice Department spokesperson Zolile Nqayi said: "The department is aware through public reporting [of the allegations against Bosasa] and it had no effect on who would be awarded a tender. Furthermore the department subscribes to the notion 'everyone is innocent until proven guilty'."

A total of R80 million was budgeted for the contract in this financial year, but it was likely that not all of it would be spent as the department and Sondolo are still concluding a service-level agreement.

"Checks were conducted on the company with the National Treasury and it was cleared at the time of the award. In any case, this tender is independent of developments elsewhere and there was therefore no legal basis to exclude Sondolo from the tender process," said Nqayi.

Prisons Graft: Bosasa's Empire of Influence
20 November

The company at the centre of South Africa's prison corruption scandal is closely connected to powerful individuals on the political landscape, including the country's new spy boss, Gibson Njenje.

A number of them were also close to Thabo Mbeki's presidency.

Bosasa Operations, exposed this week in Parliament for allegedly bribing top prison officials to secure contracts worth more than R1.7 billion, makes a killing from government business. This includes work for the departments of Correctional Services, Justice, Home Affairs, Transport and the provincial governments of Gauteng and the Eastern Cape.

Bosasa's chief executive, Gavin Watson, has close links with the governing ANC through his family's anti-apartheid struggle credentials and his brothers' post-1994 business interests.

Njenje is a founding member of Bosasa Operations and was a director of the company before being appointed head of the National Intelligence Agency (NIA) in October.

A number of people benefiting from Bosasa contracts or linked to Watson and his family had links to Mbeki's office, including the ex-president's political adviser, Titus Mafolo, and Mbeki's head of office, Lorato Phalatse, who is married to former Strategic Fuel Fund chairperson Seth Phalatse.

Watson's brother Valence is the chief executive of Vulisango Holdings, the empowerment partner of controversial mining firm Simmer & Jack. Valence Watson's business partners include Nozuko Pikoli, the wife of axed prosecutions boss Vusi Pikoli, and Siviwe Mapisa, the brother of correctional services minister Nosiviwe Mapisa-Nqakula.

Mapisa-Nqakula told the *M&G* this week that she knows Gavin Watson. "Mr Watson is a former CEO of Dyambu Holdings, a company the minister was formerly affiliated to. Mr Watson resigned from Dyambu and went on to form Bosasa. The minister has had no contact with him since then."

According to the minister, she has "no relationship with Bosasa nor has she benefited from the operations of Bosasa". She is "not aware of any relationships members of her family may have" with Bosasa.

The *M&G* can reveal that Bosasa is seeking to interdict the Special Investigating Unit (SIU) and President Jacob Zuma from continuing its investigation into tender rigging.

In its frantic efforts to halt the SIU's graft probe – which could lead to both civil and criminal charges – Bosasa claims that the SIU leaked sensitive information to the *M&G* that resulted in a "trial by press". Bosasa is referring to a series of *M&G* exposés of collusion between Bosasa and senior correctional services officials, including former prisons boss Linda Mti and the department's former chief financial officer, Patrick Gilllingham.

Zuma's involvement in the case stems from Mbeki's authorisation, as president, of the SIU probe into Bosasa. The SIU and Zuma are defending the matter.

SIU head Willie Hofmeyr shocked Parliament with sordid tales of corruption inside South Africa's prisons, disclosing details about how Bosasa put the likes of Gillingham and Mti firmly in its pocket.

Hofmeyr's briefing also raised uncomfortable questions about why Mapisa-Nqakula has been sitting on the SIU report from at least mid-September. It is the duty of the minister – Mapisa-Nqakula – or of the acting prisons commissioner, Jenny Schreiner, to launch a civil claim against Bosasa.

Hofmeyr said on Tuesday: "It is a matter that justifies the institution of legal proceedings by the department to recover damages from the company."

Mapisa-Nqakula, who was appointed by Zuma in May to head the prisons department, originally said she had to present the SIU report to Cabinet before releasing it. Her spokesperson, Sonwabo Mbananga, later told the *M&G* that this release was on hold because of Bosasa's pending legal action against the SIU.

The *M&G* now has access to the court papers filed by Bosasa against the SIU. Nowhere does it seek to interdict the SIU or Zuma from releasing the final report. Instead the applications focus on the alleged tainting of the probe due to media leaks.

Approached again after Hofmeyr's explosive briefing to Parliament, Mbananga remained adamant: the minister would still not release the report because the SIU has referred it to the National Prosecuting Authority "and therefore the contents ... are sub judice".

Bosasa's spokesperson, Papa Leshabane, denied the corruption claims, labelling Hofmeyr's briefing as "speculative, arrived at without hearing Bosasa, are disputed and will be dealt with in the appropriate forum".

Bosasa also disputes the way in which Hofmeyr dealt with the matter at Parliament. According to Leshabane, their attorneys have advised them that Hofmeyr went beyond the powers of the SIU, acted unlawfully and breached Bosasa's constitutional rights.

Although Hofmeyr evidently referred to Bosasa, Mti and Gillingham in his briefing, he didn't name them, citing pending legal action against his unit.

Hofmeyr's presentation this week vindicated the *M&G*'s revelations in February that Bosasa had access to tender documents before they were publicly advertised. Bosasa is demanding R500 000 from the *M&G* for referring to a "corrupt relationship" between the group and the Department of Correctional Services.

Bosasa's strategy to avoid penalties is two-pronged. First, it is pursuing an application for an interdict preventing the SIU from continuing its investigation until the court has made a final decision.

The application is brought by Bosasa Operations, the company's operations coordinator Angelo Agrizzi, financial coordinator Andries van Tonder, buyer Frans Vorster and Watson. The four men were given notices by the SIU to provide certain documentation during interrogation by the unit.

The applicants claim that the SIU's probe is tainted because of alleged media leaks and the handling of a seizure operation at Bosasa's premises.

In reply the SIU denies leaking information to the *M&G* and accuses Bosasa of activating a "data deletion utility" on Bosasa's servers shortly before the SIU arrived.

In the second court action the plaintiffs ask the court for a permanent order against the SIU, "declaring the entire process of the first defendant's [the SIU's] investigations into the plaintiffs to be fundamentally tainted".

Hofmeyr's presentation brought into sharp focus again Bosasa's astonishing success in winning government tenders. Even after 2007, when it became publicly known that Bosasa was under investigation for tender-rigging, the group continued to secure lucrative contracts from the Justice Department and the Eastern Cape.

The group's most recent tender is a R3.9 billion contract awarded by the Eastern Cape to Phakisa Fleet Solution, a Bosasa company, to manage the provincial fleet of vehicles.

At the time when the Bosasa group was awarded its first major prisons contract for catering in 2004, the company was owned by Watson's family trust (26%), Bosasa directors Carol Mkele (33,3%) and Joe Gumede (18,5%), and the Bosasa Employees Trust (22,2%).

Between 2004 and 2006 three companies within the group – Bosasa Operations, Sondolo IT and Phezulu Fencing – were awarded six tenders by the prisons department at a value of R1.8 billion.

The SIU's probe focused on four tenders: a catering tender for R717 million over three years; an access control tender at R237 million; a fencing contract for R587 million; and a tender for TV systems in prisons at a cost of R224 million.

Hofmeyr's probe found that in almost all cases Bosasa was involved in the drafting of tender specifications and that procurement policies were severely discounted.

From warder to prisons finance chief

Suspended senior prisons official Patrick Gillingham's opulent lifestyle, allegedly partly bankrolled by Bosasa, was laid bare this week in Parliament.

The former finance chief of the prisons department was presented as a main beneficiary in the irregular awarding of lucrative tenders. The SIU claims that he was handsomely rewarded for his loyalty to the company.

The "at least" R2.1 million of kickbacks allegedly paid to Gillingham included cars for him and his children, rugby tickets at Loftus Versfeld, an overseas trip for his daughter and a house in an exclusive Midrand estate.

Court papers before the North Gauteng High Court also mention the cars for his children, but Gillingham's lawyer Ian Small-Smith this week denied his client's guilt. "It is factually incorrect to allege that Bosasa Operations and/or any company in the Bosasa group purchased the vehicles in question. Upon proper investigations it would be revealed that not Bosasa Operations, or any company in the Bosasa group, had anything to do with the purchase of the vehicles."

Gillingham does not have a tertiary qualification.

Beeld reported in 2006 that he was managing the department's budget of more than R9 million a year with only a matric certificate. After school Gillingham joined the prisons service as a warder.

His personal and professional lives soon converged when he married the daughter of a senior prisons official in the apartheid regime.

Gillingham's career in Correctional Services bloomed. He quickly rose through the ranks to become functional services director and later KwaZulu-Natal's commissioner, before being promoted to the chief financial officer position.

In 2007 it seems Gillingham was becoming a liability. He was moved to the position of regional commissioner for Limpopo, Mpumalanga and North West – a move perceived as a demotion and linked to his involvement in the Bosasa saga that was starting to hit the headlines. In September last year he was suspended by former prisons boss Vernie Petersen after he [Petersen] was presented by the SIU with a draft report of its findings.

Gillingham has been on paid leave ever since.

During his tenure as chief financial officer, Gillingham was a confidant of both prisons boss Linda Mti and his minister Ngconde Balfour. – *with Yolandi Groenewald and Glynnis Underhill*

Chapter 17

Single-stock Futures Débâcle

Stuart Theobald

Sunday Times / Business Times

In early 2009, as the world reeled from the financial crisis and toxic assets became part of our everyday language, there was a belief that South Africa might have escaped the financial tsunami.

Then Stuart Theobald discovered single-stock futures (SSFs) – South Africa's very own version of toxic assets.

Single-stock futures are a way for investors to speculate on movements of a share price without actually buying the shares. The contract implies the shares will be bought in the future, but it can be rolled over into a new contract and effectively never settled. The investor need only put down a deposit of about 10% of the agreed future price.

His investigation into the trading of the SSFs began in late 2008, with a painstaking look at the Johannesburg Stock Exchange's records of day-to-day trading in derivatives and set it against shareholder registers. It took him weeks, but he detected patterns of trading in those spreadsheets which pointed to specific individuals who had been speculating in these toxic futures and could see the losses mounting, until they reached the billions.

But which banks and brokers were involved? His contacts in the financial markets proved their worth, and one player led to another, and on to the biggest victim of all – Absa.

Absa got wind of his plans to publish and released a stock exchange news service announcement just days before he went to press, trying to head off the story. But they underestimated what he knew – the whole picture, including estimates of losses and the names of individuals involved.

The consequences are ongoing. Absa, Nedbank, small derivatives broker Cortex and others are involved in legal action. The Financial Services Board is conducting a share price investigation – including Stuart's work as evidence. The Securities Regulation Panel is investigating Nedbank for violations of its codes. The Reserve Bank has been spurred into action.

Not bad for one journalist's investigation, and proof that investigative journalism is not always ignored.

Stuart Theobald is a financial journalist and partner in Intellidex, a research and media business that provides financial research for stories about the investment world. Until 2008 he was news editor of the *Financial Mail*. He is also the editor of *Business Day Investors Monthly*, and a contributor to the *Sunday Times* and to a variety of overseas publications.

Absa-lute Disaster! 1 February

Absa has been hit by losses of about R1 billion after a disaster in its derivatives clearing business.

The bank has had to foreclose on single-stock futures positions, a type of derivative, in a clutch of small JSE-listed companies after investors defaulted on margin calls through small private-client broker Cortex Securities.

Those investors include controversial businessman Jac de Beer, who has been the subject of a Scorpions investigation and has had a Department of Trade and Industry (DTI) order issued against him to refrain from "harmful business practices", and Jaco Verster, former CEO of Acc-Ross, a key entity in the débâcle.

De Beer is linked to golfer Ernie Els through various developments, and Els himself may be exposed to losses.

Bulelani Ngcuka, former national prosecutions director, also has a large exposure.

Absa's biggest problem is investors in Pinnacle Point – formerly called Acc-Ross, a golfing resort and hotel development company – from which the bank could have lost R900 million. Further exposures to derivatives in other companies probably top R100 million.

Absa is the latest bank to take a hit on dealings in leveraged instruments traded on the JSE's derivatives exchange, Safex.

Rand Merchant Bank (RMB) was the first, when in October last year it foreclosed on Dealstream, an unlicensed brokerage house that traded in leveraged instruments. The episode has cost RMB more than R300 million and landed it with substantial stakes in Vox Telecom, Simmer & Jack and Control Instruments.

Absa is in a bigger hole, with stakes in Pinnacle Point (28%), microlender Blue Financial Services (16%), empowerment holding company Sekunjalo (17%) and IT company ConvergeNet (10%).

Absa narrowly avoided taking up 42% in cosmetics company Beige Holdings after coming to an agreement with defaulting empowerment shareholder Thebe, a company linked to the ANC.

Absa now has no choice but to try to manage the interests in the companies to attempt to recover some of its significant credit losses. It will also pursue Cortex Securities, which in turn will pursue the underlying clients that defaulted.

While Dealstream is alleged to have engaged in fraudulent activities, Cortex does not appear to have done anything illegal in racking up the large positions, but it is liable to Absa for the default, which is sure to wipe it out.

The effect on Absa depends on how it treats the situation from an accounting perspective.

The announcement on Thursday was of the "acquisition cost" of the securities, totalling R1.4 billion.

Absa said it would "equity account" Pinnacle Point and Sekunjalo Investments. This means it does not have to reflect substantial falls in the share prices of those two companies, but rather consolidate the earnings of the companies into its income statement proportional to its interest. It will hold the stakes on its books at the market price on 31 December – its year-end.

But this is a gross distortion of economic reality. First, the market price of Pinnacle Point has fallen from 65c to 42c since the year-end. Second, the size of the stake and illiquidity in the share mean it will never be able to sell it at even the current price. The real value is more like 13c a share. At that price, the Pinnacle Point stake is worth just R161 million.

Similar, though less extensive, impairments should be made to the other stakes too. This means Absa has spent R1.4 billion for something worth just a few hundred million rands – an actual loss of at least R1 billion.

In the first half of this financial year, the Absa Capital unit made R1 billion in profits. The futures disaster will wipe that out. Absa will eventually have to impair the assets and recognise the real loss.

Pinnacle Point is the largest exposure. The consortium that held futures positions included an entity called Jansk International and former CEO Verster.

Jansk was once subject to a Financial Services Board investigation, which forced it to release a number of investors. It is known to be the vehicle used by De Beer, although British Virgin Island-registered companies, such as Jansk, are notoriously difficult to penetrate.

De Beer is noted in the Acc-Ross pre-listing statement as having had the DTI order issued against him to desist from taking money from investors to invest in companies in which he was involved. But Jansk did at some point have outside investors. Sources told *Business Times* that De Beer once boasted that the Rupert family was invested in Jansk.

Market rumour has it that Els is exposed, possibly through Jansk, or directly. *Business Times* did establish that the Ernie Els Trust is a client of Cortex. Els's brother Dirk is a co-director with De Beer of EII Developers, which developed the Nondela Golf Resort with a course designed by Els. The golfer is also associated with Pinnacle Point through his signature course at Gardener Ross Golf and Country Estate, a Pinnacle Point development in Centurion.

However, Cortex CEO Mark Weetman denied that Els was involved in the defaulting contracts. Efforts to reach Els's management team at the Dubai Desert Classic golf tournament this week were unsuccessful.

The consortium also included Ngcuka, an empowerment partner of Pinnacle Point. Ngcuka's exposure is believed to have been about R150 million.

When Cortex facilitated the trades, the shareholders' register shows the disappearance of an unnamed nominee company – which obscures the identities of the actual owners – from the shareholders' register. The JSE's Safex database simultaneously shows the creation of a large open interest in single-stock futures.

Things went along fine for a while. The share price crept up. In August last year, according to shareholder registers, a large additional slug of single-stock futures was bought when the share price was at around 91c. The margin required was 10c a share.

In November the picture changed significantly. Acc-Ross undertook a major transaction, buying Pinnacle Point by issuing shares, which left Pinnacle Point in control of the business. The number of shares in issue multiplied fourfold, which reduced the total proportion of shares sitting in single-stock futures to 27% of all the shares in issue. At that point, the share price was at 100c and the consortium was sitting on a paper profit of about R340 million.

The margin the consortium had put down with the broker had been pushed up to 15c a share, or just R190 million, for an underlying exposure to the company of R1.2 billion.

Things soon went awry. In mid-November, the share price went into freefall. Volumes in what was now called Pinnacle Point had always been small. Selling pressure forced the share price down easily.

There was another complication. The JSE, spooked by the collapse of Dealstream and RMB's exposure to Vox Telecom, pushed up the margin requirement to 20c a share. Suddenly the consortium faced a major cash-flow shock – R430 million for the fall in the share price, plus R45 million in extra margin. Some of that could have been financed from the R340 million paper profit the consortium had held earlier, although that could already have been used for other purposes.

The bottom line was that the consortium could not come up with the cash. Absa would not disclose how much, but a significant amount was outstanding.

It was December, the toughest cash-flow month for many companies.

Business Times understands the consortium is threatening court action against Absa, claiming it was about to meet the margin requirements when Absa foreclosed.

The consortium defaulted and lost the margin it had put down.

Cortex CEO Weetman, who acknowledged his firm had defaulted, said: "The risk flows through us on to Absa bank, but ultimately the client is liable [for the loss in value of the underlying position]."

In theory, the margin should cover any risk the financing bank carries, because it should cover the maximum price fall possible in a single day.

The problem was that the share price fell faster than anyone could sell the shares, breaking all the assumptions underlying Safex's margining models. Plus, there was very little liquidity in the share, so there were too few buyers in the market to sell them to. Absa was left with the shares.

The JSE determined that the slug of shares was worth far less than the market price, after it adjusted the price for the lack of liquidity. Neither the JSE, Absa nor Cortex would say what that value was.

But there is a clue to the worth, which indicates the real value of the stake.

While the consortium was defaulting, another default was taking place. Pinnacle Point CEO Wilf Robinson – coincidentally a former CEO of Absa Private Bank – had taken a large single-stock futures position himself.

The JSE's news service revealed that in February last year Robinson sold R14,6 million worth of shares and simultaneously bought futures, in which the underlying interest was R14,4 million in shares – thus raising a lot of cash that he needed to pay in tax on the shares he had been given in the company. But in December, at the same time as the consortium received a margin call, Robinson did too.

"I wasn't able to meet a margin call," Robinson told *Business Times*. Like the consortium, he defaulted, and the bank ended up with the shares.

The JSE news service records that Robinson's shares were transferred at 13c a share, realising just R2.6 million, leaving Robinson R11.8 million out of pocket. This is probably what the JSE priced the shares at for Absa – a far better indication of the value than the market price.

By that measure, the original Pinnacle Point consortium's interest fell in value from almost R1.3 billion to R165 million – a collapse of R1.1 billion. All Absa had as security on that was the margin.

Absa would not say how much it had recovered.

Business Times has reason to believe the shareholders defaulted on a margin call when the share price was around 65c. If so, Absa is owed R650 million. But there is further reason to believe that the consortium failed to cover earlier losses because the share price fell so fast.

The consortium must have been up to date when it bought the additional slug of futures in November. At that stage it put down margin of R190 million. If that was Absa's only security, it is out of pocket to the tune of R900 million. That would equate to Absa's figure of a R931.4 million "acquisition cost" – which would have included the 13c-a-share Safex price plus the bad debt.

Cortex also traded clients into futures over 42% of Beige Holdings. But in this case Absa came to a different conclusion, said the banking group's risk director David Hodnett.

"Beige is tied up and sorted out," he said. That must have required a rescue for Thebe MediCare, Beige's empowerment partner, which was sitting in the single-stock futures.

Thebe directors did not return *Business Times*'s calls. The company's controlling entity, Thebe Investments, benefits a trust which in turn benefits the ANC.

For Absa, the only option is to take on the large equity positions and try to manage them to realise some value.

Robinson said he had held discussions with Absa representatives who intend to become strategic shareholders. "We've had meetings with them as shareholders, giving them feedback on our business, but it's early days."

Hodnett confirmed that Absa would appoint a director to the board. But before Absa's announcement on Thursday, representatives of Blue Financial Services and Sekunjalo were not even aware that Absa had become a large shareholder.

If the companies do well, the share prices will rise and Absa can recover some of its lost money. But it would not have anticipated that a derivatives clearing business would morph into a private equity business, taking about R1 billion in cash with it.

Single-stock futures explained

An investor – any retail investor can do it – trades with a stock broker to buy or sell single-stock futures (SSF) contracts.

An SSF contract says the holder will take delivery of 100 underlying shares at a specified future date at a specified future set price. The contracts are traded on the JSE's derivatives exchange, Safex.

On one side of the trade is the broker and his client. The broker also has an agreement with a clearing bank, which finances the trade and hedges its risk.

The client only puts down a "margin" – a fraction of the total exposure. The bank hedges its risk by buying shares in the market, usually to the full exposure.

The margin is what Safex holds to limit the risk of the price of the shares moving. The client always has to maintain the margin, so if the share price falls, he has to deposit more money with the broker.

An example: a client buys 10 SSF contracts in Anglo American. Each contract is 100 shares, so his total exposure is to 1000 shares. The counterparty bank takes the trade and buys the 1000 shares to hedge the risk of delivering the shares at the expiry date of the SSF.

At the time of the deal, the Anglo American share price is R200, so the client has a total exposure of R200 000. The margin requirement, set by Safex, is R3800 per contract, so the client puts down R38 000.

Imagine the next day Anglo's price falls to R195. Now the total underlying exposure is R195 000, a R5000 loss. The client will be called upon to top up his margin – a "margin call" – to get it back to R38 000. If the client couldn't pay, the position would be closed, the underlying shares sold, and the bank would get back its money.

If, however, the share prices increase, say to R220, the total position will be worth R220 000. The client will have made a profit of R20 000.

The amounts would be slightly different in reality, because the bank also charges interest, and various fees are involved.

How it all went wrong

- October 2007: A consortium of investors led by Jac de Beer and Jaco Verster switch their direct holdings in Acc-Ross into single-stock futures over 65% of the company. They raise about R45 million in cash through the transaction, financed ultimately by Absa. Bulelani Ngcuka joins the consortium later.

- August 2008: A substantial additional slug of futures is acquired. The share price is at 91c. The consortium of investors is sitting on a paper profit of R230 million on an underlying exposure to 89% of the shares in the company.

- November 2008: Acc-Ross undertakes a major transaction, issuing shares to acquire Pinnacle Point. The share issue dilutes the futures concentration down to 28% of the company. The share price is at 100c, and the consortium has a R340 million paper profit, which it may have taken out of the transaction. The total exposure is R1.2 billion of which Safex holds R190 million as security. The company is renamed Pinnacle Point.

- November 2008: Later in the month, the share price starts to fall fast, along with a general market decline. The Dealstream collapse in October leads Safex to increase margins on futures. Speculators begin attacking companies that have big futures exposures, and the consortium finds itself in a major loss position.

- December 2008: By the first week of the month, the consortium is in a loss position of R430 million, and it also has to come up with R45 million of extra margin.

The consortium defaults on the margin calls, leading Cortex Securities to default to Safex. Safex turns to the clearing bank, Absa, to cover the margins.

Absa takes delivery of the shares, along with slugs of Blue Financial Services, ConvergeNet and Sekunjalo in which futures holders had also defaulted in a manner similar to the investors in Pinnacle Point.

The episode ends up costing Absa R1.4 billion on companies it acquired that are worth R300 million or less.

Beige Means Red for Absa   *8 February*

The Securities Regulation Panel (SRP) has launched an investigation into trading in shares in small pharmaceutical company Beige Holdings – and single-stock futures in general – following queries from *Business Times*. The result could land Nedbank, and possibly other banks, with more unexpected losses.

Thebe Investment Corporation (TIC) announced on Thursday that it had bought just over a third of Beige Holdings, a small listed pharmaceutical company. It acquired the stake from Absa, which had ended up with the interest when Cortex Securities defaulted on margin calls on single-stock futures, as revealed last week by *Business Times*.

At the same time Absa had also received stakes in Pinnacle Point (28%), Sekunjalo (17%), Blue Financial Services (16%) and ConvergeNet (10%). In the case of Beige shares, Thebe MediCare – a 24% subsidiary of TIC – defaulted along with some of its directors to Cortex. TIC says it had no say over the affairs of Thebe MediCare and its decision to dabble in single-stock futures.

The TIC acquisition narrowly scraped under the SRP code's rule that a shareholder has to make an offer to all other shareholders to buy their shares if it acquires 35% of a company. The rule is a major constraint on a shareholder and forces many to manage their stakes at under the 35% level. If they cross that point, they have to be prepared to acquire, and pay for,

100% of the company.

The question for the SRP is whether any shareholder has crossed that 35% level in the mess around sorting out the defaulting futures positions.

According to shareholder registers from the last quarter of 2008, Nedbank was sitting on 42% of Beige as security for its counter-party role on the single-stock futures. Earlier last year, it was sitting on 88% of Pinnacle Point Holdings. Did this require a compulsory offer to minorities? SRP executive director Richard Connellan isn't sure. "We are calling for full information on this, and we are going to look at it very carefully."

The issue turns on where the economic and voting interest in the shares lies. Technically, it should lie with the entity holding the shares – in Beige's case, it was Nedbank, which had acted as the counter-party to Cortex Securities' acquisition of single-stock futures. Nedbank did, however, sign over voting rights to Thebe MediCare, in order for it to qualify as a BEE investor in Beige, so it may be able to argue to the SRP that it did not hold the actual economic interest.

But what of Pinnacle Point? The voting rights, as far as *Business Times* was able to tell, lay with Nedbank, although it, too, may have signed over voting rights in those shares. If it did, Nedbank would be doing business with some interesting characters.

Should Nedbank be forced into making an offer to minorities, it would have to offer a price far higher than the current market price. Beige's price has halved in the last five months while Pinnacle Point has halved since its high four months ago.

The rule requires it to offer the highest price it bought shares at when it bought them in the 30 days prior to crossing the 35% threshold. Any minority shareholder would accept the offer, and Nedbank would end up owning a large piece of a company at a price far higher than it is worth.

But Absa may also be exposed. It inherited the Beige stake when Cortex defaulted, which, judging from shareholder registers, should have been a 42% interest. However, Absa financial director Jacques Schindehütte assures *Business Times* that Absa only ever had just under 35% of Beige. What happened to the balance? No one seems to know.

In written replies to our questions, TIC said it "did not hesitate to buy the shares" from Absa because it saw much value in Beige, but it did not trigger the compulsory offer because "we see value in the broad shareholding by the public in Beige". One would assume that Absa was left with the balance, but apparently it wasn't.

Absa may still have landed itself with quite a loss out of the deal. TIC is refusing to disclose what it paid for the shares, but it would probably have been less than the R62 million they are worth at the current market price. The stake, though, would have cost Absa far more and depends on when Thebe MediCare and its directors Ian Black and Yaseen Bhayat defaulted. Bhayat refused to comment when reached on his cellphone, insisting on written questions, which had not been answered by the time we went to press.

Bloodied Bosses Feel the Pinch   *1 March*

The single-stock futures débâcle has caused major headaches for banks. But many company directors have also had sleepless nights about their own exposures.

It started in 2007 when a number of small brokers and finance boutiques figured out an interesting scheme.

Directors of companies often hold large stakes in their company's shares. But, thanks to the single-stock futures market, those shares could be turned into cash while the directors continued to have exposure to the share price.

Investec directors pioneered the principle earlier, switching from underlying equity into futures in 2006.

Directors are required to make an announcement to the JSE if they acquire or dispose of any interest in an instrument linked to their shares. From those, *Business Times* has pieced together the tail of directors' woes. Those who have lost the most are:

STEINHOFF

Directors: Markus Jooste and a consortium of directors

Loss: R224m

In one of the earliest of such transactions, CEO Markus Jooste led a consortium of directors into futures in their shares in a big way. In June 2007 they collectively bought futures on 22 million shares, more than half by Jooste himself, at R22 a share.

By November 2007 things were looking tough and the consortium decided to get out of the futures by covering the positions and buying underlying shares at R20.25 a share. The loss at that point was just R33 million.

But the directors appear to have held on to their shares. According to the latest Steinhoff annual report, Jooste holds 23 million shares and other directors still have theirs. So that original futures position is now worth just R264 million – a loss of R224 million.

But the directors can be grateful they got out of the single-stock futures position and do not have to stump up the cash to cover the increased margins.

BLUE FINANCIAL SERVICES

Director: Dave van Niekerk

Loss: R100m

Former director Riaan Swart defaulted on his futures position through Cortex Securities, so Absa ended up taking more than 16% of Blue Financial Services.

But Dave van Niekerk, who founded Blue along with Swart, also took on a big single-stock futures exposure. In his case, however, he kept the cash – it was left in his brokerage account and used as a guarantee for Blue's acquisition of Credit U last year. So the trading was not for Van Niekerk himself to get a cash windfall.

That was fortunate, as the Blue share price fell dramatically – from a high of 690c in August last year to 308c now.

Van Niekerk's total futures trading position – including earlier futures trading – ended up losing more than R100 million.

He announced the closing out of the futures position last week, settling the amount outstanding, and no longer has a large futures position.

Van Niekerk holds a large direct position in Blue and the R100 million in losses is not a large proportion.

Swart, however, defaulted on his position when margin calls were made. He has now settled with Absa by handing over 23 million shares.

AFRICAN DAWN

Directors: Marius van Tonder, Connie van Nieuwkerk, Steven de Bruyn,
        De Wet Vivier.

Loss: R80m

Directors of African Dawn have long dabbled in futures in the company shares. But they collectively took a very large exposure towards the end of last year when they bailed out the holders of large contract-for-difference (CFD) positions in their shares. CFDs have a similar economic structure to single-stock futures, but are not traded on the JSE.

Afdawn made an announcement two weeks ago, after being instructed to do so by the JSE, revealing that the directors had switched their holdings in single-stock futures into CFDs in October last year. At the time they did not think they had to tell the market, despite clear rules that directors must disclose any trade.

The JSE is still looking into this and may impose fines on the directors.

Switching to CFDs meant directors could reduce their margins – CFDs usually have smaller margins than single-stock futures – and release more cash to themselves.

At that point the directors had accumulated a CFD exposure on 20 million shares, then worth R72 million. But the share price did not play ball. By the end of the year it had lost a quarter of its value.

However, on 8 January the directors entered into a strange transaction. They bailed out of their CFDs and bought the underlying shares. But it was not only their own CFDs – they bought the CFD positions of a number of other holders, too, to the tune of a further 29 million shares. Stranger still, they bought the underlying equity at 358c a share, on a day when the share price closed at 270c. This amounted to a very generous bail-out of deeply underwater CFDs.

African Dawn CEO Marius van Tonder said the directors were worried about the overhang that a number of distressed CFD holders would mean for the share price, and the bail-out introduced a solid holder.

Van Tonder added that the directors were bullish on the shares and they wanted a bigger stake. Four or five other shareholders participated in a consortium to bail out the underwater CFDs.

The consortium had to raise finance for the purchase, although he added that the directors had accumulated value since listing the company at 7c a share.

The bail-out must have come as a relief to the broker that wrote the CFD contracts – Watermark Securities. It would have been nervous about its clients meeting the margin calls as the shares fell in value.

But the directors' sense of generosity has done them no favours. The stake they took on is now worth just R94 million – a loss of R80 million.

CAPE EMPOWERMENT TRUST

Director: Shaun Rai

Loss: R40m

Chairman Shaun Rai remembers the good times, when the company share price was on the climb. "The year before [2007] we all bought single-stock futures – those were the good times. We lost a lot of money in the bad times," he said.

He and other directors traded single-stock futures through Cortex and CFDs through Nedbank.

In July 2007 Rai accumulated a number of single-stock futures positions, in some cases selling the underlying equity first. A few months later he and some other directors bought CFDs. Buying the futures got him 18 million shares, then worth R44.7 million, although he raised R23 million by selling shares he held.

For the CFDs, he sold underlying equity and entered into contracts covering roughly double the amount of the sales. So all the transactions added up to him selling shares, then entering contracts that doubled his exposure.

All this was while the share price was at its peak. By November last year it had fallen from 260c a share to just 60c. That meant significant paper losses for Rai. On 12 November he took the pain and bought the underlying shares and settled the leveraged exposure.

The shares he ended up with are worth R27 million. But at the time of the derivatives trades he had exposure of R67 million in total. To finance the difference, he said he had to sell a range of assets.

BEIGE HOLDINGS

Directors: Yaseen Bhayat and Ian Black

Loss: R33m

Thebe MediCare was the empowerment partner of Beige Holdings. In turn, Yaseen Bhayat and Ian Black were the major shareholders in Thebe MediCare.

Thebe MediCare decided to switch its exposure to Beige by switching from direct equities into single-stock futures covering 187 million shares, of which Bhayat and Black's proportional interest added up to 120 million shares. Bhayat and Black had additional exposure to futures in Beige covering another 52 million shares. The futures valued the equity at 29c a share, so the combined exposure was R50 million.

The pair sold the underlying shares, raising cash in the transaction, having put down about R5 million as margin.

But things went badly wrong. By December last year, the shares traded as low as 10c, at the same time as margins were pushed up by the JSE. Bhayat and Black couldn't come up with the extra cash and defaulted on the margin calls. The cash they raised from the transactions had obviously been used up.

In December, the futures positions were closed out at 10c a share although the close-out was only on 106 million shares. It is not known what happened to the rest. But, at 10c, the loss on the original position is about R33 million.

The default meant Absa ended up with the shares, which it then sold to Thebe Investments, which had held about 25% of Thebe MediCare.

Thebe Investments bought the shares, it said, because it saw great value in Beige. It surely did not appreciate the loss it would have taken, along with the directors, as a shareholder of Thebe MediCare.

HUGE GROUP

Directors: James Herbst, Anton Potgieter, Arie Morelis and Vincent Mokhele

Loss: R48m

Directors in Huge Group, a telecoms company, were very enthusiastic users of single-stock futures.

After listing in 2007, the directors, particularly CEO James Herbst, frequently switched their underlying equity exposure into single-stock futures exposures. As a group, they sold about 15 million shares, raising more than R72 million. Then they entered futures contracts for about the same number of shares and exposure.

By October last year, however, there had been a change of heart.

The directors began buying out the futures and taking back the underlying shares. At that point the share price started sliding – from around R4 to December lows of 105c. The unwinding continued until February this year.

The directors effectively borrowed money against their shares, but have now paid it all back. Along the way, the shares have become far less valuable – the 15 million shares are now worth R24 million.

PINNACLE POINT

Director: Wilf Robinson

Loss: R12m

Trading in Pinnacle Point futures was done mainly by outside investors, but CEO Wilf Robinson did take a futures position by selling underlying shares in February last year – to raise cash to pay taxes. But the share price went south and in December he defaulted on a margin call, leading to a forced sale of the shares at far less than they were worth when he got the single-stock futures exposure. The difference added up to R12 million.

How they cashed in ...

Say you hold R1 million worth of shares and need to borrow cash against them. Banks would take the shares as security to make a loan, but would only lend a fraction of the value of the shares. So, sell the shares and buy futures instead.

Futures are a promise to take delivery of shares at a set price at a predetermined future date. You have to put down a margin on the underlying exposure – until recently, it was about 10% of the value of the exposure. So you could get R1 million for selling your shares, and then put down R100 000 to buy the futures.

Effectively, your underlying exposure has not changed, but you have R900 000 in cash. Though the structure has the form and effect of a loan, none of the players in single-stock futures, from the JSE to the boutiques who did the structures for directors, thought about compliance with the National Credit Act, which governs lending.

The problem is that the margin has to be maintained. So if share prices fall, you have to top it up to cover any fall in the underlying share price. No problem if you keep that cash in hand. Big problem if you spend it. And a few directors did spend – some on game farms, some on more futures, so magnifying their exposure – a great recipe for disaster.

Single-Stock Futures Débâcle Points to Price Manipulation   *8 March*

An investigation into single-stock futures trading has revealed strong circumstantial evidence that share prices have been manipulated to try to boost profits on trade in the derivative instruments. This could see traders facing prosecution.

Following its own investigations, the JSE has referred various trades in companies linked to single-stock futures to the Financial Services Board (FSB) for investigation and possible prosecution.

As was first revealed in *Business Times*, brokerage Cortex Securities and its clients defaulted on single-stock futures positions in the companies Pinnacle Point, Blue Financial Services, ConvergeNet, Sekunjalo and Beige Holdings.

The defaults occurred because of "margin calls".

Single-stock futures allow investors to take large exposures in a share by only putting down a fraction of the amount involved. This fraction is called the "margin" and has to be maintained by the investor – if share prices fall, the margin has to be "topped up".

The margin requirement is set by Safex, the JSE's derivatives exchange. Each day, Safex "marks to market" the value of the positions and specifies a "variation margin" that brokers must deposit with Safex if share prices have fallen. If they have increased, Safex gives cash back to the broker. Marking to market means adjusting the value of the positions to the price on the market.

Safex uses the closing share price each day to set the variation margin. If the closing price is high, the investor gets a reduction in margin requirement and cash back from Safex. There is therefore a large incentive for investors to try to ensure closing prices are as high as possible.

That is fairly easy to do in shares with low liquidity – you put in a high-priced offer to buy shares near the close of the market, and get a transaction through at that price, which then sets the closing price.

Further investigation was undertaken into whether price-manipulating transactions took place in companies in which large single-stock futures positions were held.

Traders stand to profit a great deal if they can ensure the closing price is high.

Only the JSE has full information on such trades, particularly on which brokers were trading. However, the relationship was scrutinised between the closing prices of certain shares and the highest daily trade in those shares.

If the closing price was the same as the highest daily trade, it would suggest that the highest price trade had been made right at the end of the day.

An analysis of trades over an 18-month period – from mid-2007 to late 2008 – revealed anomalies.

The companies selected were those known to have had large single-stock futures activity: the Cortex quintet, as well as Cape Empowerment Trust, Simmer & Jack, Vox Telecom, African Dawn, Huge Group and Peregrine. Two "control" companies were added – South Ocean Holdings and PSG Group – which have similar volumes of trade and market cap as companies being analysed but which are not known for much futures trading activity.

Volumes are important. If there is almost no trade, it is normal for the high price to match the closing price often – there being very little price movement during the day.

On the other hand, it would be rare for the closing price to match the high price in large, liquid companies.

Top of the list were four of the five companies in which Cortex Securities had put investors into large single-stock futures positions. Also quite high up were Huge, Vox, Cape Empowerment Trust and Blue. Control dummy South Ocean was also high up, probably because trade is very thin in the share.

Why would a bullish investor trade systematically just before the close of the market? The most obvious reason is to set the closing price high.

Cortex clients had amassed single-stock futures exposures in these companies running into billions of rands. In Pinnacle Point, the "open position" – the underlying shares being held against single-stock futures contracts – was worth about R1.2 billion. If the share price closed just one cent higher, holders of the single-stock futures would receive R12 million in cash from the variation margin.

Pinnacle Point was then examined in more detail, by looking at each trade in the first week of October last year, a period in which the rest of the market was falling fast but the Pinnacle share price was increasing.

The evidence was supportive: most of the high-priced trades came during the closing auctions.

Some of these trades were ridiculous. On 1 October, there was a trade just before the auction, of 77 shares worth about R70. The trading fees would have cost more. On 2 October a trade of 5000 shares pushed the share price up 4% to 95c, and the total trade cost R4750. That difference in the closing price, however, meant single-stock futures holders received R48 million in margin. The interest on that alone would have covered the cost of the trade.

Games were probably also being played by other traders who wanted to force prices down. If they could get prices down, it could trigger a margin call for which the underlying investors would have to cough up. If they defaulted, forced sales would follow and the short position could make a lot of profit.

Indeed, in some trades in early November last year it appears that efforts were made to drive down the price of Pinnacle Point shares. That would obviously not be in the interests of Cortex's clients, and it is believed Cortex drew the JSE's attention to various seller activities in that month.

The cases the FSB is investigating may refer to these short sellers, rather than those who were trying to hold the share price up. Trading periods being probed by the FSB suggest this possibility.

The evidence is circumstantial, though, and it would be hard to make it stick by legal standards.

The JSE's surveillance department believes manipulation took place and Shaun Davis, general manager of surveillance, said the exchange has referred evidence to the FSB, which investigates and recommends cases for prosecution.

"We have reviewed trading in a number of shares underlying single-stock futures and have referred the outcome of some reviews to the FSB," said Davis.

The FSB said it was investigating trade in Pinnacle Point, Huge Group, Vox Telecom and Cape Empowerment Trust, but not Beige, Sekunjalo or ConvergeNet, suggesting that the JSE did not feel it had compelling evidence about trade in those companies.

The FSB can refer cases for criminal prosecution or use its enforcement committee to hand out fines.

The statistical study here provides supporting evidence, but the JSE has far more data at its fingertips to study trader behaviour.

Sources said JSE surveillance department staff have been ensconced at Cortex Securities, along with a team from Absa, Cortex's clearing bank.

In the case of Pinnacle Point, another source pointed to Jac de Beer, the man behind the single-stock futures in Pinnacle Point. Entities linked to De Beer, including Jansk International and Quattro Trust, are on the Pinnacle Point shareholder register as small, direct holders, but are believed to be the main entities in the single-stock futures position. The source said these entities were used to support the share price.

In the case of Beige Holdings, the futures positions were held by Thebe MediCare, in which the dominant shareholders are Ian Black and Yaseen Bhayat. There is no evidence linking them to the trade in Beige. It is quite possible that underlying investors were the ones trading the shares to get higher closing prices.

For technical reasons, Cortex could not have done any trade directly. Cortex is only a derivatives member of the JSE, not an equity trading member, so at least one other broker with an equities trading licence would have been involved.

Supporting a share price is not on its own illegal. Investors could argue that they believed the shares were worth more and wanted to buy. But pushing a price up simply to ensure a high closing price would be illegal.

Cortex Securities managing director Mark Weetman refused to comment.

PART FOUR

Crime and Punishment

Chapter 18

The Station Strangler

Lavern de Vries and Warda Meyer

Cape Argus, Weekend Argus

In 1995 Norman Avzal Simons was convicted of murder. His victim was a 10-year-old boy called Elroy van Rooyen, who went missing at a railway station in Cape Town.

Simons was sent to prison for life and local people believed that, at last, the Station Strangler was behind bars.

For almost a decade the bodies of young boys had been found at various sites around Cape Town, many of them last spotted at railway stations. Was this little boy the 22nd victim of the man dubbed the Station Strangler? And was Norman Simons the Strangler? Was he guilty of 22 murders, just one murder or even, perhaps, no murders at all – a case of a wrongful conviction?

Lavern de Vries was wondering about the case as she listened to another man wrongfully convicted of murder at the annual Power Reporting investigative journalism conference at Wits University in 2009. Raphael Rowe described how he had been convicted at the age of 18 of a murder he did not commit, and spent 12 years in prison before he was acquitted and released. He now works as a reporter for the BBC's *Panorama* programme and investigates these cases himself.

"On the way back to Cape Town I imagined all sorts of ways of pitching the Station Strangler story to my editor without him thinking I was crazy," says De Vries. But when she got back to work she discovered her editor had been thinking along the same lines.

Gasant Abarder asked her to join up with Warda Meyer and review a case that went back 20 years, a really cold case.

Warda already knew the story. She was a journalism student at the Peninsula Technikon when the killings caused panic in the Western Cape. She had met Simons and knew his advocate, Koos Louw.

For weeks they sifted through piles of documents, spent their evenings looking for the families of victims and witnesses, read the never-before-seen notes Simons wrote during his trial, and trawled through court records and testimonies from police officers working on the case.

Simons was arrested after the police issued an identikit picture of the man they were looking for. And he confessed, which must be the most compelling evidence in any crime investigation. But though the police may have thought they had found their serial killer, they never charged Simons with any of the other murders.

The case is still unresolved. But new forensic techniques could at last answer the question, did Norman Simons kill Elroy van Rooyen? And was Simons the Station Strangler?

The series of articles moved the Western Cape MEC for community safety to call for the reopening of the Station Strangler murders.

Lavern de Vries started out as a general reporter for the *Cape Argus* before becoming its crime reporter in 2008. She had previously worked for a number of different publications as a general news reporter, including Voice of the Cape radio station, *People's Post* and the *Big Issue*.

Warda Meyer has been a broadcast journalist since the late 1990s, working for a variety of radio stations in Cape Town. In 2009 she moved into print and currently works for the *Weekend Argus*. She writes, among other things, about politics and crime, gang violence and urban unrest.

A Killer was Abducting Kids   *11 December*

Let's start with the facts.

There are two boys, Elroy and Rayno van Rooyen, both aged 10, Elroy a few months older. It is the early afternoon, 11 March 1994, and the two are looking to make some pocket money at Pick n Pay in Strand, pushing trolleys for shoppers. A stranger offers them R10 to carry boxes to an unspecified destination in the direction of the railway station. The boxes are empty.

Rayno goes along with it for a time. Then he gets spooked. He departs, leaving Elroy alone in the company of the generous benefactor.

Observing them is local resident Fouzhia Hercules, who wonders just what the boys are doing with the man.

Fast-forward a couple of hours. A young friend of Elroy van Rooyen sees Elroy on a train at Faure station, apparently alone, and travelling who knows where.

Eight days later the savagely mutilated corpse of Elroy van Rooyen is found in a shallow grave at Kuilsriver. His hands are bound. He is lying face down in the sand, half undressed, strangled with his own tracksuit pants.

Another Station Strangler murder, number 22 in a series of horrors that started in 1986 when the body of 14-year-old Jonathan Claasen was discovered.

By the time Elroy van Rooyen's violated corpse is discovered, the search for the so-called Station Strangler serial killer is the largest and most intensive in South African criminal history.

The mood in Mitchells Plain, the centre of the Strangler's activity, is dangerous – mobs are scouring the area looking for targets so they can take the law into their own hands. South Africa's first democratic elections are barely a month away and the Western Cape is the only province in the country where the ruling National Party has any hope of keeping power – at least if it can convince people of their bona fides in government.

Then a breakthrough comes. First police compile and publish a new police identikit based on the observations of Fouzhia Hercules and Rayno van Rooyen. Then they get a call that points them to an individual who allegedly has a history of booking himself into psychiatric institutions for depression, either shortly before or shortly after the killings in the Station Strangler sequence, and who bears a strong resemblance to the composite identikit.

Norman Avzal Simons, a Standard 3 teacher at a Mitchells Plain school, was arrested on 15 April 1994.

In his later confession, Simons said he had been raped by his own older brother when he was about the same age as the Strangler's victims, and he had never come to terms with the trauma. Simons said he was inhabited by an older brother who had raped him in childhood. He said he heard voices telling him to kill.

Simons also closely matched the serial-killer profile drawn up in 1992 by psychologist Micki Pistorius, a protégée of Robert Ressler, the doyen of serial-killer profiling in the FBI. Pistorius said the killer would be around 28 years old, that he would likely be a teacher, a priest or a policeman, and that he would have been sodomised himself between the ages of 8 and 14.

There is no doubt in the mind of then-police captain JD Kotze, later a top member of the now defunct Directorate of Special Investigations (the Scorpions), that the police got the right man – even though they failed to find forensic evidence connecting Simons with any of the other killings, and in the end Simons was charged only with the murder of Van Rooyen.

Simons was convicted by the Cape High Court in June 1995. Initially sentenced to 25 years, the sentence was commuted to life imprisonment by the Supreme Court of Appeal in March 1998, largely on the basis of the untested possibility of Simons being guilty of the Station Strangler murders, and therefore constituting an ongoing danger to society.

Full stop? Not quite.

Simons's lawyer, Advocate Koos Louw, a former magistrate, is convinced Simons is innocent. Louw has made it a personal crusade to have the case re-opened, and to secure what he sees as justice for his client.

According to Louw, the case is haunted by anomalies, apparent inconsistencies and contradictions, throwing doubt on Simons's conviction for the Elroy van Rooyen killing, and on his possible connection to the Station Strangler's eight-year orgy of murder.

Central to Louw's case is the virtual absence of any positive evidence linking Simons to the murder of Elroy van Rooyen.

No forensic or DNA evidence was led to connect Simons to the killing. The only scientific evidence interrogated in the court record excludes Simons as a suspect in two of the other Station Strangler killings. Reference is made to the serological comparison of semen samples taken from Simons with samples found at two crime scenes.

Both are connected with blood type A, but whereas the crime scene samples are those of a "secretor", Simons is a "non-secretor".

What this means is that Simons was shown to be part of the 20% of the population who through a quirk of genomes do not imprint their genetic profile (such as blood group) in bodily fluids such as semen and saliva, while the crime-scene semen was left by somebody who, like 80% of the population, leaves such imprints.

Behind the complicated science there lies a simple and incontrovertible truth: that you cannot be a secretor and a non-secretor at the same time, and therefore it could not have been Simons who left the semen at the crime scenes in question.

In other words – though this does not have any bearing on the Van Rooyen murder, where no semen deposit was found – if the semen was indeed that of the serial killer and all the victims were slain by the same murderer, the serial killer could not have been Simons.

No other scientific evidence was led. In the end what was crucial in securing the conviction in court was the fact that the court allowed into evidence the confession extracted from Simons under police interrogation after his arrest in April 1994. But then subsequently, on 16 April 1994, Simons repudiated the confession.

In an affidavit deposed before a magistrate, he claimed it had been extracted under extreme pressure in interrogation – much of which was targeted on his homosexuality.

Some credence could be given to Simons's denial in the notes in police investigations dockets, where it emerges that – apparently possessed by the need to confess – Simons led police to supposed crime scenes where no bodies were found.

It is also noted that Simons was uncertain of the location of the Melton Rose railway station, the station closest to the place where Van Rooyen's body was found. Police investigators were also not able to connect the dots between the sighting of Elroy van Rooyen in the company of the stranger in Strand, and his sandy grave near the Melton Rose railway station. All they had was the eyewitness identification given by Fouzhia Hercules.

Hercules does not absolutely confirm that the man she saw was Simons. She told the court and confirmed to Independent Newspapers that she chose the man who looked most like the man she saw that fateful day. And in the parade, Elroy's cousin, Rayno, was unable to pick out the man who led the boys towards the railway station.

"They Have Not Found the Man Who Did It"

Norman Avzal Simons, the man branded the Station Strangler, has broken his silence 14 years after his conviction for one of the murders. He still maintains he is innocent.

Cape Town's most notorious serial killer cut a bloody swathe of terror across the city that left 22 young victims dead during the late 1980s and early 1990s.

Simons was sentenced to 25 years in prison in 1995 for the kidnapping and killing of victim number 22, 10-year-old Elroy van Rooyen. No evidence was led to connect him to any of the other Station Strangler murders. In 1998, though no evidence to this effect was tested in court, the Supreme Court of Appeal in Bloemfontein expressed the opinion that he could have been responsible for the other 21 killings.

Simons's personal notes and diary entries written during his trial and inside prison have been released to the *Cape Argus*.

Today, the *Cape Argus* begins a cold-case investigation series which will continue in tomorrow and Sunday's editions of the *Weekend Argus*. The question at the heart of the investigation is: who killed the other 21 Station Strangler victims?

In his most recent diary entry, written on the back of notes Simons made during his trial, he writes: "My inner being has been trampled upon. By [*sic*] having me as a scapegoat has not helped the society-at-large, because they have not found the person who did these terrible things to the kids."

Simons says he is still called the Station Strangler by fellow inmates.

"Walking about in the prison, being called the Station Strangler, is not a 'beautiful' thing, but I have to 'live' with it," he writes.

Simons maintained his innocence throughout his trial and his advocate, Koos Louw, has been fighting a 15-year crusade to prove his client's innocence.

Simons was born in Cape Town to Stanley Nombewu and Evelyne Simons. He lived in Joburg and the Eastern Cape and moved back to Cape Town as a teenager to live with his mother.

He worked as an intern in a children's home and qualified as a teacher in 1992. From 1991 he started regularly booking himself into psychiatric institutions, where he was diagnosed with depression and personality disorders.

Simons's history of mental illness dates back to the year his older brother was killed in a stabbing incident. While being questioned about the Strangler murders, he claimed his brother had sodomised him, though he has since admitted that he had lied about this.

Simons is serving time at the Drakenstein Correctional Centre, a low-security prison outside Paarl.

He refers to state witness Fouzhia Hercules, who identified Simons as the man she had seen with Elroy on the day he disappeared. Her testimony was the state's trump card that secured Simons's conviction.

Writing from the confines of his single cell, he says he knows that "justice will prevail".

"The world out there, I believe, still do [*sic*] have their doubts about my innocence. I have been dealt a heavy blow and a scar that can never be erased," he says.

"[My friends and family] don't need this in their lives, just because of a lady who said that I'm a 'strangler' and the lots [*sic*] of propaganda in newspapers. It won't be long, soon it will all be over, for God will silence all my enemies."

Louw and his wife, Rynette, are his only visitors at the prison.

"My children met Simons during 1994 and 1995 while he lived with us. My son was about 10 years old when we took Simons in. I would never have allowed him to stay in our home if I for one second doubted his innocence. We trusted him completely," says Rynette Louw.

The Many Faces of the Strangler *12 December*

He had long hair. He had short hair. He was tall and slight. He was short and muscular. He had a round face, he had a long face. He was light-skinned. He was dark-skinned. He had missing teeth. He had no teeth missing. He was a lone presence as insubstantial as a shadow. He was five men on a murderous rampage.

The Station Strangler had as many shapes as fear itself.

By early 1994, after eight years of horror on the Cape Flats, the police and the public alike still had no good idea of who the Station Strangler was, how he spoke or what he looked like. Evidence was fragmentary and sometimes inconsistent.

One victim, Jeremy Smith, 12, found in the bush near Weltevrede Road, was missing an ear, apparently severed by the killer.

Another, Neville Samaai, 13, had a hole cut in his trousers with a pair of scissors when the body was found.

Neither detail was repeated at any other crime scene.

Yet all the time the body count was rising. In the first three months of 1994 alone, the decomposed bodies of 11 Strangler victims were dug out of shallow graves, many in bushes, most in desolate dunes, throughout the length and breadth of Mitchells Plain.

By the time Norman Avzal Simons was arrested in April of that year the Strangler had claimed a total of 22 victims in a cycle of sickening violence against children that started in 1986.

But here is the problem.

If there was only one Station Strangler, it was highly unlikely it was Norman Avzal Simons. He bore little resemblance to most of the identikits. He matched few of the physical descriptions given to police investigators.

Nor was there any similarity between his dress, demeanour or the car he drove – a Mazda – and those connected in evidence with the Strangler.

Moreover, after his arrest – first on the umbrella Station Strangler investigation docket, then subsequently for the murder of Elroy van Rooyen, 10, alone – Simons was scientifically tested against physical evidence collected from the various crime scenes.

Police were trying to link their suspect to at least some of the long series of brutal murders. It was explicitly their intention to gather sufficient evidence to allow them to charge him as the Station Strangler, not for the murder of Elroy van Rooyen alone.

The list of forensic dead-ends includes the following:

- A fingerprint found at the scene where a still-unidentified boy, aged about 13, was discovered, near Weltevrede Road, Mitchells Plain. At the same crime scene a scrap of paper was discovered beside the body, reading: "Many more in store." Neither the fingerprint nor the handwriting was that of Simons.

- A second fingerprint was lifted at the scene where the corpse of Neville Samaai, 13, was discovered. This too checked negative against that of Simons.

- Also at the Samaai crime scene a copy of *Huisgenoot* was found with a crossword puzzle half completed. The handwriting did not match that of Simons.

- Blood and semen were found around the body of Jeremy Smith, 12. They did not match those of Simons.

- Blood and semen samples were found at the scene of the killing of Calvin Spires, 9. They classified serologically as blood type A, but were deposited by a "secretor". Simons is a "non-secretor" and this excludes the possibility of a match.

- A handwritten note, the content of which has not been made public, was discovered near the body of Elino Sprinkle, 11. The handwriting was different from that of Simons.

- A car moving suspiciously in the Weltevrede vicinity where Sprinkle's body was found was reported to police. It was identified as a Volkswagen Jetta and the registration number was given to police. The registration did not connect back to any friend or connection of Simons. Nor did Simons match with eyewitness reports of Strangler sightings.

- The second identified victim of the Strangler, Yusuf Hoffman, 14, who died in 1987, was seen in the company of a man who referred to himself as "John" and wore a gold ring on the middle finger of his left hand. "John" was a tall, coloured male with a light complexion. Simons is of medium height and is dark.

- Samuel Nqaba, 15, victim number six, was last seen getting into an olive-green Valiant station wagon with a tall black man with a long face, aged between 20 and 25, wearing square-shaped dark glasses.

- Denver Ghaza was murdered after getting into the car of a man with a long cut on the left side of his face, stretching from the nose at an angle down the cheek. The man was smoking and bought a beer while in the company of Ghaza. The man was – unusually for the Cape Flats – apparently unable to speak Afrikaans with any fluency. Though Simons is scarred on the face, the scar is a burn, not a cut. He is fluent in Afrikaans.

Two boys playing with the murdered Sprinkle just before he was abducted, testified to a story that breaks completely with the Strangler pattern. They claim they were approached by five men while on their way to Kapteinsklip railway station.

One of the men was described as being short and having his lower front teeth missing. This man allegedly put a rope around Elino's neck, then dragged him into the bushes. This was the last time the boy was seen alive.

In all, as police searched with increasing desperation for evidence and leads in an eight-year investigation, identikit artists compiled more than 10 composite images. All of them gave a markedly different impression of the Strangler's appearance.

But, balanced against all the questions, as Strangler investigator JD Kotze points out, the killings stopped after Simons was arrested.

There were no more bodies found that definitely bore the distinctive "signature" or unambiguously manifested the modus operandi of the Station Strangler. "Serial killers don't change their MOs [modi operandi], they might try to perfect their fantasies," Kotze says, "but they don't change their MOs."

Even so, there may have been more than one Strangler. The Strangler's MO, as recorded, was relatively variable and relatively unspecific.

Even the murderously sexual drive that is usually definitive of serial killers was not always evident.

Some victims were sodomised, others were not. All that really runs through the sequence is the fact that the dead children were lying face down in the sand, hands bound, and they had been strangled.

The possibility of copycat killers, inspired by the first Strangler, having indulged their own fantasies in imitation cannot be excluded.

Why City Detective Ruled Out Simons in String of Murders

One of the most seasoned investigators of the Station Strangler murders broke ranks in giving evidence to an inquest at the Mitchells Plain Magistrate's Court in 2008.

The inquest was into the killing of six boys identified as victims.

In the course of its hearings, the court considered whether it could find sufficient evidence to recommend that charges be brought against Norman Avzal Simons – in the end finding that though there was some prima facie evidence, there was no reasonable prospect of any successful prosecution.

But before this, it heard the testimony of Inspector Don Engelbrecht, a police sergeant at the time.

Engelbrecht thought that Norman Simons was not the Station Strangler and, moreover, that he did not kill Elroy van Rooyen.

According to the court transcript, Engelbrecht questioned Simons on 13 April, the day after his arrest, after which he ruled Simons out as a suspect based, in part, on the following:

A witness in the Elino Sprinkle murder case said a VW Jetta, registration CA 722 331, was seen near the bushes where the boy was found dead. The witness also said he saw a person and heard screaming. After following up the lead, Engelbrecht could find no link between Simons and the Jetta.

Police discovered a handwritten note half a metre away from one of the bodies. The note read: "Many more in store, number 14, station wrangler." The note had a fingerprint but the print found on the note did not match that of Simons. The note, according to Engelbrecht, must have come from the killer because the exact number of murdered boys was 14 – a fact only he would know as media reports had, until then, carried incorrect figures.

In preparation for Simons's case, an officer showed Engelbrecht which places Simons had identified as murder scenes or burial grounds, but none of the places that Simons had identified matched any of the murder scenes Engelbrecht knew of and had visited.

Two of the victims had semen traces. The same person left semen on the two boys but the semen didn't match Simons's. Simons never mentioned any of the children in his confession.

"I read the so-called admission, the statement he gave to the magistrate and the pointing out and it didn't change my opinion," Engelbrecht said.

Furthermore, the modus operandi of the killer also largely influenced his opinion: "Few people know what the modus operandi was. And in all the cases where there was testimony from children, the same method was followed.

"And there are more children that are alive that survived an attack – two boys, grown men today, are in their 20s and married. They survived an attack, the same method, basically everything was the same, and by chance one of them knew Simons and when I spoke to them, they said, 'No, it's not Simons, it's another person.'"

At the time of the inquest in July last year, Engelbrecht said that police were still investigating the description offered by the two survivors – that of a black man of medium build who could speak Afrikaans and another language.

Police refused the *Weekend Argus* access to Engelbrecht.

We were told that we could speak to him in his personal capacity on a range of topics including "his garden, his life" but under no circumstances would we be able to interview him on the investigations into the Strangler.

Top Policeman Still Sure Simons
Was Serial Killer

The scenery may have changed but former murder and robbery detective "JD" Kotze still knows how to find his way around the bushes in Kleinvlei.

A few metres from a graveyard, Kotze points to some sandy dunes. This is the spot where, 15 years ago, the decomposed corpse of 10-year-old Elroy van Rooyen was found.

"The case traumatised a lot of us. Many of our guys were medically boarded for stress afterwards," he says, recalling the Station Strangler murders. "We had to deal with what these people had gone through, the families' hurt."

Kotze, later a chief special investigator with the now-defunct Directorate of Special Operations, recalls that in 1994 then murder and robbery chief, Colonel Leonard Knipe, put him in charge of investigations into the Station Strangler killings.

"It was a difficult case. We concentrated on the murders of the '90s ... there were several dead-ends in the first series of murders and a lot of tip-offs in the second spate."

One of the biggest challenges arose from the fact that, when found, the corpses were generally in an advanced state of decomposition.

"There wasn't very much to work with." That and the lack of reliable witnesses to the sequence of abductions and killings.

"It was like looking for the devil," Kotze says.

The investigating team's break finally came when a police informant fingered a man who frequented psychiatric institutions as possibly being the serial killer.

After following Norman Simons, and observing that it was sometimes only after midnight when he returned to Kenilworth Clinic – where Simons was booked in at the time – the team decided to approach him for questioning.

The team formed the impression Simons had several of the characteristics in a profile put together by psychological profiler Micki Pistorius.

"In many serial killing cases the perpetrators were either molested or abused, or something went wrong in their childhoods ... they kill because they want a sense of control and they want to live out their fantasies," says Kotze.

Reflecting on a case which he says he chooses not to think about "because I don't want to relive it", Kotze says he has empathy for Simons. "I knew how he was abused … based on what he said; we followed up leads, and we discovered that he was treated for homosexual-related sexual illnesses. That was never brought into court.

"I don't know why, but the indication I got was that the abuse was ongoing."

Kotze firmly believes Simons really was the Station Strangler. "My opinion, and this is only my opinion, is that although there were no facts to convict him, Simons, on the other cases, it is my belief that he was the killer.

"Although Rayno [van Rooyen] didn't identify him on the parade, he did say that he saw the person and he described the man's clothing and the number he had in the line-up. Inherently, children tell the truth. Fouzhia [Hercules]'s testimony was also tested in court and it stood up. We were lucky that we had an adult that could identify him."

Of the semen that was found on two of the victims, Kotze maintains Simons's semen was not conclusively ruled out as a match.

And the fact that Simons's handwriting didn't match the note found on one of the victims also doesn't sway Kotze.

"You'll never find a case where someone is convicted solely based on their handwriting. It's not like a fingerprint; it's not an exact science."

For Kotze the clincher is that the murders stopped after Simons was arrested. That is proof enough for him.

After Simons's arrest, Kotze recalls, he was called out to several crime scenes which detectives suspected might be connected to the Strangler. But none of these convinced Kotze.

"In my experience, serial killers don't change their MOs. They might try to perfect their fantasies, though, but they don't change their MOs."

And the Strangler's MO: according to Kotze, he would approach the victim in such a way as to win his trust, then lure him away to some desolate area of sandy dunes near a railway station.

Once there the killer would force the boy to lie face down in the sand – with a sand mound underneath his stomach, so the buttocks were raised.

He would then simultaneously rape and strangle the victim, until the life drained away.

Asked what he would ask Simons if he had the opportunity to speak to him, Kotze says, "I'd appeal to him to come out and tell the truth and admit to what he's done, so that the parents of the other children can get closure."

"I was Strangler Victim"   13 December

A man who believes he was one of the notorious Station Strangler's first victims is hoping answers to the Cape's worst serial killings will emerge as police have a new suspect in the case – a convicted murderer and rapist from Johannesburg.

In an exclusive interview with *Weekend Argus*, Mitchells Plain resident Wayne Petersen described how he and a friend were probably the first known Station Strangler victims – and escaped to tell the tale.

Petersen, now 33, was abducted, with a playmate, near his home in Beacon Valley, Mitchells Plain, on 27 August 1986 and raped twice in bushes near a Philippi informal settlement.

Petersen revealed that earlier this year police told him they had found a suspect in Johannesburg. This man, who has been convicted of murder and sexual crimes, apparently used the same modus operandi as that of Petersen's assailant, the same as the one the Strangler used to lure other victims to their fate.

A seasoned police officer who investigated the Station Strangler murders also believes that Petersen and his friend were the first victims of the notorious killer.

A month after Petersen and his friend escaped from their attacker, Jonathan Claasen, the first officially recorded Strangler murder victim, disappeared – on 3 September 1986. His body was found face down in a shallow grave in the dunes. He had been sodomised.

Petersen, too, was approached by a stranger asking for help with carrying banana boxes.

"A man walked up to us. He asked us if we would help him carry banana boxes. He said the boxes were further down the road. He offered us R10 each to help him," Petersen recalled this weekend.

At the time R10 was a lot of money for 10-year-old boys and the duo agreed. The man told them he was known as "Huis".

Petersen described "Huis" as a stocky black man, with scars that "looked like scratch marks" on one cheek. He had short dark hair, a sharp nose, large eyes and thick lips.

When the boys asked where the boxes were, the man repeated they were a little way further on … then further and further, as he lured them into the bushes near Philippi.

At some time during the long walk, the man dropped back, walking behind them in the bush.

"Before we knew it, there was a rope tied around our necks. He had thrown it over us from the back and choked us … We couldn't breathe. He told us to continue walking or he would kill us.

"I thought I was going to die."

Finally they stopped near a tree, the two boys still roped together, the man with the end of the rope in his hands. There the man raped the boys.

Petersen said that their assailant, who spoke fluent Afrikaans, later led them to an informal settlement near Philippi.

"He said he came to that area, that people knew him and he would have to speak a black language now," Petersen recalled.

The man sexually assaulted the boys again and then fell asleep, giving the pair a chance to untie their bonds and escape.

After they had found their way home, their parents took them to the Mitchells Plain police station.

The officer investigating their case, a Detective Constable Falken, since retired, accompanied the boys to the informal settlement, says Petersen. But the police did not get out of their cars because of political unrest in the area at the time.

Petersen says: "We were the first kids. He saw he could get away with it with us, so he started with more. All I want is for something to be done. I want to know if he was locked up, or whether he's still out there."

Petersen has attended at least three identity parades but has never been able to identify his assailant. He was not asked to participate in any ID parade featuring Norman Simons.

Then earlier this year detectives approached Petersen and revealed they had found a possible suspect in Johannesburg, a man convicted of a series of murders, rapes and abductions in that city. Apparently this man also has a scar on his face and had also lured his young victims, several under 15, with the pretence of helping him carry boxes.

It is understood this man, who reportedly was in Cape Town at the time of the Station Strangler's killing spree, was never questioned about the Strangler murders.

Petersen told *Weekend Argus* he was traumatised by his experience and had become withdrawn after the abduction. To this day he was uncomfortable around men.

His secret was so closely guarded that even his wife had not known what happened to him until this weekend.

Hunt for Strangler Offered Compelling Platform for NP

As South Africa approached the most important watershed in the country's history, the hunt for the Western Cape's first known serial killer came to be distorted through the fracturing lens of the politics of the day.

In the lead-up to the 1994 elections, the National Party was looking to reinvent itself as the political home of the Western Cape's coloured majority – and, by attracting the coloured vote, to fend off the electoral threat posed by a nationally rampant ANC.

Prominent Capetonian Ryland Fisher, a journalist at the time, remembers the political climate:

"There were those who used the race card in a very serious way. They played on the fact that the coloured community was afraid of black people and what they would do.

"Within that environment I think it was possible for the NP to use this case in a way of showing how black people would turn against coloured people. In a way, they used the fact that Simons's father was a black man."

In the first quarter of 1994, then premier Hernus Kriel posted a R100 000 reward, later increased to R250 000, for information leading to the arrest and conviction of the Station Strangler.

He publicly vowed his police would catch the killer and bring him to justice.

The NP published full-page pictures of the Strangler identikit image in the local newspapers. It distributed shock-horror pamphlets emblazoned with the same picture, darkly predicting an ANC government would set criminals like this free on bail.

The Strangler became the ultimate bogeyman, as the NP whipped up a frenzy around its core election issue – the so-called *swart gevaar*.

Even 13 years later, when Simons was brought from prison to testify at an inquest, he was fitted with a bullet-proof vest in case a member of the public tried to take the law into their own hands.

In this climate the pressure was all but crushing on investigators to crack the case before the country went to the polls on 27 April. When Norman Avzal Simons was arrested on 12 April, they appeared to have done just that.

"It was really a ploy to get the coloured vote," Patricia de Lille, leader of the Independent Democrats, said. "This arrest came just too suddenly ... All of a sudden before the election Simons was arrested. It was like the Jews voting for Hitler," she said.

But Simons's lawyer, Koos Louw, believes the pressure may have led investigators to cut corners and ignore or suppress contradictions in the evidence they encountered.

The case only went to trial, Louw said, because of "a perceived fear of civil unrest that would follow if they admitted their errors".

One key contradiction arises, ironically, out of an initiative by Simons to join the police as a reservist. On the same day 10-year-old Elroy van Rooyen was abducted from the Strand – about two hours before – Simons had a photograph taken at a police station as part of his application to join the reserve. In the photograph he has short hair. In the police identikit compiled on the basis of eyewitness testimony to the abduction by Fouzhia Hercules and Elroy's cousin Rayno, however, the suspect is shown as wearing his hair long, in an Afro style.

Police have consistently explained away the anomaly, suggesting Simons might have combed his hair flat for the photograph – thus giving the impression of short hair – but no evidence around the seeming disparity was tested in court.

There are also indications that, as they prepared their case against Simons for prosecution, police may not have not noticed, or cared to notice, murders that appeared to bear many of the hallmarks of the Station Strangler killings.

In August 1994, for instance, the half-naked body of 15-year-old schoolboy Nicolaas Michael Dippenaar was found on the premises of a primary school in Namaqualand. Dippenaar was found with his hands tied behind his back, his black denim trousers pulled down to his ankles.

The torso was positioned with the stomach down in the sand; there was a rope mark around the neck where the boy was strangled at the same time as being sodomised.

Approached for comment on the NP's political strategies in the 1994 elections, Kriel told Independent Newspapers: "I can't remember."

Chapter 19

Dead Men Tell No Tales

Fred Kockott
Sunday Tribune

Crime is always in the headlines in South Africa and in 2009 there were reports of a new and controversial shoot-to-kill policy.

This was not news in Durban, where the *Sunday Tribune* was reporting on the death toll of shoot-outs between criminal suspects and the police as early as February. Were they being eliminated instead of being brought to justice before the courts?

Eight months later, Fred Kockott found himself sitting in the office of a lawyer and on his desk was a copy of a High Court interdict restraining the police from unlawfully killing taxi boss Bongani Mkhize. It had been to no avail. Mkhize died, shot by the police bullets just weeks after obtaining the order.

The difficulty in investigating the story was that six of Mkhize's colleagues had already died in similar circumstances. Almost every source felt threatened, especially those who could give evidence in court.

The investigation highlighted serious shortcomings in the Independent Complaints Directorate (ICD), which had originally cleared police of any wrongdoing in nearly all of these cases.

The ICD has renewed its investigations and recalled all related police dockets as part of a broader probe that now looks set to become a test case for the watchdog body.

Fred Kockott cut his teeth as a journalist in the 1980s in KwaZulu-Natal, establishing the Concord news agency which served the independent press in South Africa as well as foreign press agencies. He changed course in the 1990s, setting up the Phemba Kahle agency, a music school and various art and craft projects. He returned to journalism in 2002. He was runner-up for the first Taco Kuiper Award.

Taxi Boss Shooting:
Sleuth Smells a Rat

The family of a slain KwaZulu-Natal taxi boss believe police could be covering up the circumstances of his killing, and have instructed their lawyer to disclose the preliminary findings of an independent forensic ballistic expert, to challenge the official version.

The death of taxi boss Bongani Elphas Mkhize in a hail of police Swat team bullets on Durban's Umgeni Road on 3 February came in direct defiance of a High Court order interdicting the South African Police Service from doing precisely that – killing him.

The order was granted after six Mkhize associates in the KwaMaphumulo Taxi Association had already died at the hands of police probing the ambush murder, in August last year, of SAPS colleague Superintendent Zethembe Chonco.

KZN monitor Mary de Haas said these killings and the subsequent exoneration of police in Independent Complaints Directorate (ICD) probes raised the spectre of the police "enjoying carte blanche licence to kill without repercussion".

But not only civil society is expressing alarm. KZN's public transport manager, Advocate Simo Chamane, said with all suspects in the Chonco murder case dead, his murder might remain a mystery.

In the police version of the Mkhize killing, the cops were shooting in retaliation after Mkhize, alone in his car at the time, opened fire on them.

But the preliminary findings of independent ballistic forensics expert Jacobus Steyl suggest it is unlikely that Mkhize opened fire on pursuing police. A former policeman, Steyl is regularly called on as a credible ballistics expert for court proceedings.

Steyl's investigations show that the windows of Mkhize's luxury Lexus remained closed throughout the shooting. Moreover, the pattern of shots into the body of his car show that the cops started firing from behind the vehicle, and continued firing as they drew up alongside the driver's door, where the final shots were fired, leaving bloodstains on the driver's headrest.

If Steyl's preliminary reconstruction is correct, it would mean that – to support the police version – Mkhize would have had to open fire, backwards, while driving in the opposite direction.

Steyl also notes that no ballistic evidence has yet come to light to establish that an unlicensed 9mm handgun photographed beside Mkhize inside the car had, in fact, been used to shoot at police. He suspects a so-called "primer residue" test, which would establish this, has not even been performed.

Attorney Petrus Coetzee told the *Sunday Tribune* that the Mkhize family believe he was murdered in a planned hit and the unlicensed firearm subsequently planted.

Steyl's preliminary findings regarding the earlier killings of Mkhize's associates also raised questions about police versions.

Earlier this year, the ICD said the findings of their investigations into the killings of the Chonco murder suspects were "unsubstantiated" because there had been no witnesses.

On Mkhize's death, the ICD have declared that it could not divulge any information because investigations were at a sensitive stage.

Coetzee described as "a mockery of justice" the fact that in a country "where the constitution is supreme and guarantees everyone access to information, a deceased's family had to engage an attorney to obtain progress reports of investigation into the police shooting of their husband and father".

Coetzee also noted that while journalists had been able to interview eyewitnesses to the Mkhize killing – as is evident in newspaper reports where witnesses were named – neither the police nor the ICD had seen fit to do so.

KZN head of detectives Commissioner Pat Brown said since the Mkhize family were planning legal action against police, their questions would be dealt with at the inquest.

Coetzee said the Mkhize case smacked of a cover-up "through lack of investigation".

"You can have an inquest only once a prosecutor is satisfied a criminal docket has been properly investigated. This is clearly not the case here."

What Really Happened

Before he died in a hail of police bullets, KwaMaphumulo taxi boss Bongani Mkhize made one of the most startling interventions in the annals of South African law.

He secured a High Court interdict forbidding the police to kill him. They killed him anyway – less than three months after the restraining order was granted.

"It is arrest that concerns me, causes me to fear for my life ... I verily believe my life is in danger from members of the South African police," Mkhize wrote in his application to the High Court.

This was after six of his associates had been killed by police investigating the murder of their colleague, Superintendent Zethembe Chonco.

The High Court order did Mkhize little good. He died in a hail of police bullets in broad daylight on Durban's Umgeni Road on 3 February this year.

According to the police, Mkhize opened fire on arresting officers and was killed as they shot back.

It was not detectives seeking suspects in the Chonco murder case who killed Zondi, though, but a heavily armed contingent from the National Intervention Unit, the SAPS's premier specialised Swat team.

Now, eight months after the killing, police have yet to disclose any details of their investigations into the incident.

At the time they indicated that Mkhize was sought in connection with another murder, that of a traditional leader close to both the police and the taxi industry, Inkosi Mbongeleni Zondi.

They have since confirmed that the murder docket on Chonco has been closed after the deaths of all wanted suspects in the case.

But the Mkhize killing is not going away. The dead taxi boss's family, their lawyer Petrus Coetzee and independent forensic ballistic expert Jacobus Steyl have accused the police and the Independent Complaints Directorate of not properly investigating the shootings of Mkhize and his taxi association colleagues.

Coetzee said the Mkhize family suspected a cover-up.

KwaZulu-Natal's general manager of public transport, Advocate Simo Chamane, has also expressed concern. "All we've got are reports from police that these suspects were killed either trying to fight back with the police or trying to go for their guns. We never did get to the bottom of who was behind Chonco's murder."

In his application for High Court protection in October 2008, Mkhize claimed he had received information that he was suspected of having orchestrated Chonco's murder, and was the last surviving person on a list of suspects the police had decided to eliminate.

Chonco, station commissioner of Kranskop police station, had been appointed to head investigations into violence related to taxi route disputes, including murders arising from disputes between Mkhize's KwaMaphumulo Taxi Association and the Stanger Taxi Association.

Chonco was ambushed on 27 August 2008 while travelling between Kranskop and Stanger, transporting suspects to court.

In the wake of the Chonco killing, members of the KwaMaphumulo Taxi Association were targeted as suspects.

"One by one they die – thugs pay the price for cop's murder," read the headlines in a *Daily Sun* article dated 18 October last year and included in Mkhize's application.

"When a top cop [Chonco] was shot dead in an ambush, his angry colleagues vowed to avenge his death. And this is what's happening. Today the seventh suspect lies dead." The newspaper went on to quote unnamed police sources as saying that an eighth suspect, a taxi boss, was on the run.

Mkhize said he learned he was on a list of suspects in the Chonco case from an associate, Moses Dlamini, who was interrogated, and allegedly severely assaulted, by the police a day after Chonco's murder.

In opposing the granting of the interdict, the KZN head of organised crime, Johan Booysens, said Mkhize was not a suspect in the Chonco murder case, and scotched Mkhize's hit-list fears.

But Mkhize was far from reassured. He went on to allege that the existence of a list of Chonco murder suspects had also been confirmed in a meeting with then KwaZulu-Natal MEC for community safety liaison Bheki Cele, now national police commissioner. This meeting was called after the deaths of five members of the KwaMaphumulo Taxi Association at the hands of police investigating Chonco's murder.

In his affidavit opposing Mkhize's application for a protection order, Cele denied confirming the existence of a list of Chonco murder suspects, but never disputed warning Mkhize and two colleagues that there was "a war out there" and that "when the waters are muddy, crocodiles will hunt [amanzi adungekile izingwenya ziyathanda ukubhukuda kuwona]".

Rather than be hunted, Mkhize said in his application, "I have offered to hand myself over ... I am prepared to be interrogated in the presence of my legal representative."

He never got the chance.

Other than to state that Mkhize had been "positively linked" to Zondi's murder the previous week, the police have not answered queries about how a heavily armed National Intervention Unit task team came to be tailing him that day.

Coetzee has filed a notice of intention to sue the police for damages on behalf of the Mkhize family.

Does It All Point to a Big Police Cover-Up?

Some policemen have got some serious explaining to do, says independent ballistics expert Jacobus Steyl, who is conducting forensic investigations into the KwaMaphumulo Taxi Association chairman Bongani Mkhize and several of his associates.

Steyl said his examination of Mkhize's vehicle and post-mortem results cast serious doubt on the police version that Mkhize, driving alone, had shot at a heavily armed National Intervention Unit task team on Durban's Umgeni Road on 3 February this year.

For a start, all the windows of Mkhize's car were closed when he died under a hail of police bullets, a finding corroborated by independent pathologist Reggie Perumal.

Steyl said his preliminary findings indicated that the police had started firing at Mkhize from behind.

"Some of the shots were aimed quite low ... but there are also shots at a higher section of the vehicle that went in through the boot and above," said Steyl. "Then the shots turned to the door behind the driver, but angled towards the driver, and then straight to the driver," said Steyl.

Perumal said the post-mortem findings showed Mkhize's body had been riddled with bullets, and bullet fragments ... mostly from heavy-calibre rifles, such as R4s or R5s, "but he did not die from these shots. He died from two shots with a 9mm in the direction of the head."

Steyl said no police 9mm firearms were handed to the Independent Complaints Directorate until after post-mortem findings that Mkhize had died of two 9mm gunshots around the neck and head.

Steyl said, in terms of standard police procedure, when a firearm is fired by a policeman and someone is killed or injured, that firearm has to be handed in immediately for ballistic tests.

Perumal said while the wounds on Mkhize's arms showed that his arms were in a forward position at the time of sustaining these wounds, this could not overrule the possibility that Mkhize had been firing at police prior to or after being hit in the arm.

But he did confirm Steyl's findings that the windows of Mkhize's car were closed at the time.

Steyl said this suggested an unlikely scenario in which Mkhize had driven with one hand, pointed the firearm over his shoulder and shot through his back windscreen at a heavily armed police Swat team.

He said that to determine whether Mkhize had fired shots, primer residue tests should have been done.

"When a shot gets fired, primer, a compound which starts the ignition in the cartridge, spreads about a metre from the person firing," said Steyl.

So, with the windows closed, Mkhize's body and clothing would have been "covered all over" with the residue.

Steyl, a former policeman, said that, despite eight months having lapsed since the incident, he had yet to receive any feedback from either the police or the Independent Complaints Directorate about any aspect of their investigations into Mkhize's death or the earlier killings of other suspects in the Chonco murder case.

Regarding earlier killings, Steyl said when he examined the Hyundai Tucson in which Magojela Ndimande and Thokozane Tembe were travelling when they were killed by police on 17 September, he retrieved a bullet casing on the dashboard console and so believed no thorough forensic ballistic investigation had taken place.

Inspection of the vehicle also showed that all windows had been closed at the time of this alleged shoot-out. As in Mkhize's case, there also was no indication that shots had been fired through the closed windows from the inside out.

As to the police version that the suspects had used AK47 assault rifles to fire at them, Steyl said it was odd that no pictures of such weapons had been taken at the scene.

Steyl said at the scene of the killing of Mzumeni Johannes Luthuli (aka Kopolota) and Nathi Wilson Mthembu, on 21 September, the home-owner still had some vital ballistic evidence, including cartridges and a bullet recovered in the house.

"She is reluctant to hand these to the police. She wants to give them to the ICD but, almost a year down the line, does not know who to contact. I have not been able to advise her, as they have not told me who is conducting the investigation," said Steyl.

The ICD has said that it has completed investigations in the killings of all the Chonco murder suspects, cleared the police of any culpability, and referred the matters back to the police to complete as inquest dockets.

"This is ridiculous," said Steyl. "How can the ICD come to such a conclusion when no proper investigation has taken place, and then leave the matter in the hands of police to take further?

"I have not even had the opportunity to share with them some of my preliminary findings, and there are still exhibits out there."

Taxi Body Tried to Rein in Police

Even before Bongani Mkhize made his High Court application, lawyers acting for the KwaMaphumulo Taxi Association petitioned police top brass to stop what they believed was a systematic campaign of violence and intimidation against the association's members.

Shortly after the 3 September killing of Lindelani Buthelezi, the first suspect in the murder of Superintendent Chonco to die, as well as a string of alleged brutal assaults during interrogations, the lawyers wrote to the KZN provincial head of detectives, Commissioner Pat Brown.

The lawyers said the police appeared to have abandoned the rule of law in conducting their investigations. They went on to assure him that the association viewed the murder of Chonco in a most serious light and committed the association's members to cooperating with the police in their investigations. They undertook to surrender to the police any member wanted for questioning.

In a later letter, lawyer Nathi Shozi warned that police appeared to be "conducting the investigation as a law unto themselves ... They have virtual licence to arrest and detain at will, to interrogate and to assault and even to kill."

Mkhize, as chairman of the taxi association, also arranged for well-known independent forensic and ballistic expert Jacobus Steyl to investigate the shootings of alleged suspects in the Chonco murder. The suspects died at the hands of the police.

Mkhize "Sick With Stress"

In the weeks before he got a High Court protection order, Bongani Elphas Mkhize was "getting sick with stress", a family representative told *Weekend Argus* last week.

Then, when the court order was granted interdicting police from killing him, Mkhize relaxed – until he received a phone call to tip him off that police were allegedly hatching a plan to take him out on the pretext that he was wanted for the murder of Inkosi Mbongeleni Zondi. The following day, Mkhize died at the hands of a police Swat team.

One of Mkhize's daughters – who does not wish to be named – insists her father was unarmed that day, and believes police planted a gun in his car to support the official version that Mkhize opened fire on pursuing police.

Police claimed Mkhize had been "positively linked" to Zondi's murder the previous week.

They said Mkhize failed to stop when police tried to pull him over, shooting at them instead.

"My father? Never. He was not that kind of man. He was a very humble, soft-spoken man, but very serious," his daughter said.

"He grew up in Kranskop, and worked for an insurance company for a while before he started running taxis in Joburg. He then moved back to Kranskop, and was running five long-distance taxis. He was interested in starting a trucking business.

"He did carry a gun, but it was a licensed firearm. I know that he did not have it with him that day."

Both forensic ballistic expert Jacobus Steyl and independent pathologist Reggie Perumal said Mkhize's body was riddled with multiple gunshot wounds, metal fragments and glass shrapnel when they examined it. They also concurred that all his car windows had been closed at the time he sustained these wounds.

The Independent Complaints Directorate declined to comment, saying that, because its inquiry was at a "sensitive stage, no information can be divulged without jeopardising the investigation".

ICD Takes Over Probe of Taxi-Men Killings

6 December

The watchdog Independent Complaints Directorate (ICD) has taken over police investigations into the February killing of taxi boss Bongani Mkhize and earlier police shootings of six of his colleagues.

This follows a *Sunday Tribune* probe revealing that there might have been a police cover-up through "non-investigation" of circumstances surrounding Mkhize's death and the earlier killings of seven of his colleagues suspected to have been involved in the murder of top cop Superintendent Zethembe Chonco.

The ICD had publicly declared that its investigations of the killings of the Chonco murder suspects had cleared the police of any culpability, and had referred the cases back to the police to complete as inquest dockets.

But now the ICD is reviewing the cases, and has recalled all the dockets from the police as part of a broader probe to assess the possibility that the killings are connected.

This follows a meeting of top ICD representatives with Petrus Coetzee, a lawyer representing the Mkhize family, and an independent forensic ballistic expert, Jacobus Steyl, both of whom have publicly expressed concern that the death of Mkhize and all the suspects in the Chonco murder case had not been investigated properly.

ICD national spokesman Moses Dlamini this week confirmed the body's decision to review these cases in the light of new evidence having emerged, including preliminary findings of Steyl's ballistic examinations of Mkhize's car and scenes of the shootings of four suspects in the Chonco murder case.

The ICD also confirmed that advertisements would now be placed in newspapers for witnesses to the shooting of Mkhize.

When Mkhize approached the court for protection late last year, six associates in the KwaMaphumulo Taxi Association had already been shot dead by police as suspects in the Chonco murder investigation.

In all cases, police said they had been either threatened or attacked first, and the suspects had died as police fired back in retaliation.

In recent correspondence with Commissioner Pat Brown, head of detectives in KwaZulu-Natal, and the ICD, Coetzee highlighted several apparent failures of both police investigators and the directorate in getting to the bottom of the killings of Mkhize and his colleagues.

This included interviewing no witnesses to Mkhize's shooting, despite the shooting having happened in broad daylight on a busy Durban street.

Coetzee said while newspapers at the time had quoted eyewitnesses to the killing, no attempt appeared to have been made to contact such witnesses by either police or the ICD.

Why Were No Witnesses Interviewed?

16 December

Bongani Mkhize, the chairman of the KwaMaphumulo Taxi Association, secured the protection of the High Court in November last year to prevent the Durban Organised Crime Unit from "eliminating" him.

Despite the interdict being granted, Mkhize died in a hail of police bullets on Durban's Umgeni Road on 3 February.

Police said at the time that Mkhize had been connected to the murder of Inkosi Mbongeleni Zondi, who had died ten days previously in a drive-by shooting in Umlazi. They also said Mkhize shot at them in an attempt to evade arrest.

An Independent Newspapers probe revealed that there had possibly been a police cover-up through "non-investigation" of circumstances surrounding Mkhize's death and the earlier deaths of six of his colleagues, all suspected of having been involved in the murder of a top police officer, Superintendent Zethembe Chonco.

It seems that the shootings were investigated independently by different police investigation officers and the dockets then referred to different public prosecutors for the purpose of holding inquests.

In correspondence with Commissioner Pat Brown, head of detectives in KwaZulu-Natal, and the ICD, lawyer Petrus Coetzee, representing the Mkhize family, highlighted several apparent failures of both police investigators and the ICD in getting to the bottom of the killings, including the fact that no witnesses were interviewed, despite the shooting having happened in broad daylight on a busy Durban street.

Coetzee said while newspapers quoted eyewitnesses to the killing, no attempt seemed to have been made to contact such witnesses by either police or the ICD.

Mkhize's family also suspects a cover-up.

Coetzee said he was impressed by the responses of ICD acting provincial head Len John to concerns that he and Steyl had raised when the men met last week, and the ICD's renewed interest.

Coetzee said the ICD had agreed to forward all these related dockets "at an appropriate stage of these investigations" to the director of public prosecutors (DPP) for a senior representative to study as part a broader probe into the killings of Mkhize and his six colleagues.

Steyl confirmed that he had handed over to the ICD ballistic evidence he had recovered in his probe into the police shooting of four suspects in the Chonco murder case.

This included a bullet casing Steyl had retrieved on the dashboard console of the Hyundai Tucson in which Magojela Ndimande and Thokozane Tembe were travelling when they were killed by police on the N3 near Merrivale on 17 September last year.

Steyl also handed over three bullets he had found during his inspection of a house in Mandeni where Mzumeni Johannes Luthuli (aka Kopolota) and Nathi Wilson Mthembu, also allegedly Chonco murder suspects, had been killed by police on 21 September last year.

"One 9mm bullet and a 5.56mm bullet from an R4 or R5 rifle were found on the bloodstained carpet and another 9mm bullet in a cupboard," said Steyl.

He added that while he had yet to get access to the results of the post-mortem examinations, his examination of this scene indicated that the two men had possibly been shot in the head by police standing almost directly above them.

"It's encouraging that the ICD is taking over and recalling all the other dockets, but it's still a concern that nine months have lapsed since Mkhize's shooting."

Vested Interests in KZN Taxi Industry "A Threat to Stability"

Government officials and politicians' vested interest in the taxi industry, and associated violence arising from disputes over routes and permits, have become a serious threat to peace and stability, says KwaZulu-Natal's general manager of public transport, Advocate Simo Chamane.

Chamane said officials at all levels, including senior civil servants and policemen at station level, were responsible for many deaths "because of direct or indirect involvement in the taxi industry".

"It is very dangerous. In its present form the taxi industry is a threat to security, and peace and stability," said Chamane.

The murder of Superintendent Zethembe Chonco, and the subsequent police killing of all suspects in the Chonco murder investigation, Chamane said, were a setback in dealing with the taxi-related conflict in KZN. Chamane said Chonco had been involved in various sensitive investigations, including the theft of 43 guns – among court exhibits in murder cases – from KwaMaphumulo police station.

It was suspected that this theft might have been an inside job.

Chamane said Chonco had also made good progress in solving murders related to the conflict between the KwaMaphumulo and Stanger taxi associations – "to such an extent that the killings had ended", said Chamane.

"Chonco was arresting people across the spectrum. Now we will never know why he was killed, as the police case is closed, with all the suspects dead."

KwaZulu-Natal violence monitor Mary de Haas said: "The question will also always arise: Were they really his killers?

Sources

Chapter 1
http://secure.financialmail.co.za/09/0612/cover/coverstory.htm
http://www.timeslive.co.za/multimedia/archive/00256/mainpage-0111_256379a.pdf

Chapter 2
http://www.mg.co.za/article/2009-02-13-tearful-niehaus-admits-fraud

Chapter 3
http://www.mg.co.za/article/2009-09-18-semenya-saga-chuenes-trail-of-lies

Chapter 4
http://www.etv.co.za/extended/index/3rd_degree

Chapter 5
http://www.citypress.co.za/SouthAfrica/News/I-want-my-f-pardon-20091219

Chapter 6
http://www.politicsweb.co.za/politicsweb/view/politicsweb/en/page71619?oid=125134&sn=Detail

Chapter 7
http://www.iol.co.za/index.php?set_id=1&click_id=594&art_id=vn20090612053316296C646957

Chapter 8
http://blogs.dispatch.co.za/dying/category/stories/

Chapter 9
http://www.mg.co.za/article/2009-07-25-waste-company-at-centre-of-toxic-storm

Chapter 10
http://blogs.dispatch.co.za/brokenhomes/overview/

Chapter 11
http://www.sabc3.co.za/shows/3912

Chapter 12
http://beta.mnet.co.za/carteblanche/Default.aspx

Chapter 13
http://www.timeslive.co.za/sundaytimes/article82688.ece

Chapter 14
http://www.politicsweb.co.za/politicsweb/view/politicsweb/en/
page71619?oid=138904&sn=Detail

Chapter 15
http://net-145-057.mweb.co.za/Companies/Eskom-CEO-ignored-
warnings-20090911

Chapter 16
http://www.mg.co.za/article/2009-01-23-kitchen-confidential

Chapter 17
http://www.timeslive.co.za/sundaytimes/article108708.ece

Chapter 18
http://www.iol.co.za/index.php?art_id=vn20100205123616795C312497

Chapter 19
http://www.iol.co.za/index.php?set_id=1&click_id=13&art_
id=vn20090208111556426C402490